I0793220

IMAGES
of America

RAYMOND AND CASCO

On the Cover: Silas Frank Jordan was the road commissioner of Casco for seven years. His crew and teams are shown here in 1911 building the Mill Road, today called Route 11. Foreman Jordan is shown on the left with some of his workers, from left to right, Milton Hall, Charles Lord, and Leroy Tenney. (Raymond Casco Historical Society.)

IMAGES
of America

RAYMOND AND CASCO

Martha Watkins Glassford
and Pamela Watkins Grant

ARCADIA
PUBLISHING

ISBN 978-0-7385-7398-4

Published by Arcadia Publishing
Charleston, South Carolina

Printed in the United States of America

Library of Congress Control Number: 2010930354

For all general information, please contact Arcadia Publishing:
Telephone 843-853-2070
Fax 843-853-0044
E-mail sales@arcadiapublishing.com
For customer service and orders:
Toll-Free 1-888-313-2665

Visit us on the Internet at www.arcadiapublishing.com

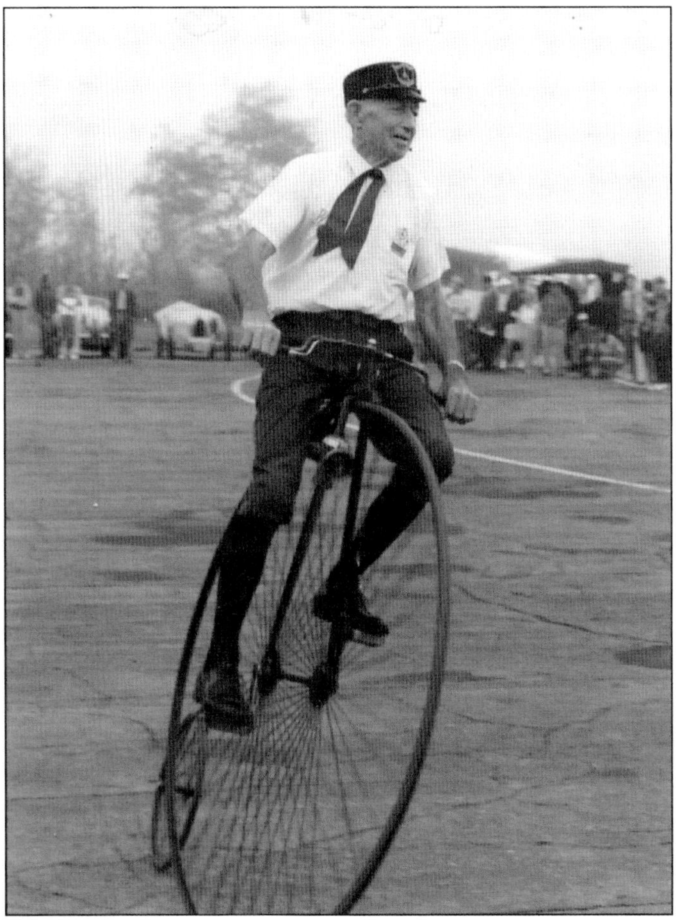

This book is dedicated to Ernest H. Knight, who spent many years researching Raymondtown, which led to the founding of the Raymond Casco Historical Society 40 years ago. Without his journey to preserve our history, this book would not have been possible.

Contents

ACKNOWLEDGMENTS

We would like to extend our sincere gratitude to the many people, too numerous to mention here individually, who have shared their time, pictures, and stories for this book. Our deepest appreciation goes to the Raymond Casco Historical Society. Unless otherwise noted, all images have come from the Raymond Casco Historical Society.

INTRODUCTION

The voices that were heard in the air belonged to the members of the General Court of Massachusetts Bay Colony, who were voting a grant of land to a company of men who had been under Capt. William Raymont from Beverly, Massachusetts. The cries of these men were due to a failed expedition in 1690 to end the French and Indian raids on the Massachusetts Bay Colony. The end result of this expedition was the granting of a township to survivors or descendents.

On January 30, 1767, after many years of failed attempts to settle land and boundary disputes, the Beverly proprietors granted land to the heirs of those men in Cumberland County, adjoining the Great Sebago Pond to New Marblehead.

As the story goes, two men came together at the outlet of Great Sebago Pond, Capt. Joseph Dingley and Dominicus Jordan. In the night, Captain Dingley paddled across the bay and, upon hearing the sound of a babbling brook, he took landfall and followed the brook to an open field. Captain Dingley received the 100 acres and built his house prior to 1770. In response to an offer by the proprietors of a free 100 acres if a mill was built, Captain Dingley picked a spot on another brook that runs into Sebago Lake and commenced to build his mill. This brook carries his name today, the Dingley Brook.

About 18 years later, the proprietors were still selling land. Lewis Gay was the first man to buy land in Cumberland County, for five shillings. He settled at one of the most scenic locations in Raymondtown on Quaker Ridge. By 1794, a total of 31 families had settled in Raymondtown. Around 1810, Richard Manning came to Raymondtown as a proprietor's agent, and eventually, his name was on a high percentage of the 100-acre lots.

Many of the early settlers kept stories of what life was like, and it helps us here today in the telling of their stories in photographs and print. The families were large in the early years. Jacob S. Watkins had 14 children, Daniel Cook had 11 children, William Decker had 9 children, Dominicus Jordan had 8 children, and Elijah Cook had a total of 20 children. Having a large family was common throughout Raymondtown.

We hope you see through our eyes the strength and courage it took to cut a life out of a wilderness loaded with bobcats, bears, and rattlesnakes. People froze to death during the cold winters, and there were Indians to cope with at that time. They could hear fish jump from the water, the cries of wild animals in the night, and the hiss of a rattler. The land was cleared of massive trees, and the hardworking early settlers of our towns built roads, homes, and businesses.

One

Raymondtown

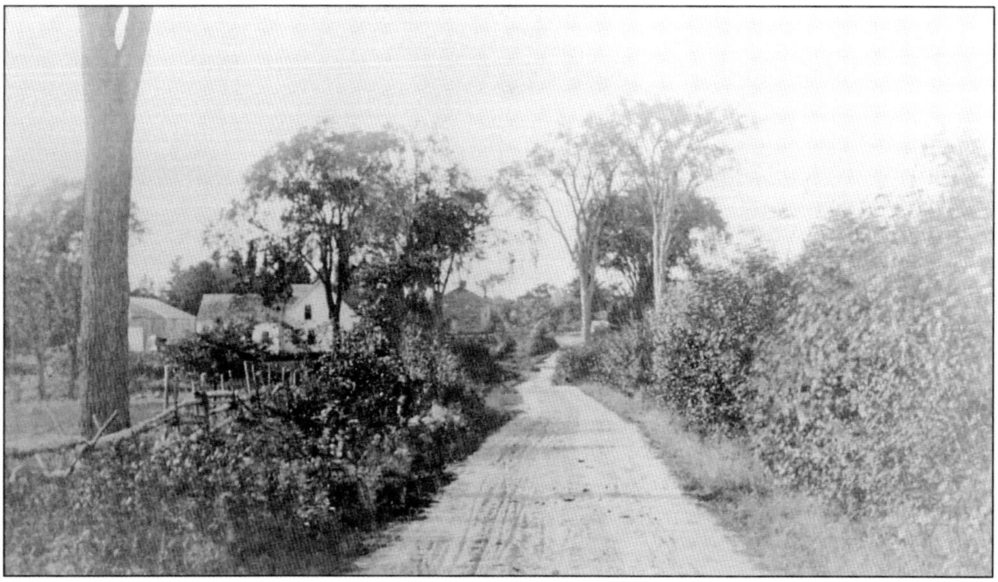

In 1770, Capt. Joseph Dingley made his nocturnal dash across Sebago Lake and came ashore by an open inlet to the lake. Following the brook to a field, he built a home close to what is known now as the Bridgton Road, or Route 302. In South Casco he cleared the land for a large farm. He and his son Samuel built a stone bridge that spanned the brook for easy travel. He had 10 years to build a sawmill; during this time, he built his second home near Dingley Brook at the outlet of Thomas Pond. He gave Samuel his first home, which became known as Stone Bridge Farm due to the building of the stone bridge.

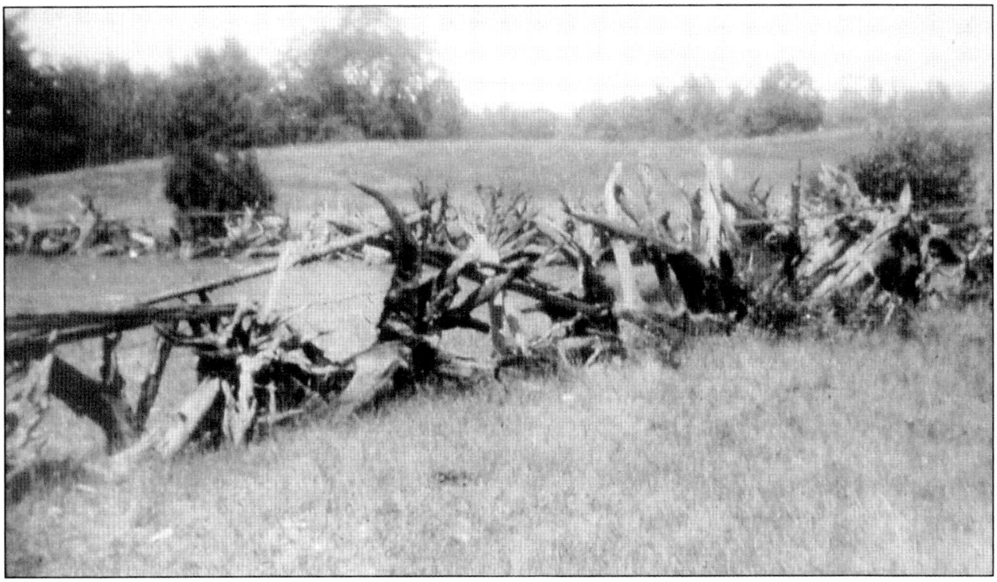

Rocks were not prevalent in much of Raymondtown, which meant boundary lines were often constructed of trees. One of the terms of the original land grant of 1767 called for the clearing of four acres of land within 15 months, so with limited time and primitive means of cutting the trees, stumps were often lined side-by-side for boundary lines or for fences to hold in animals.

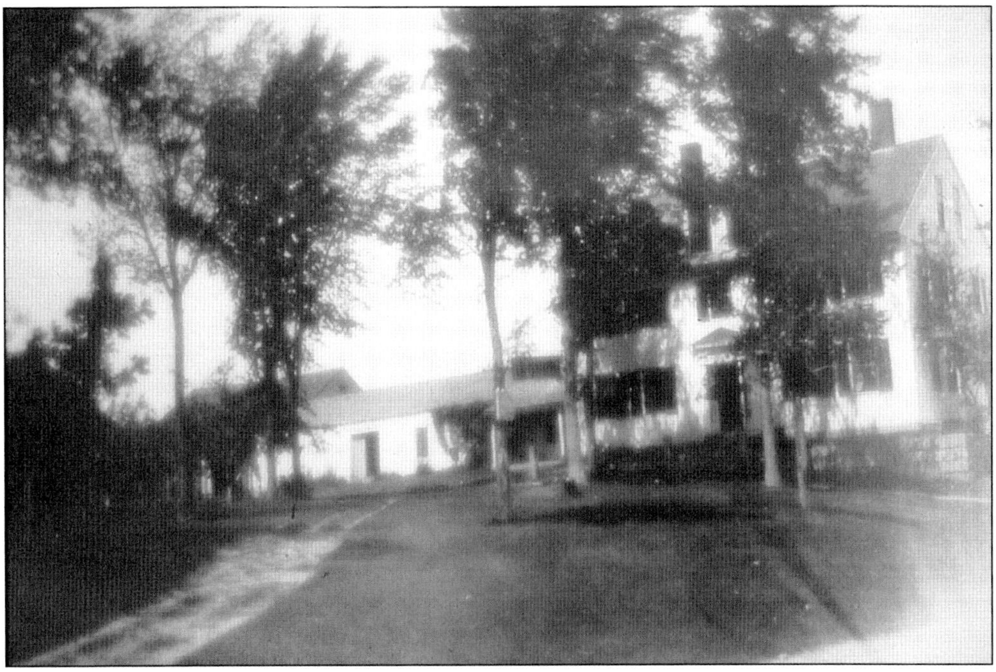

Located behind what is now Key Bank on Route 302 in Raymond is the Crockett House. The ell of this house was presumably one of the first houses in Raymondtown. Built in 1771 by Dominicus Jordan, the main house was built by Dominicus's son Nathan Jordan in 1800. The Jordans once used it as a stagecoach tavern. Charles Crockett purchased the house in 1900 and took in guests. He used the woodshed as a fishing tackle room and had the walls covered with life-sized paper cutouts of salmon.

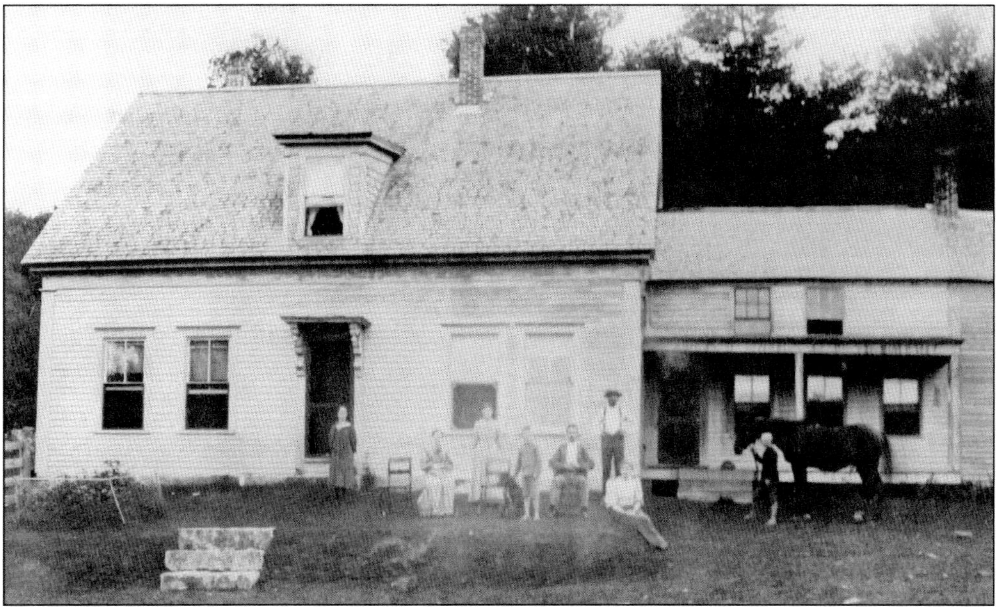

The old Lewis Gay homestead came down through his descendents over the years. Lewis Gay came to Raymondtown in the late 1700s and was the first man to buy land in Cumberland County. His deed was dated March 29, 1794, entitling him to 100 acres on Quaker Ridge, lot 13 in the fourth range. This would be about two miles north of the present village of South Casco. He built the Friends Meetinghouse on Quaker Ridge. Lewis and his wife, Mary (Murch), are both buried in the Dingley Cemetery.

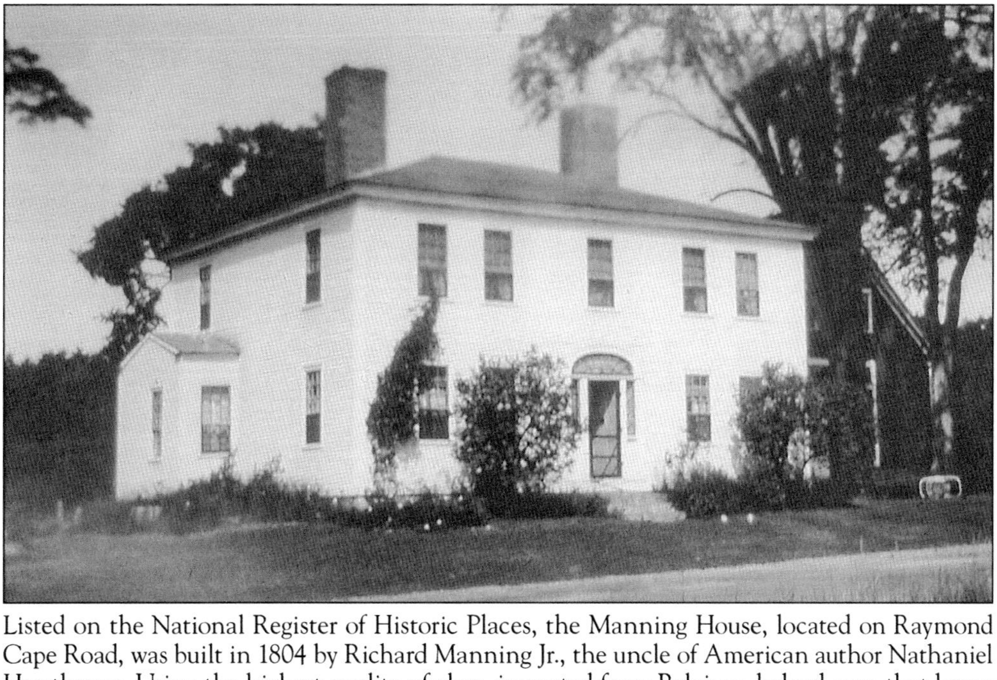

Listed on the National Register of Historic Places, the Manning House, located on Raymond Cape Road, was built in 1804 by Richard Manning Jr., the uncle of American author Nathaniel Hawthorne. Using the highest quality of glass, imported from Belgium, helped earn that home the name "Manning's Folly." In 1871, Andrew and MaryAnn (Dingley) Libby resided there, and in the early 1900s, J. Frank and Grace E. (Watkins) Welch took in boarders.

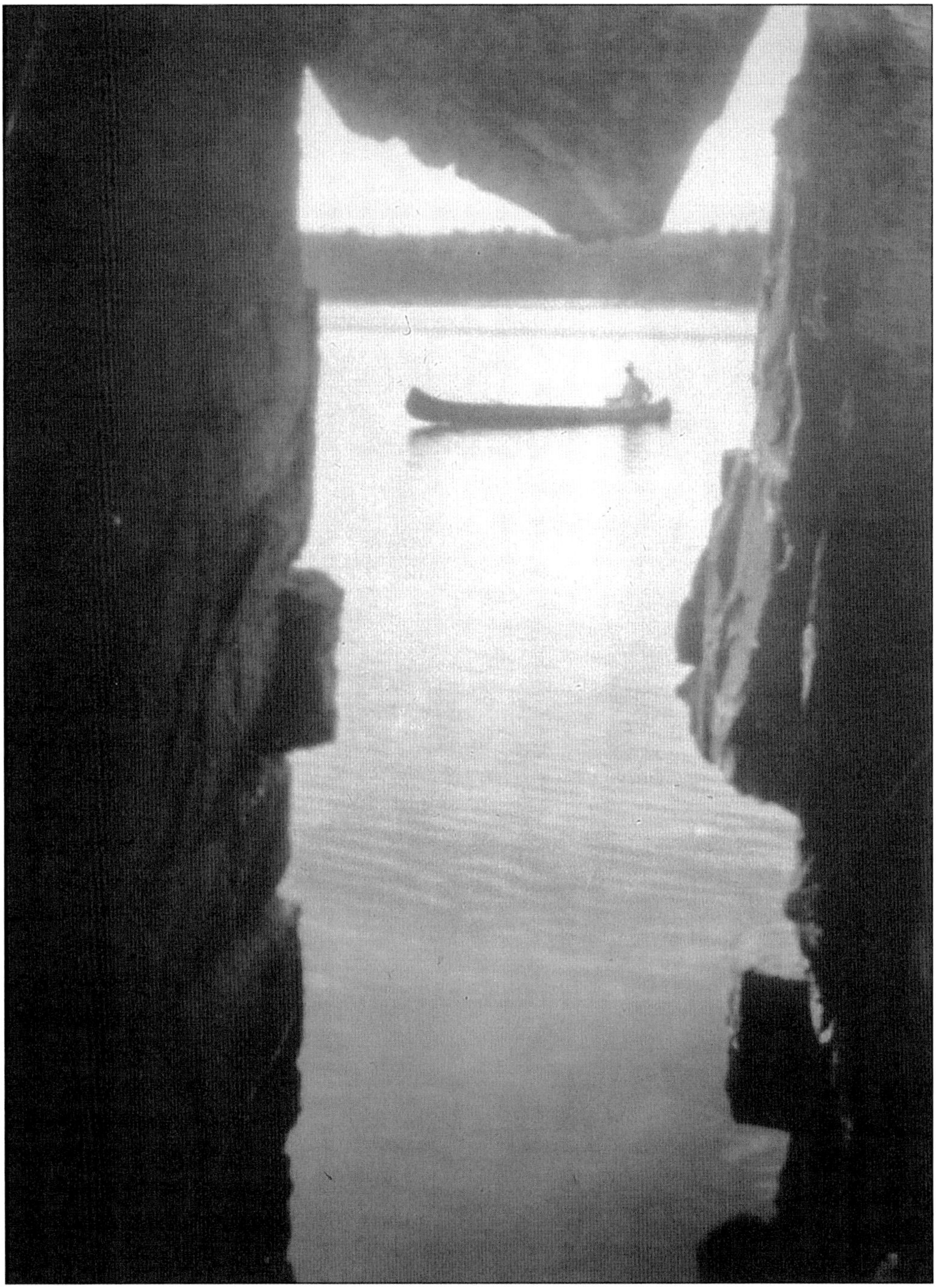

The life of the young Nathaniel Hawthorne was spent in Raymondtown exploring this cave under the rock of the "Images" on the shore of Great Sebago Pond. As a boy, he carved his name in the cave, now known as "Hawthorne's Cave." Nathaniel Hawthorne spent much of his time here as a boy from 1813 to 1825. In his diary, he wrote, "These were the freest and happiest days of his life." He grew up to become one of the nation's best-known novelists of the 19th century.

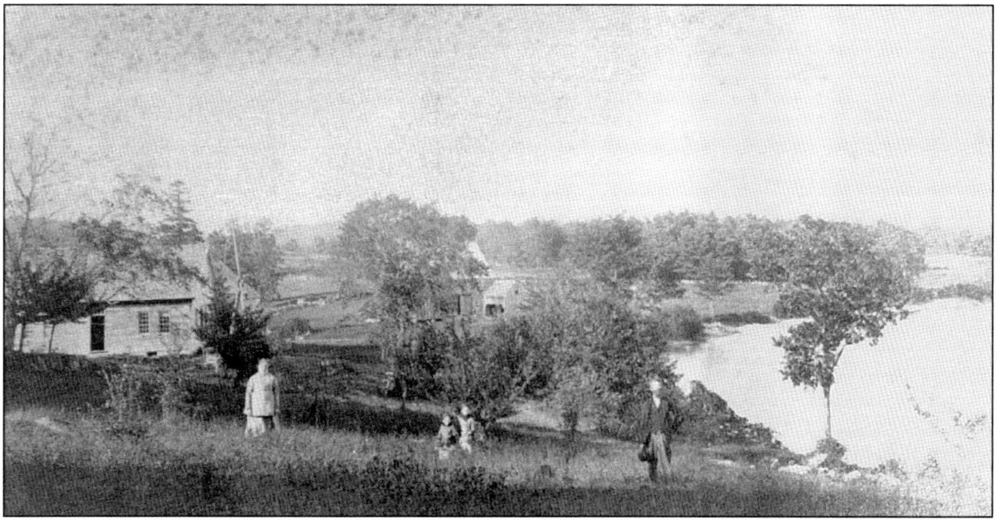

This is the home of Jacob S. Watkins, who settled in Raymondtown in 1810. He received his 100 acres through the king's grant of William Raymont through the Beverly proprietors. Watkins built his home on the shores of Thomas Pond in South Casco where he and his wife, Maria (Wheelwright), raised 14 children. Descendants of Jacob and Maria Watkins live on this land to this day.

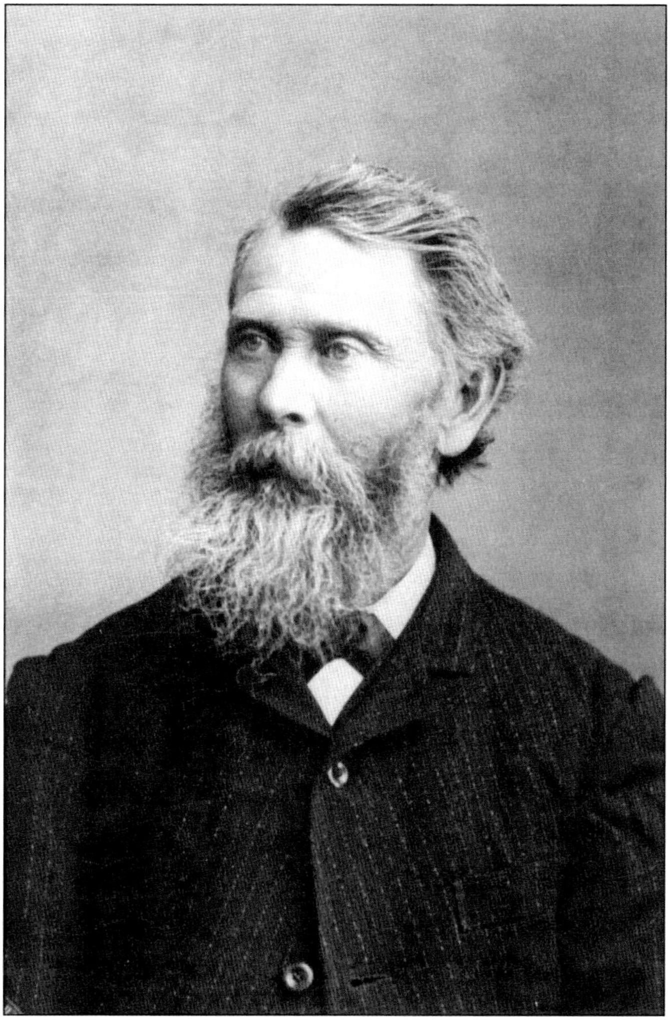

Jacob S. Watkins was born in 1783 and lived on the shores of Thomas Pond on Quaker Ridge in South Casco. He farmed the land and was a brick maker. He was also a cobbler, making the family footwear; his cobbler's bench is still in the family's possession today. Jacob had his brickyard on the pond formed by Dingley Brook at the outlet of Thomas Pond. Nathaniel Hawthorne writes of sitting on his favorite rock, fishing and watching Jacob making bricks.

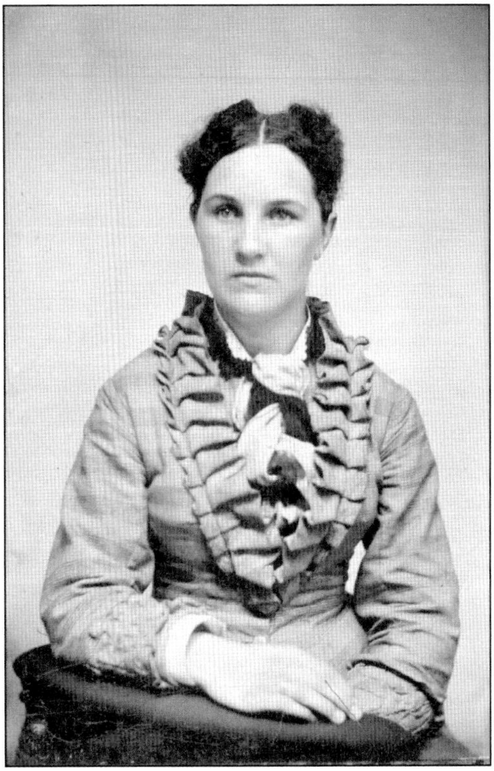

Maria Wheelwright Watkins was born in 1806 and came to Raymondtown in 1810 with her husband Jacob. They lived on the shores of Thomas Pond on Quaker Ridge Road. Together, they raised 14 children, and many of her sons and grandsons have served in various capacities in the town of Casco, including selectman, tax collector, and superintendent of schools. Well over 100 descendants of Jacob and Maria Watkins still live in Casco today.

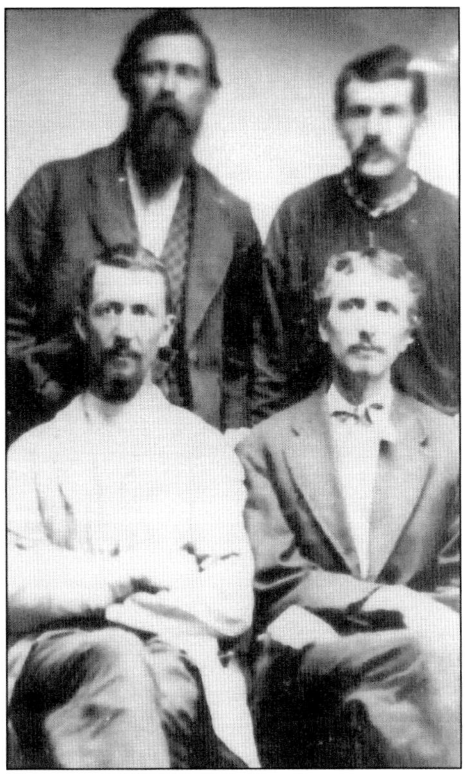

Shown here are two sons and two grandsons of Jacob and Maria Watkins. Standing on the left is Orin, who at one time worked on the Oxford and Cumberland Canal running a canal boat. Standing on the right is George, and two of his sons, Bill (left) and Winfield, are sitting. All of the Watkins children were well liked and respected in the town of Casco.

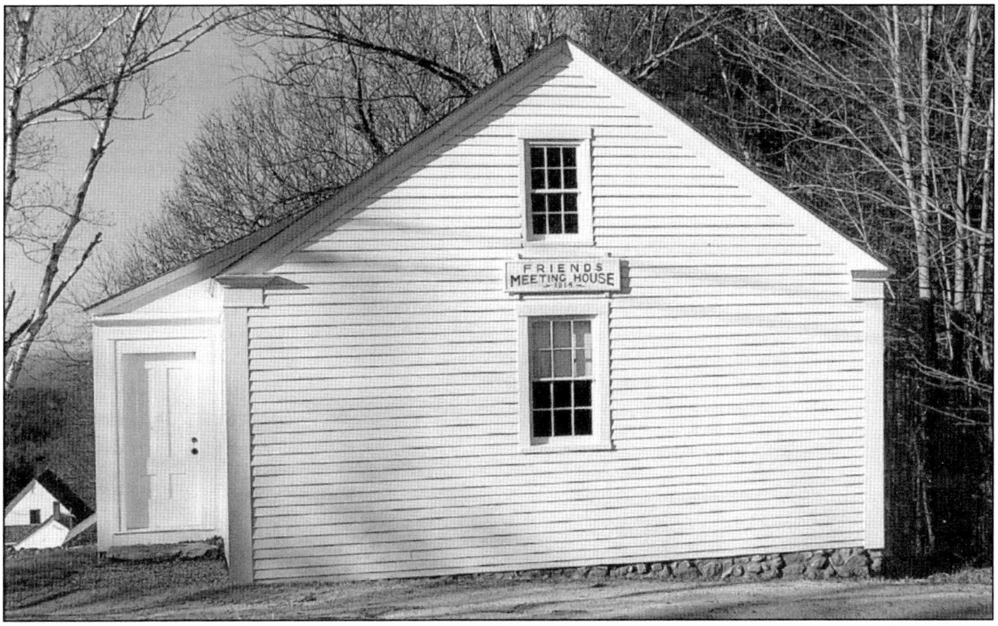

Built in 1814 and listed on the National Register of Historic Places in September 1975, the Friends Meetinghouse was built by Lewis Gay and other Quakers who had come from Windham and settled on Quaker Ridge. Monthly meetings were held at the home of Daniel Cook Jr. before the meetinghouse was built. The building was regularly used for Quaker meetings until the 1920s. The first Quaker family on Quaker Ridge was that of Obadiah Gould. The community grew steadily with the addition of families from Windham with names such as Cook and Hall.

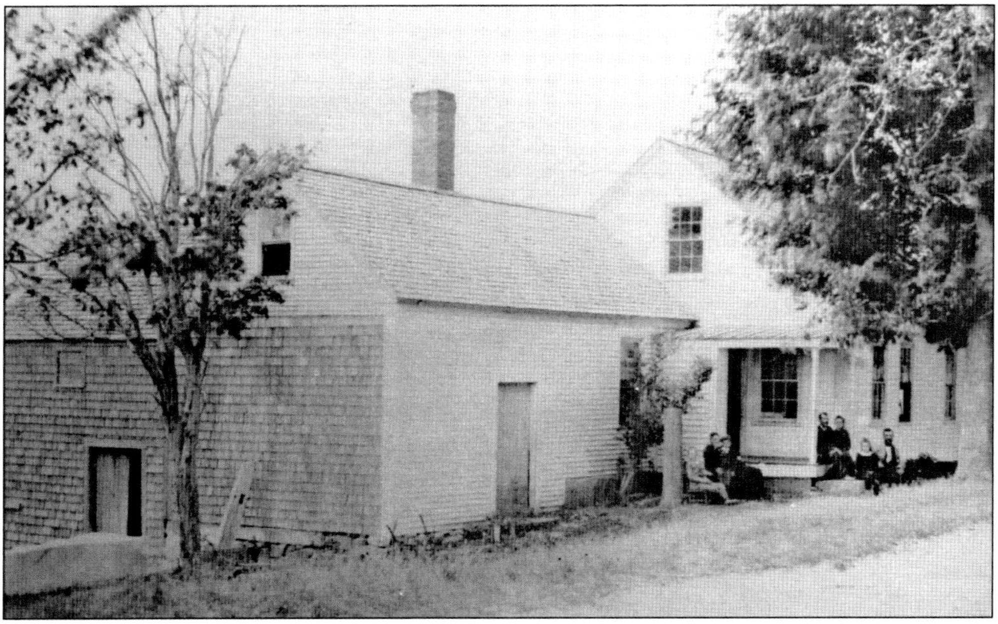

In April 1790, Elijah Cook received from George Piece, the land agent in Otisfield, a deed to lot 20 in the 7th range. From Elijah, his twin sister, Mary, and her husband, Obadiah Gould, purchased a part of the land, and in 1801, they moved from Windham, becoming the first settlers on Quaker Ridge.

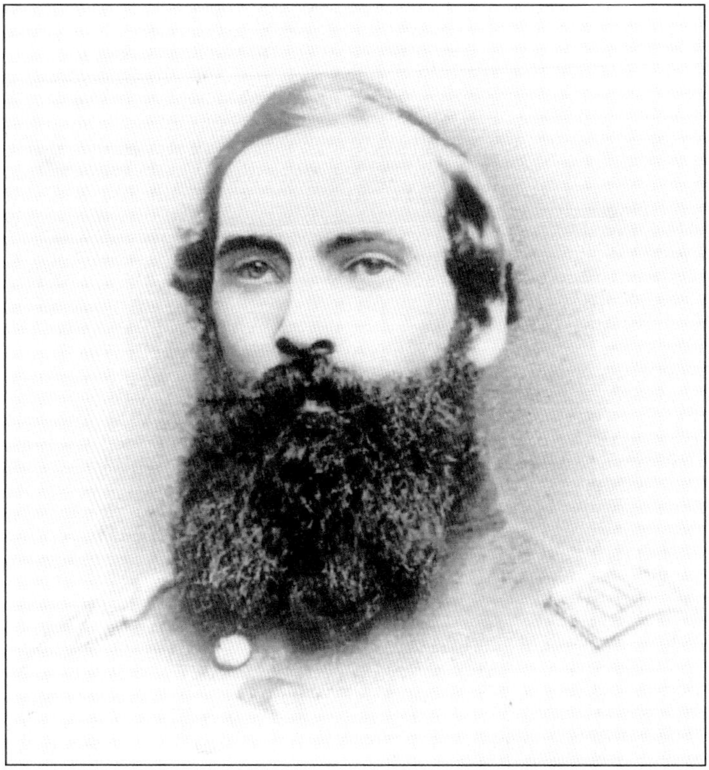

Burbank Spiller (1835–1863), of East Raymond, was a schoolteacher and young widower with a baby daughter when the Civil War began. He was one of two dozen local men who joined the 5th Regiment Maine Volunteer Infantry, one of the earliest formed in the state. The 5th Maine mustered into service on June 24, 1861. By January of the next year, Burbank had been promoted to captain. He died in battle one month later. The men of the 5th Maine Regiment gave his daughter Lucinda "Lulu" Spiller the title "Daughter of the Regiment" in honor of her father.

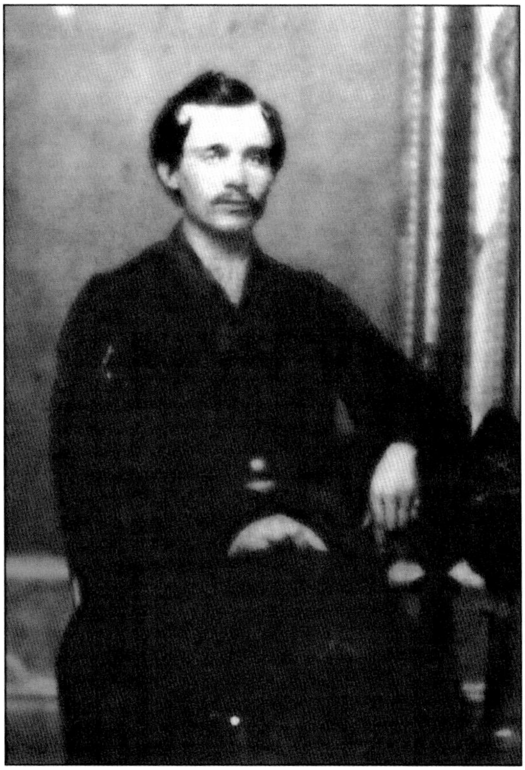

Born in 1842 in Raymond, Alvin E. Plummer was mustered into the 1st District of Columbia Cavalry on February 28, 1864. From January to March, eight companies of the 1st DC were organized in Augusta and ordered to report to Norfolk, Virginia, for special services to the Department of War. Alvin was taken prisoner at Sycamore Church on September 16, 1864, in an incident known as the "Beefsteak Raid," when more than 2,000 cattle and 300 Union soldiers were captured by the Confederate army.

The bloodiest day of the Civil War occurred with the Battle of Antietam in mid-September 1862, and as a result, there was a surge of patriotism in the towns of Raymond and Casco. About 44 men mustered into the 25th Maine Infantry, including Jeremiah Tripp Jr. (born 1830) for a term of nine months. He re-enlisted as a substitute volunteer for a draftee who lived in the neighboring town of Poland. He died March 25, 1865, from wounds he received at the Battle of Ford Steadman in Virginia.

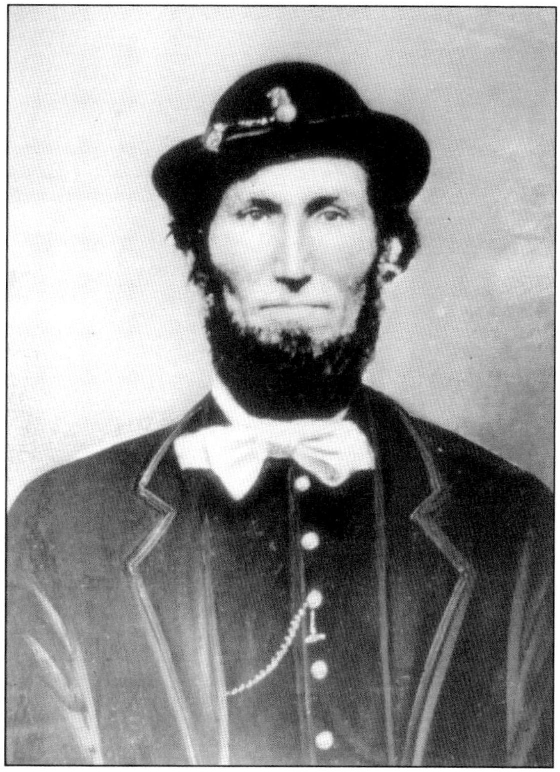

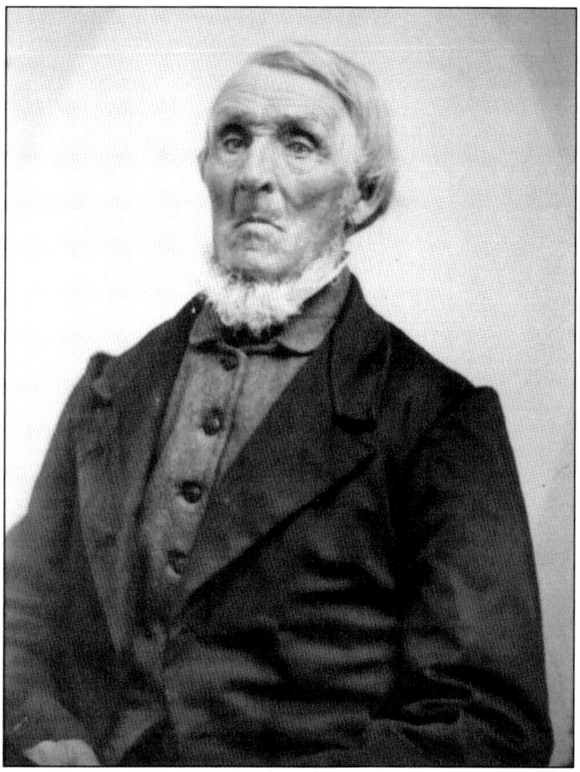

Richard Cook was born in 1828 to Richard and Mary (Mayberry) Cook. Richard married Martha Leach. They lived in Cooks Mills where he, along with his sons, ran a spool strip mill. He was also the postmaster of the Cooks Mills Post Office, which was located in part of his home.

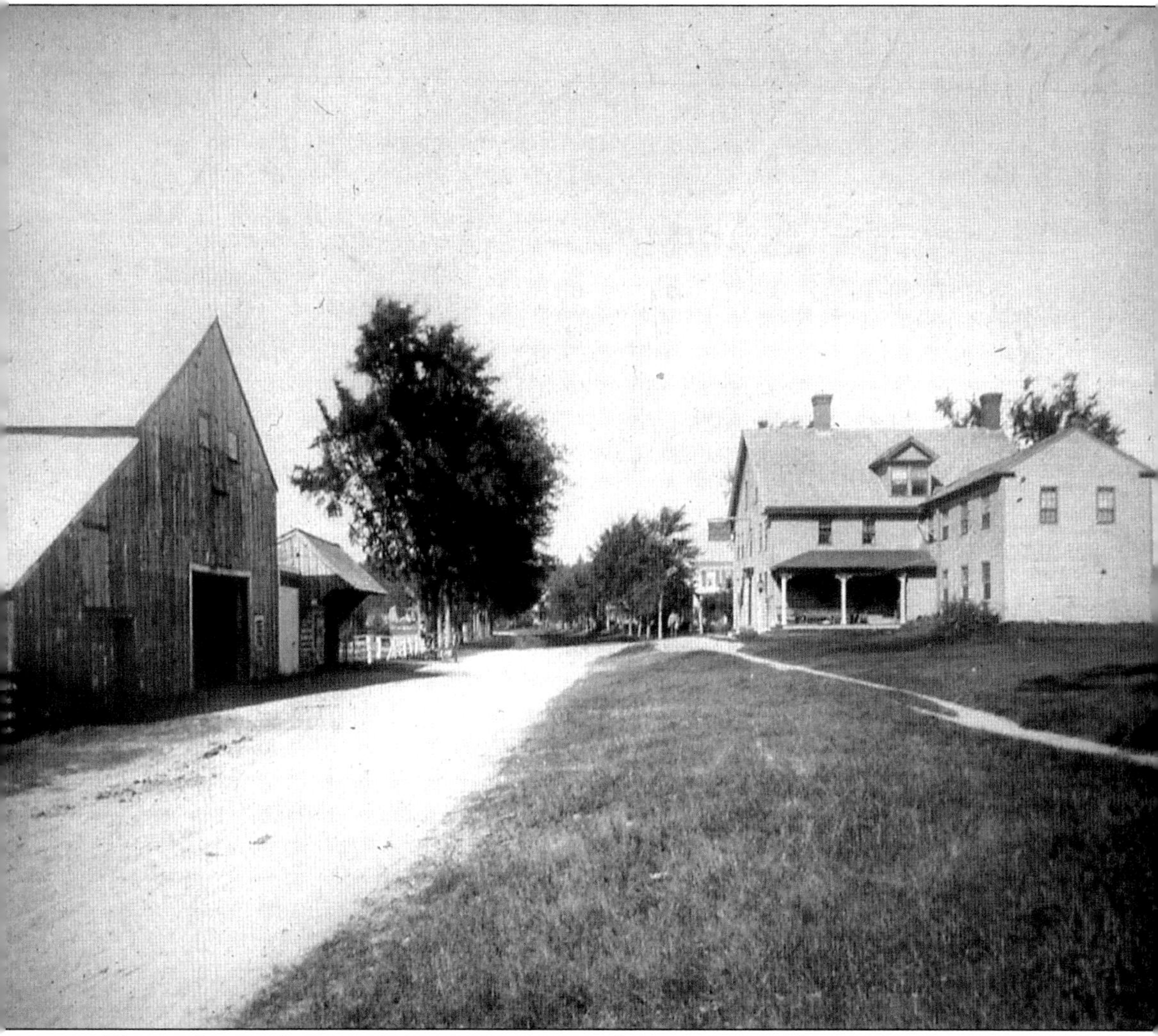

Eli Longley was born in 1762 in Bolton, Massachusetts. In 1816, he was living in Waterford, Maine. That year was exceptionally cold and came to be known as "1800 and froze to death." It was said that every month of that year there was either snow or a frost. In 1818 Longley settled in Raymondtown, where he built the Lafayette House Hotel and a tavern, barn, and store. In this picture the hotel is on the right and Longley's barn is on the left. The first town meeting in Raymondtown was in 1803 and was held for several years thereafter in Samuel Dingley's barn, in what is now South Casco. After Longley finished his new barn in Raymond Village around 1820, town meetings were held there. It was understood that Raymond Village was a more central location than South Casco, so the town meetings were held there for the next 30 years.

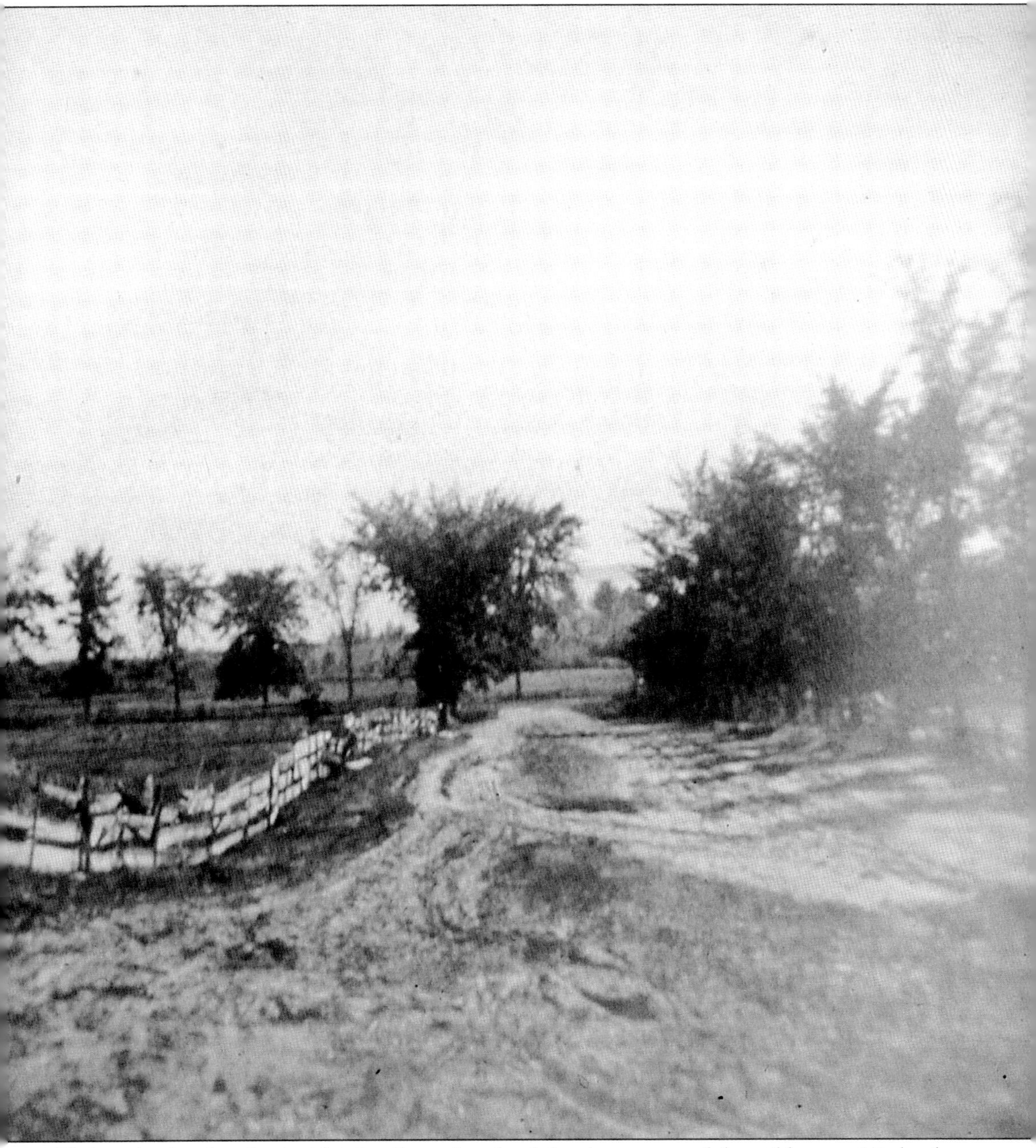

Eli Longley lived and raised his family on farmland that he cut out of the wilderness. His land was to become a considerable section of the Meadow Road, now Route 121. Longley was a man with a vision for the prosperity of his neighbors and the future of Raymondtown. He is buried in the Longley Cemetery in Raymond.

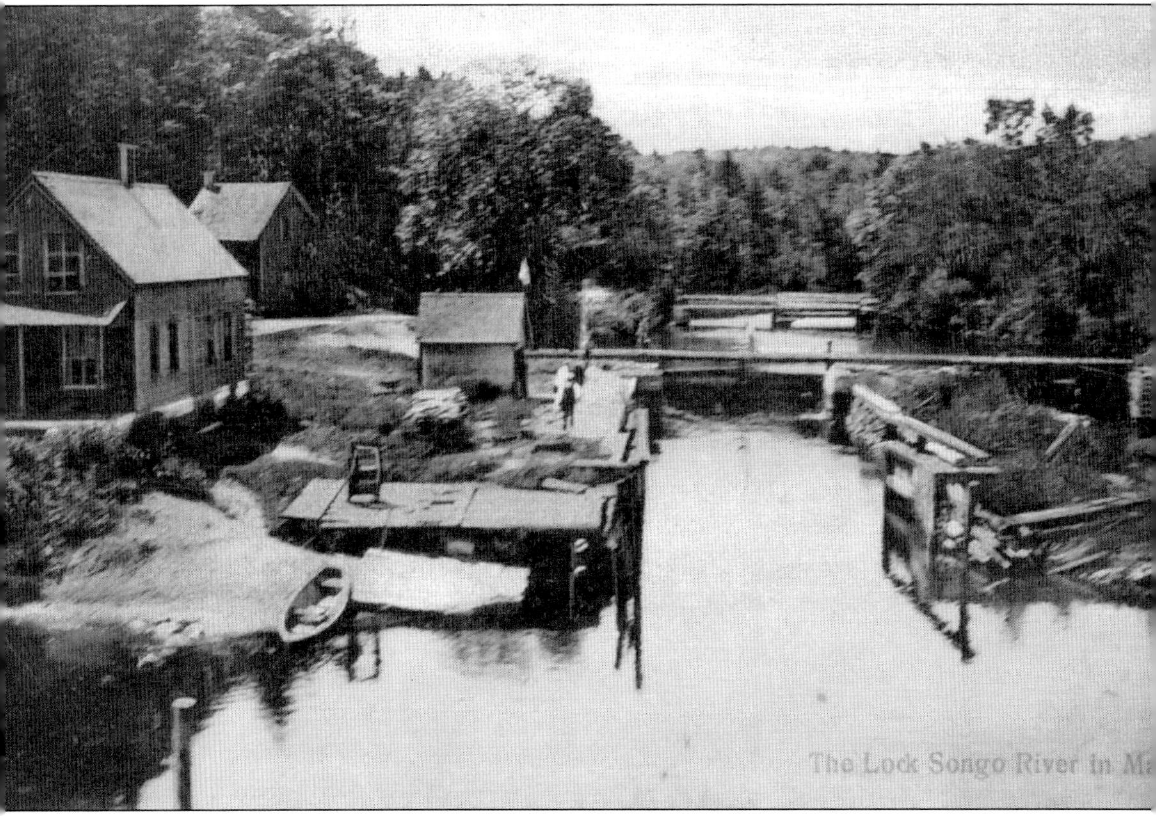

Songo Locks was at one time within the boundaries of Raymondtown, but now it is located in Naples. However, Songo Locks has always had close ties to Raymond and Casco because of the Cumberland and Oxford Canal operations being the main means of transportation of goods. Building on the locks was begun in 1828 and completed in 1830 at a cost of $260,000. The 50-mile waterway went from Portland Harbor to the head of Long Lake in Harrison. Essentially unchanged for 180 years, manpower is still the only way of operating the locks.

Two

RAYMOND

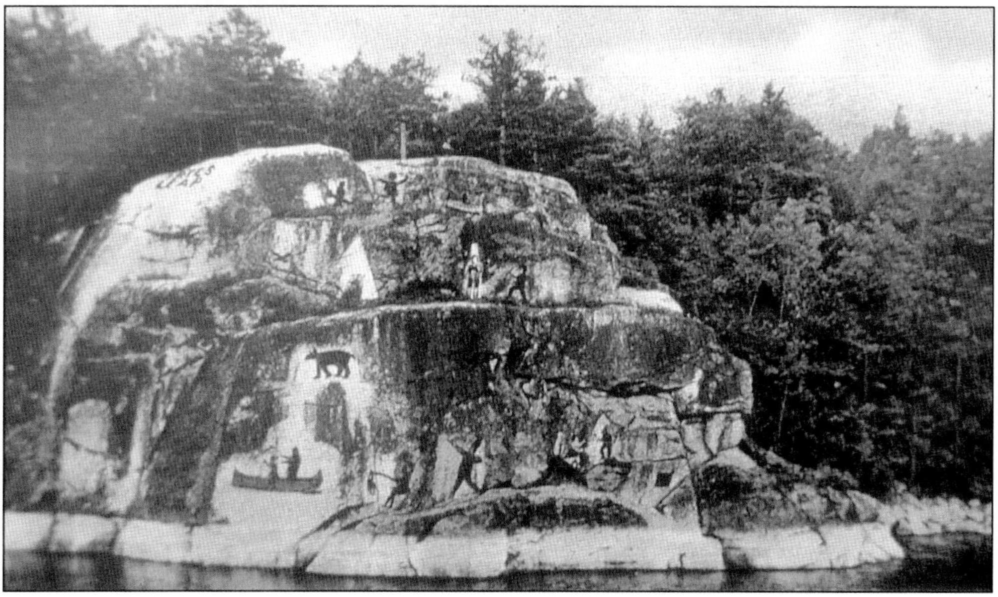

Frye's Leap, or the "Images," is a legendary spot of massive rock in Sebago Lake in what is called the "Gut," which is between Raymond Cape and Frye Island. Pursuing Indians cornered Captain Frye, so he jumped from these rocks and escaped to the island. In later years, as an attraction to passengers on steamboats, the paintings on the rocks were reinforced in bright colors. To further intrigue the tourists coming by steamboat, a man or boy was hired to live in a tent on the top and appear in full regalia and, with blood-curling whoops, fire a gun in the air. Today, the paintings have all but disappeared.

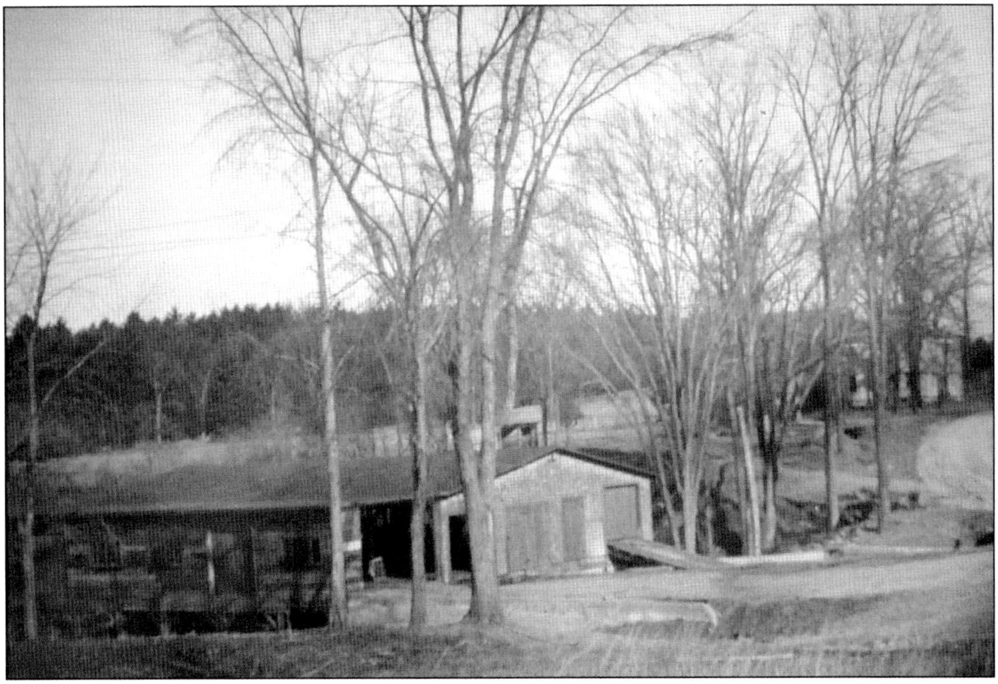

After petitioning for another 100 acres of land, Capt. Joseph Dingley built his home and sawmill on Dingley Brook. Dingley gave his first home to his son Samuel and his wife, Keziah Proctor. Captain Dingley's daughter Sarah married Peter Staples, and they lived about halfway between Captain Dingley and Samuel. Captain Dingley was said to have disliked both choices of mates his children made. After having lost some corn from his corncrib, the captain set a bear trap. One morning, he looked out and, lo and behold, he had trapped the culprit, his son-in-law Peter Staples. Dingley went about his chores and, later in the day, he let Peter go.

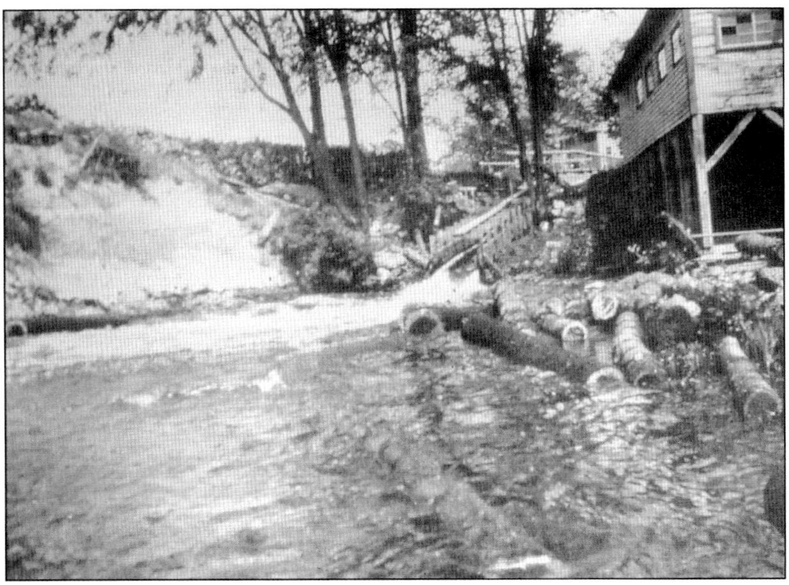

Shown here is the "flume" at Dingley Brook in South Casco. Located on the back side of the mill's building, the flume was made of wood and would have been used to slide the stripped logs down into the brook and from there into Sebago Lake.

On the corner of Main and Mill Streets, before it was Jordan and Eager Store or the post office, was the Skillin Harness Shop owned by Lyndon O. Skillin. Harness shops were small local businesses conducted in, or nearby, the homes of a person with those skills. It looks like there were quite a few patrons waiting to get their business taken care of.

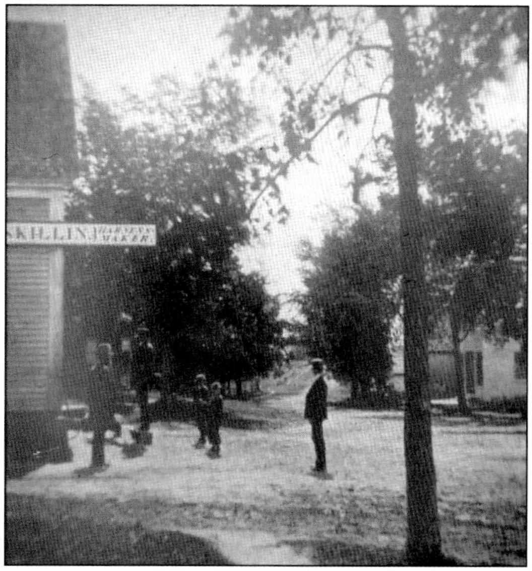

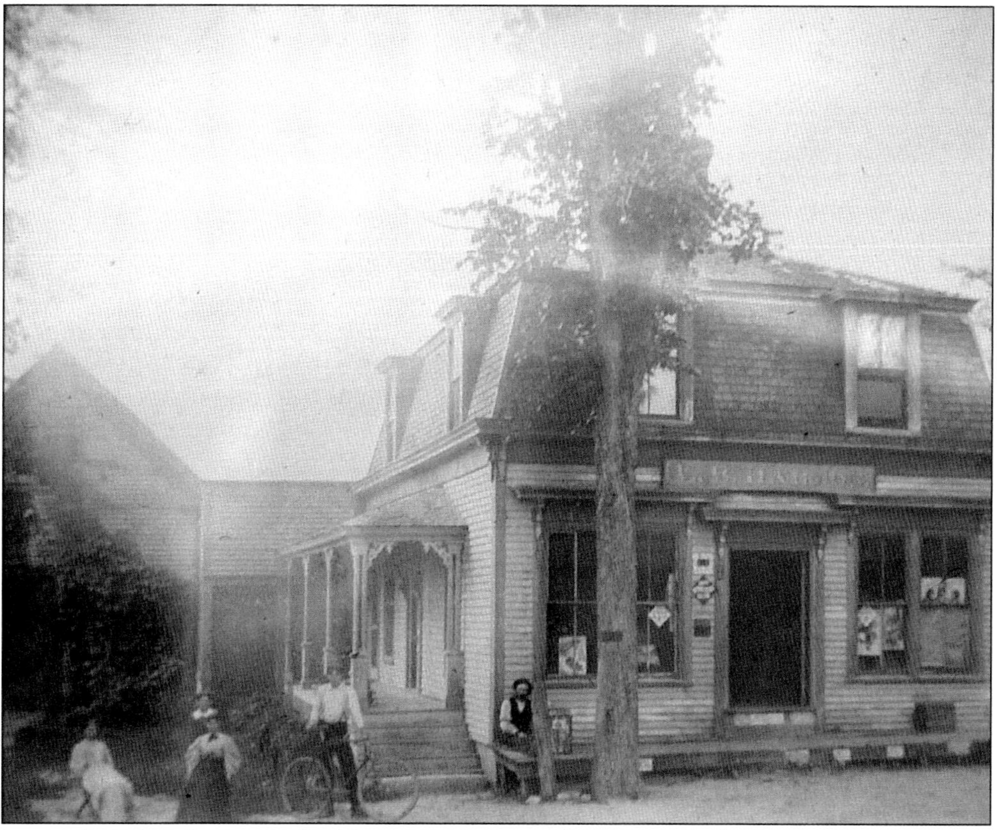

Located on Main Street, this building was at one time known as Marsh's Store, Jordan and Eager Store, and at the time of this picture, the E.B. Harmon Store. This building was an early relay station for the first telephones in Raymond. It had a rack on the side of the building that held large rectangular glass jars with lead plates and sulphuric acid, which were batteries for powering the messages through the wires.

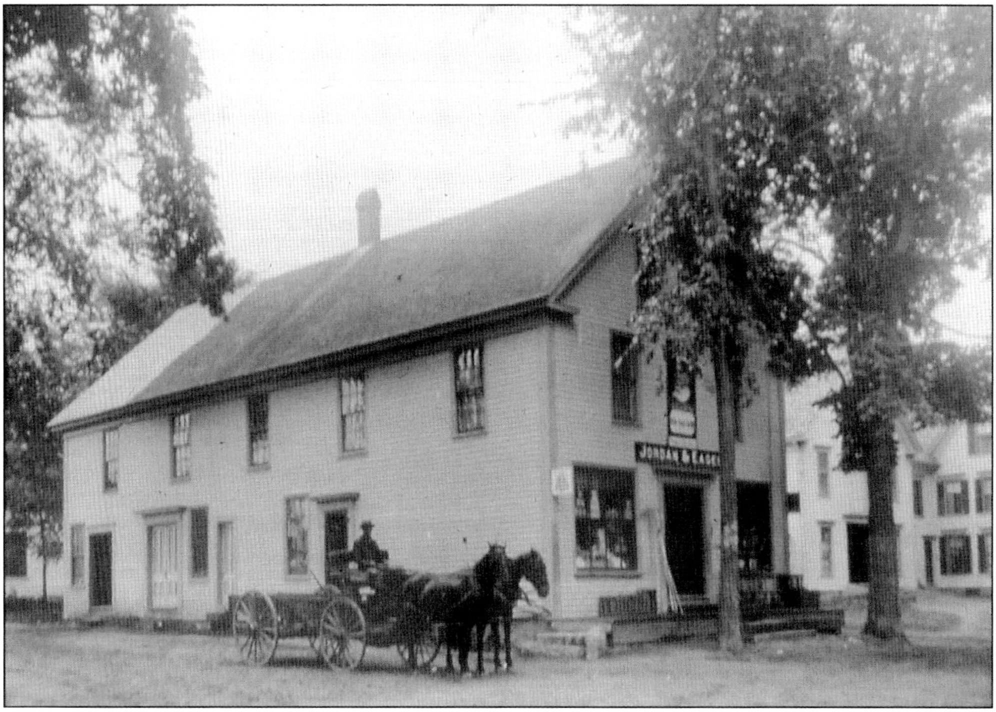

On the corner of Main and Mill Street was the Jordan and Eager Store, with the entrance platform practically in the street. The post office was attached to the side of this building at one time. On the second floor was the Knights of Pythias Lodge Hall. Charles Jordan and his brother-in-law Frank Eager operated it until it burned down in the fire of 1914.

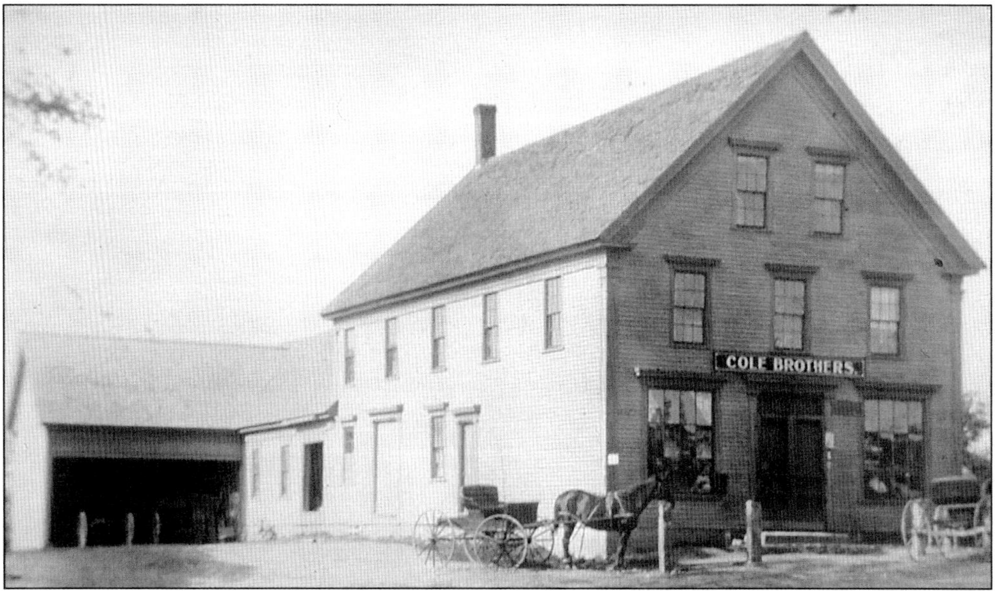

The only store in East Raymond was in the home of H.J. and O.B. Lane, which was in operation in the mid-1860s. Henry was an active participant in town and business affairs. The Cole brothers then had ownership of the store from about 1911 to 1918. The Everett and Alva Clough family purchased it in 1929, and their descendents are still operating it today.

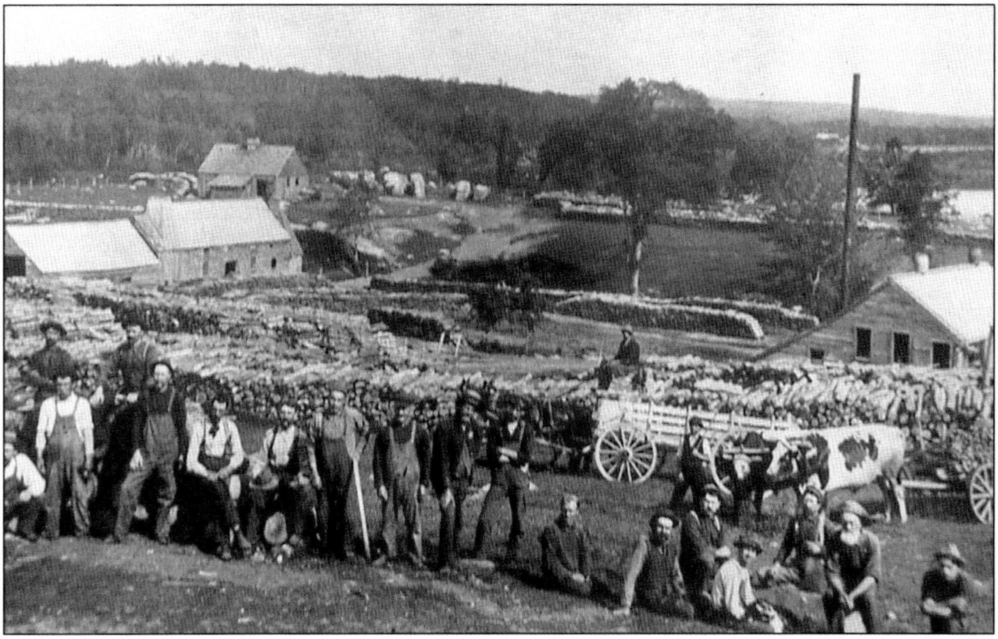

While not in Raymond, the Suckervill Mills were on the Gray line, just off Egypt Road, and gave employment to many Raymond people. With a steam-driven sawmill and a cooper shop, it was quite a complex at the upper end of Little Sebago Lake.

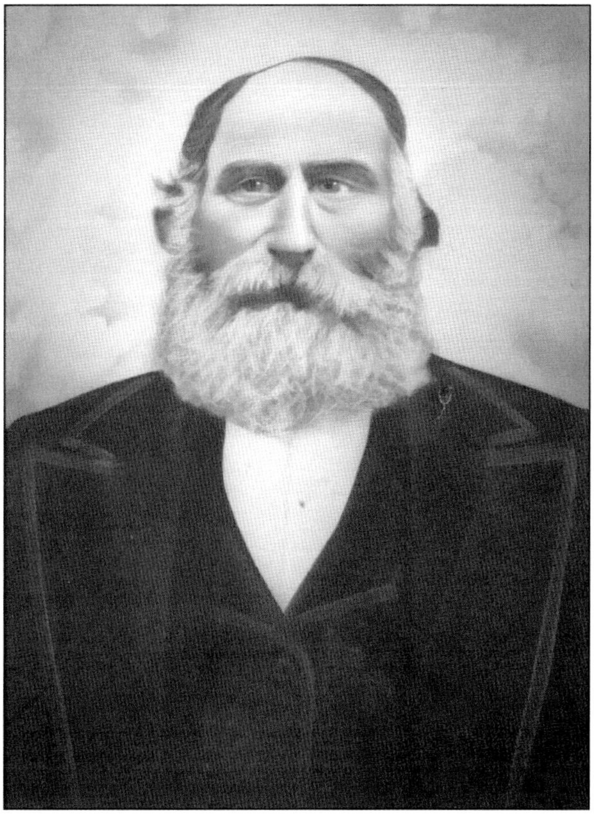

Two miles north of East Raymond, there once was a thriving community, which was called Greenville by the people of Little Rattlesnake Pond (now Raymond Pond). This image shows Elias Bartlett, who operated one of the mills on the outlet. Bartlett's Store, a school, a post office, and a dance hall were also located in this area. There were also several other mills operating in the vicinity.

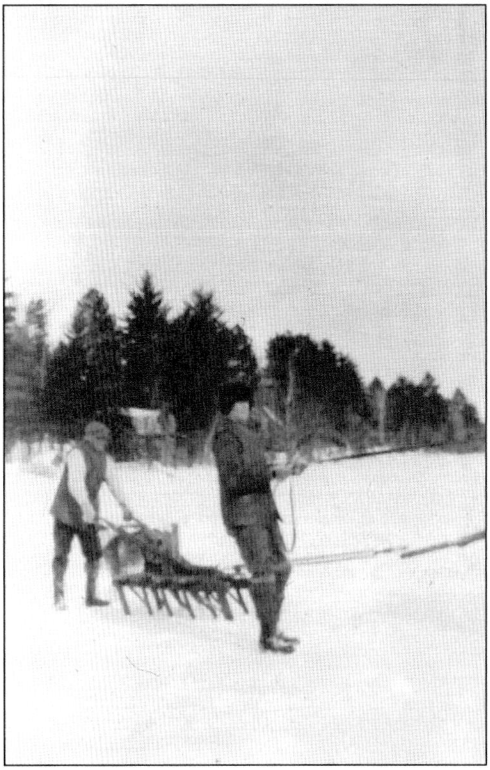

Cutting ice in Raymond and other towns was a big industry in Maine from the 1870s into the 1900s. Once the ice could support the weight, it was repeatedly scraped of snow. When the ice was at least a foot thick, it was scored and cut with big ice saws. The saws were about four feet long with a tapered blade and a handle at one end. This picture shows Irving Hayden cutting ice.

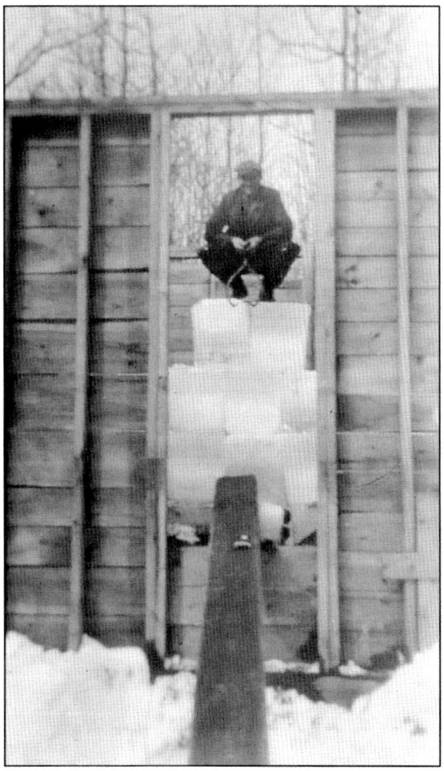

The ice blocks were taken to the icehouse and insulated with 12 or more inches of sawdust. When spring and summer came, the blocks were shipped either in sawdust or hay to markets all over the world. From 1870 to 1890, there were only two years when Maine shipped less than one million tons of ice.

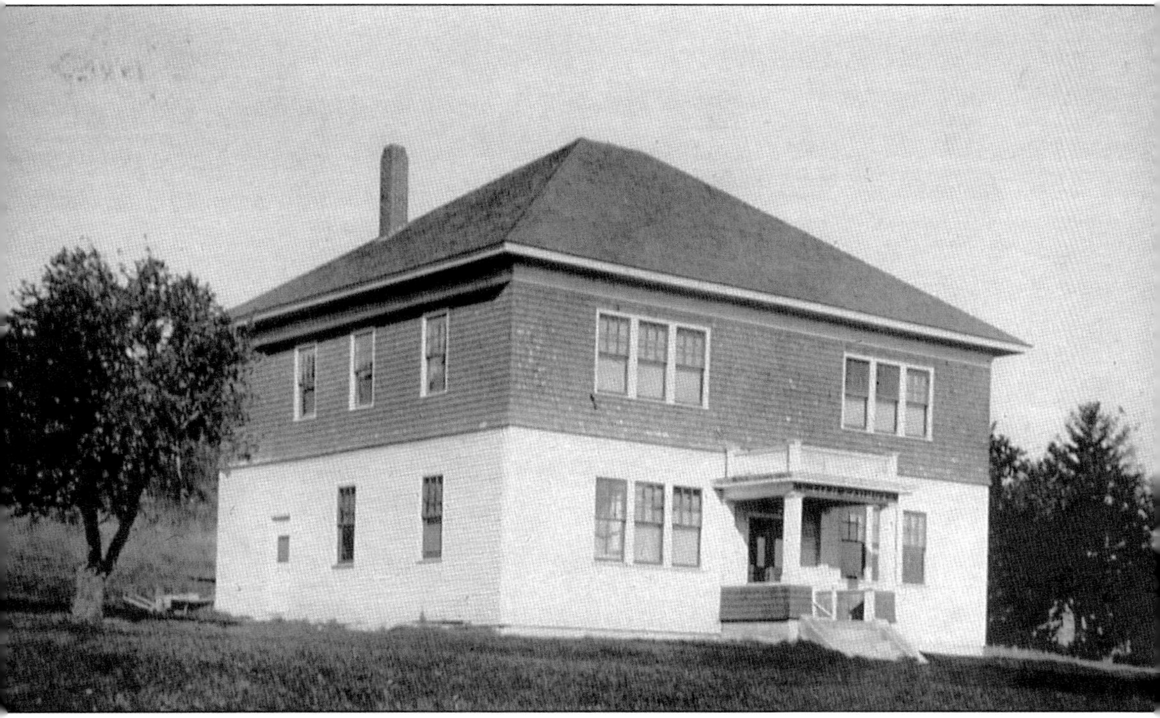

Forhan Hall was a center for civic and social activities and was built by Henry C. Forhan for the benefit and use of the town. The hall had a partial basement, which was used as housing for the Raymond Fire Department. Forhan lived next door and operated the corn shop on what is now called Indian Point, by the Jordan River. Forhan Hall burned about 1940.

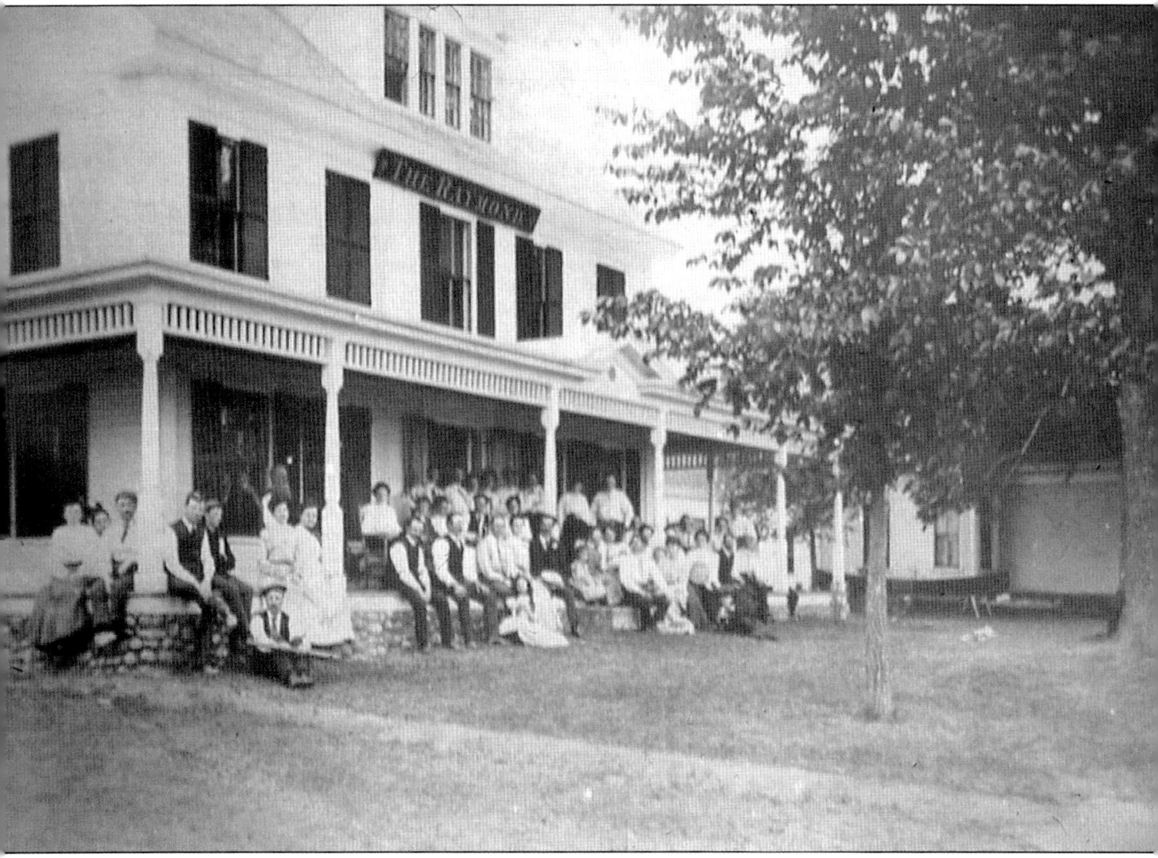

One of the largest and most attractive places for summer guests in Raymond Village was the Elm Tree Inn, situated on the corner of Meadow Road and Main Street. From its original intent, as a dwelling for "Mill" Jesse Plummer, a large ell was added for additional rooms connecting to the barn, which after became a store operated by Vince Clark. It was also used as a summer training and vacation base for a group of opera singers from New York, employees of a musical entrepreneur by the name of Regneas. One of the many changes to the original Jess Plummer place was when it was named "The Raymond" and converted to a popular summer vacation boarding house.

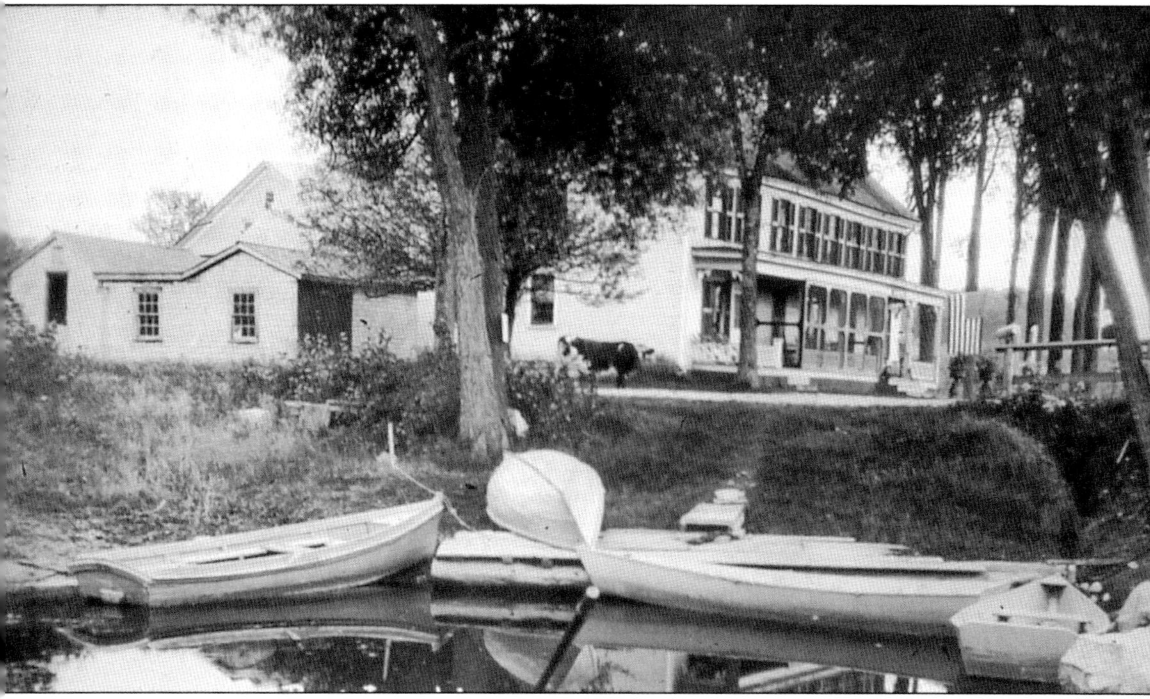

One of the many popular businesses catering to summer vacationers and year-round boarders was the Pleasant View House. Located on the corner of Route 302 and Route 85, at one time it was operated by a Mr. Fulton, who added a general store for the neighborhood. Dr. Lloy, a local dentist, operated it as well as several other places in town. It is now the Good Life Market.

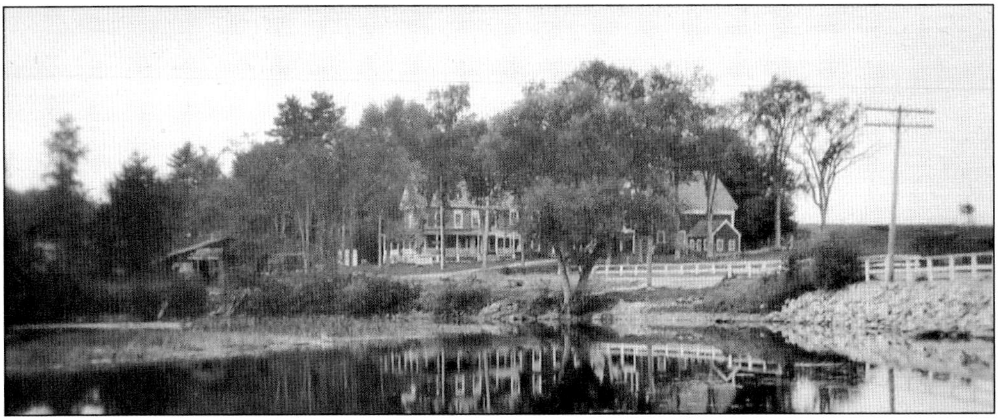

Raymond Inn, known as "Sam Withham's," was a center of activity until it was destroyed by fire. Sam was involved in many things in Raymond. The house was used for social organizations, and the ell of the house was used for dances and entertainment. The home was converted to the summer vacation trade. Withham also had a brickyard across the street from the house.

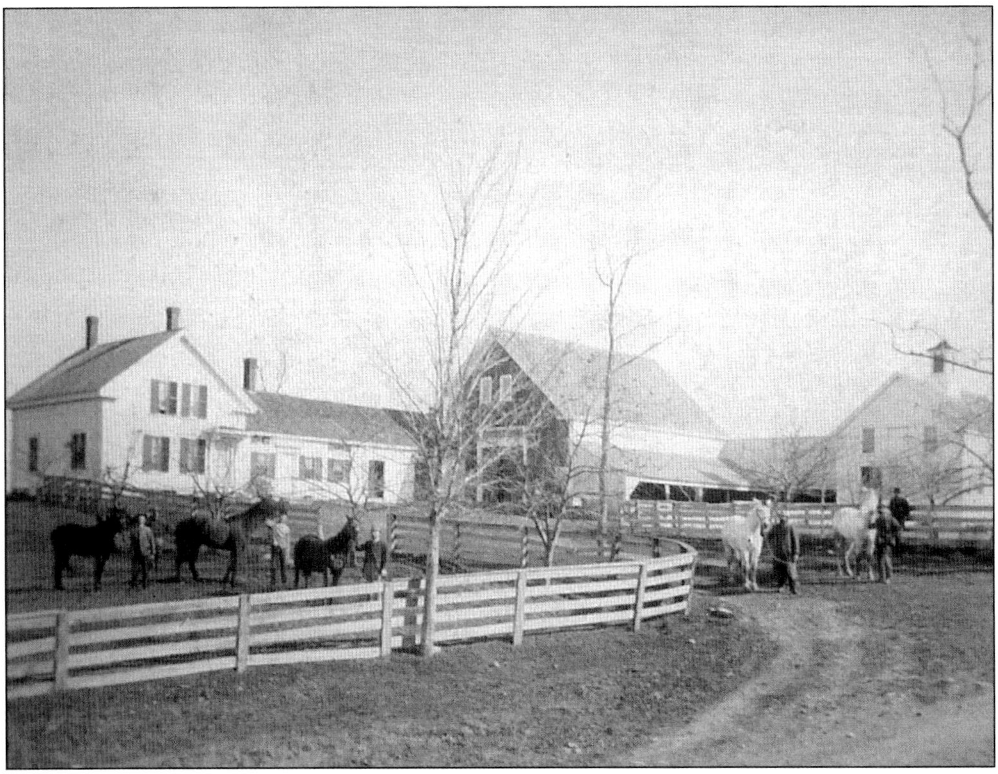

The Wilson brothers, Alfred, Charles, and Gardner, grew up on the family farm located on the corner of the Valley Road and North Raymond Road, where the Ganderbrook Christian Camp now stands. One or more of these brothers went west after the Civil War to make their fortunes and then returned home to carry out their dreams.

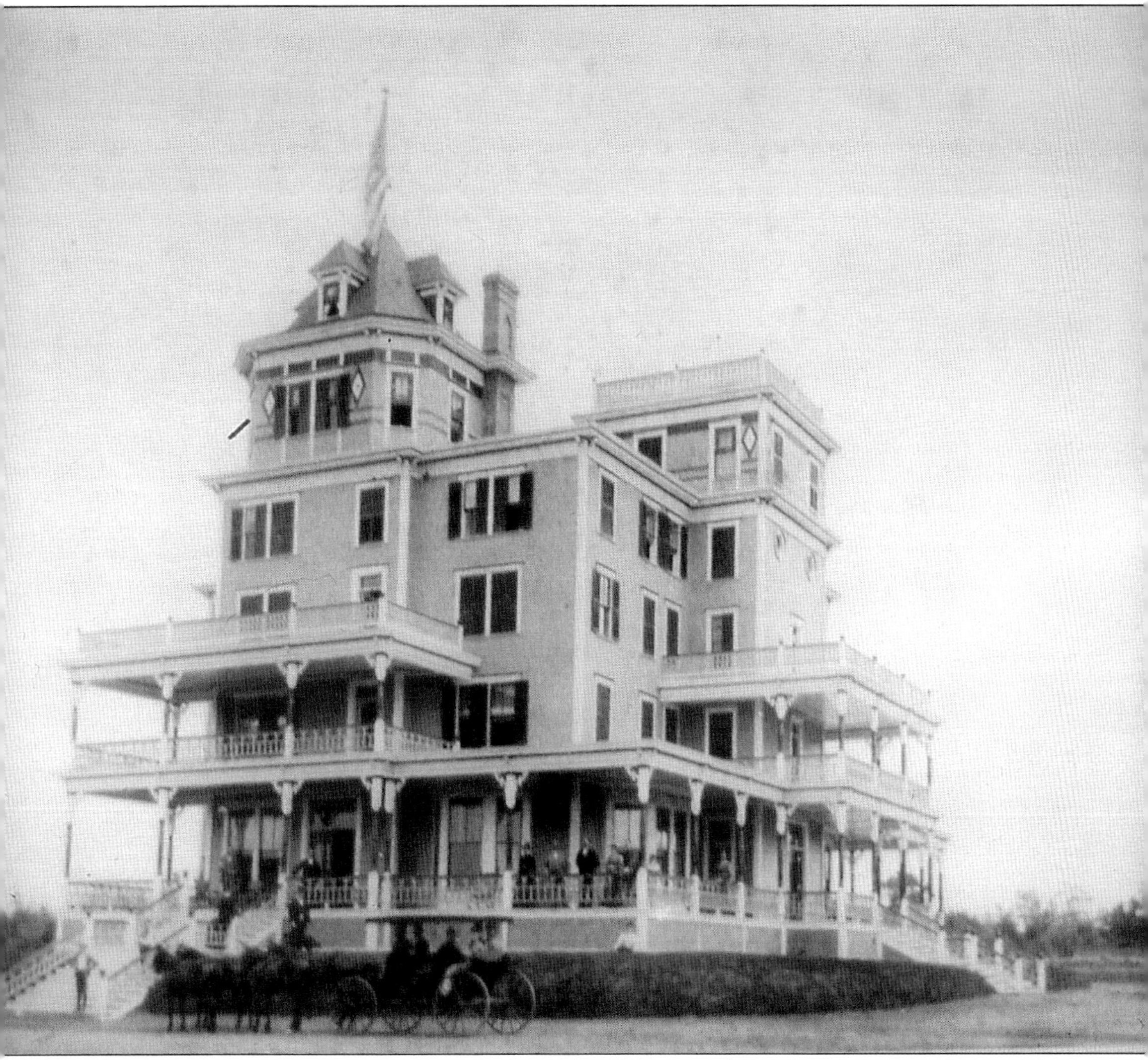

The Wilson Spring Hotel was a massive five-story hotel built on the Wilson brothers' homestead in the 1880s. It was in competition with the Poland Spring House hotel as a year-round resort and bottler of fine spring water. It had all the conveniences of the times—year-round heating, lighting that was provided by gas, and piping for spring water on all the floors. It had limited success and was burned about 1895.

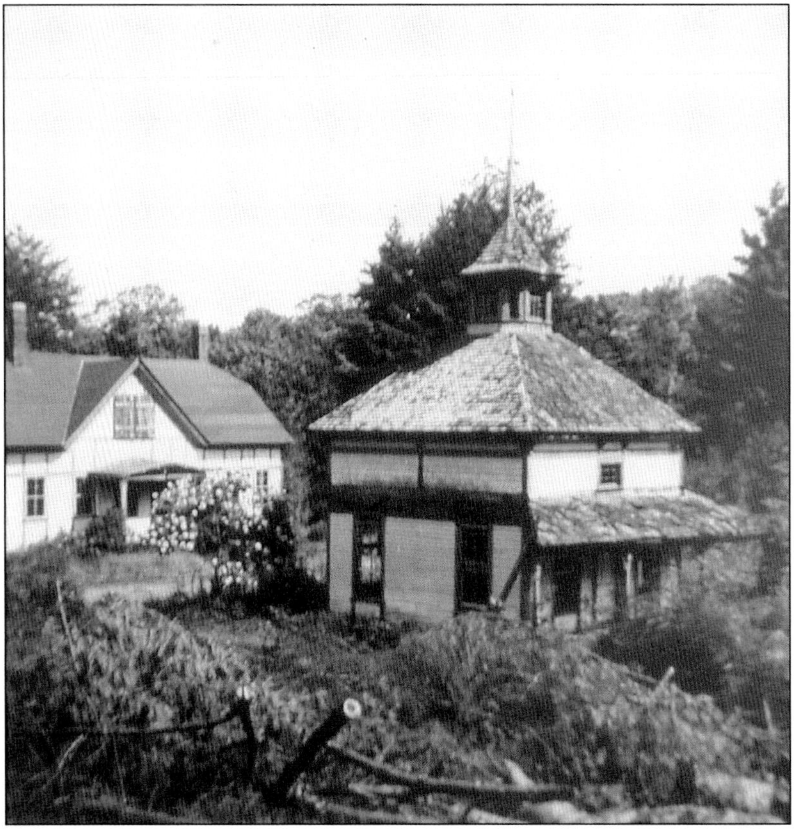

The springhouse of the Wilson Spring Hotel was across the road from the hotel. With its fine spring water from a natural spring, the house was a popular place to get a refreshing drink of pure water. The small panes of glass in the cupola were various shades of color that reflected inside when the sun came out.

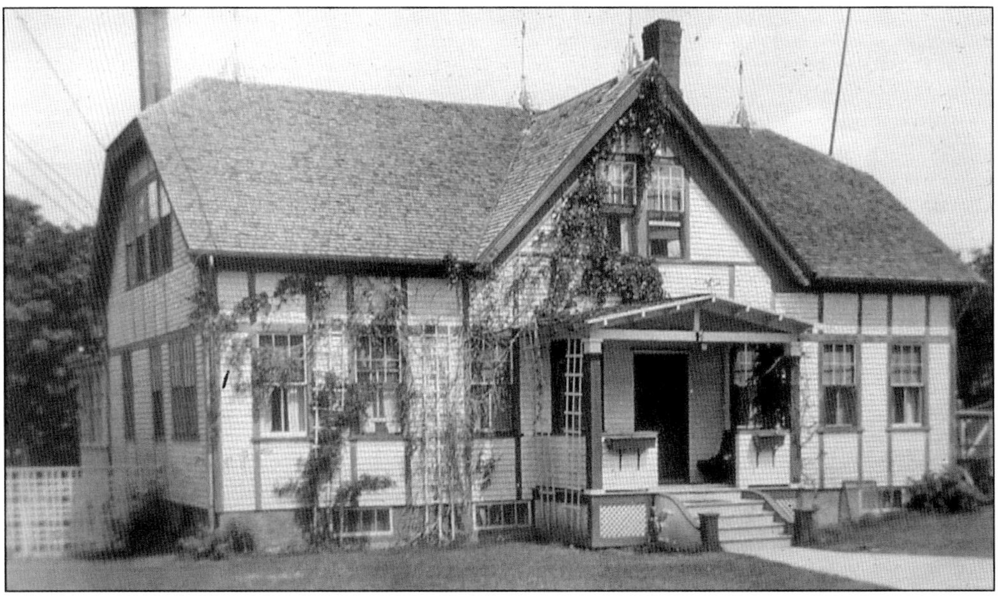

The bottling plant of the Wilson Spring Hotel was built with all the latest equipment manufactured in Belgium, and the best operators were brought from England. Standard drinks of the day, ginger ale, sarsaparilla, and root beer, were more flavorful due to the superior spring water. The water was bottled and shipped to cities across the country where pure water was at a premium.

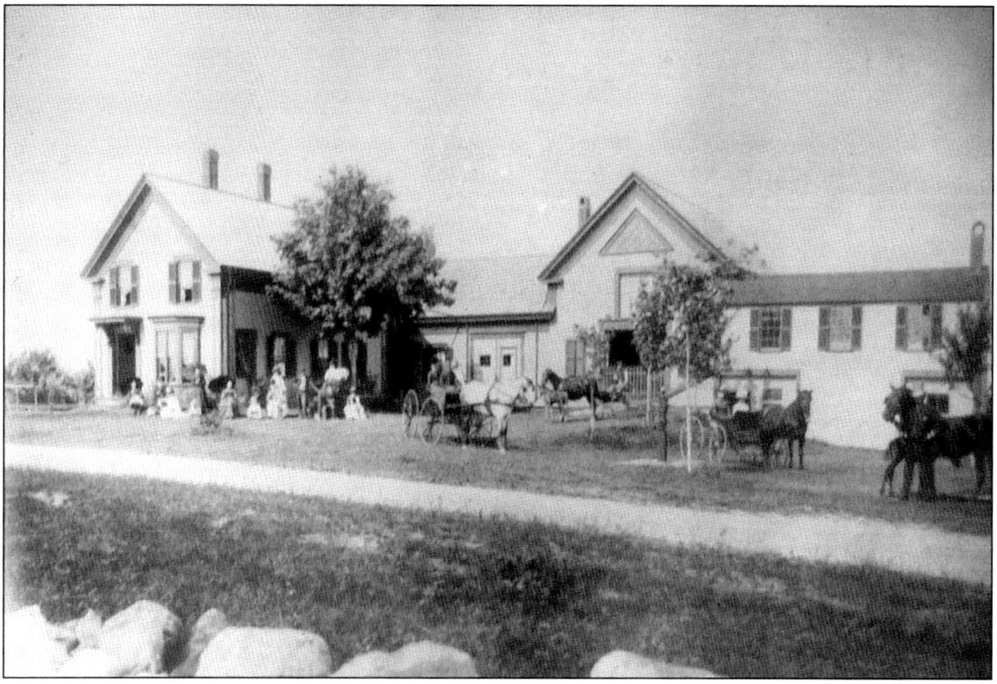

The Raymond Spring House in North Raymond was the residence of the Charles E. and Hatty Small family until the 1880s, when they started taking in boarders and promoting their spring water. A small springhouse was built at a source about 300 feet behind the homestead. They operated the inn and sold spring water for about 20 years until 1911, when the inn was closed.

In the 1920s, there was a progressive movement in the nation concerned with the physical condition of children. The newly formed Cumberland County Public Health Association would have a nurse travel to different towns, checking the height, weight, and overall physical condition of the children. This picture was taken at the East Raymond School.

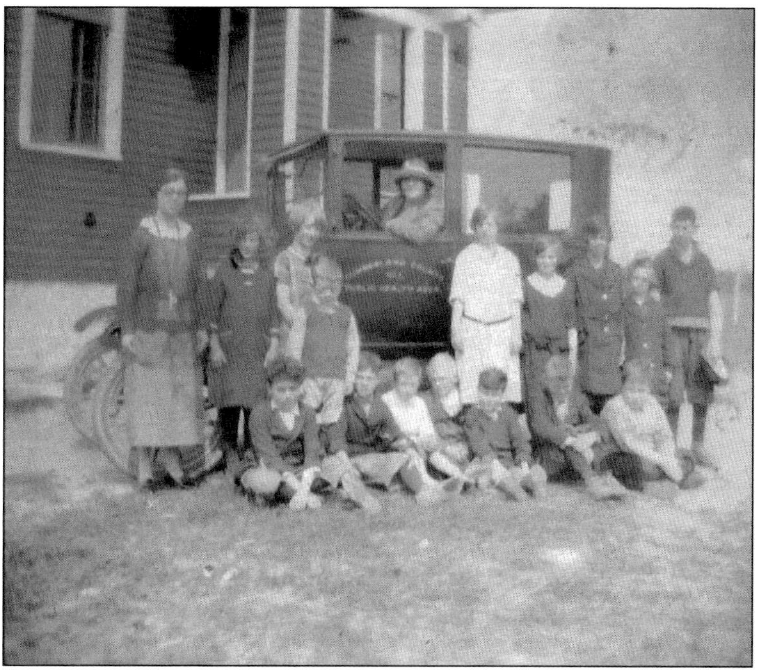

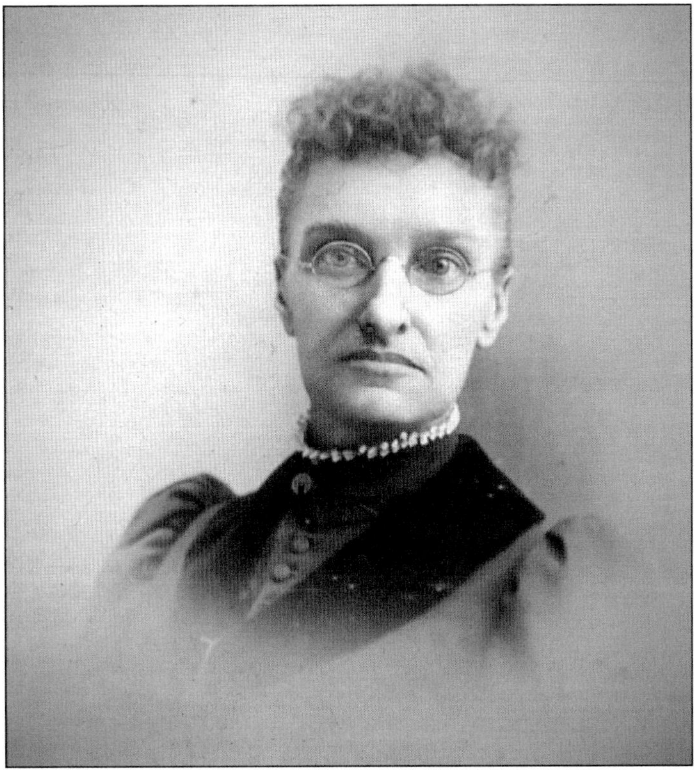

Ellen Jane Small was born November 12, 1841, in Raymond. She was the daughter of George J. Small and Eleanor B. (Patten) Small. Ellen Small gave money for the East Raymond School to be built. The East Raymond School was erected and presented to the town by her in early 1908, and then opened on December 2, 1908. Honorable Payson Smith, the state superintendent of schools, came to Raymond to speak at the dedication of the new school.

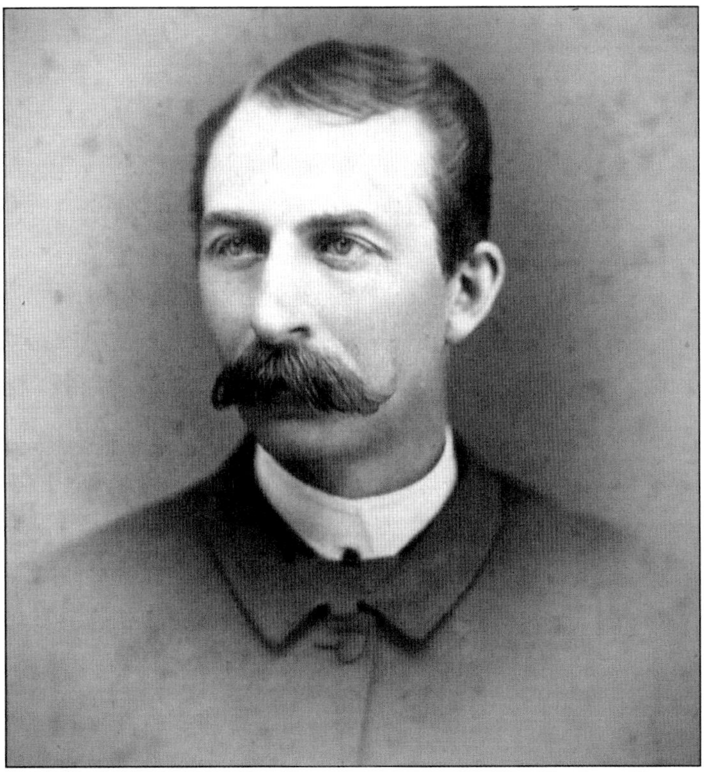

Born in 1851, Isaac D. Jordan was a highly intelligent man and a well-respected citizen of Raymond. He taught school for a number of winters and worked on the family farm during the summer. The 225-acre farm was a showplace under his care, with well-kept fences, meadows, and orchids. He contributed funds for the Jordan Small School, which was named after him and Ellen Jane Small and erected in 1925.

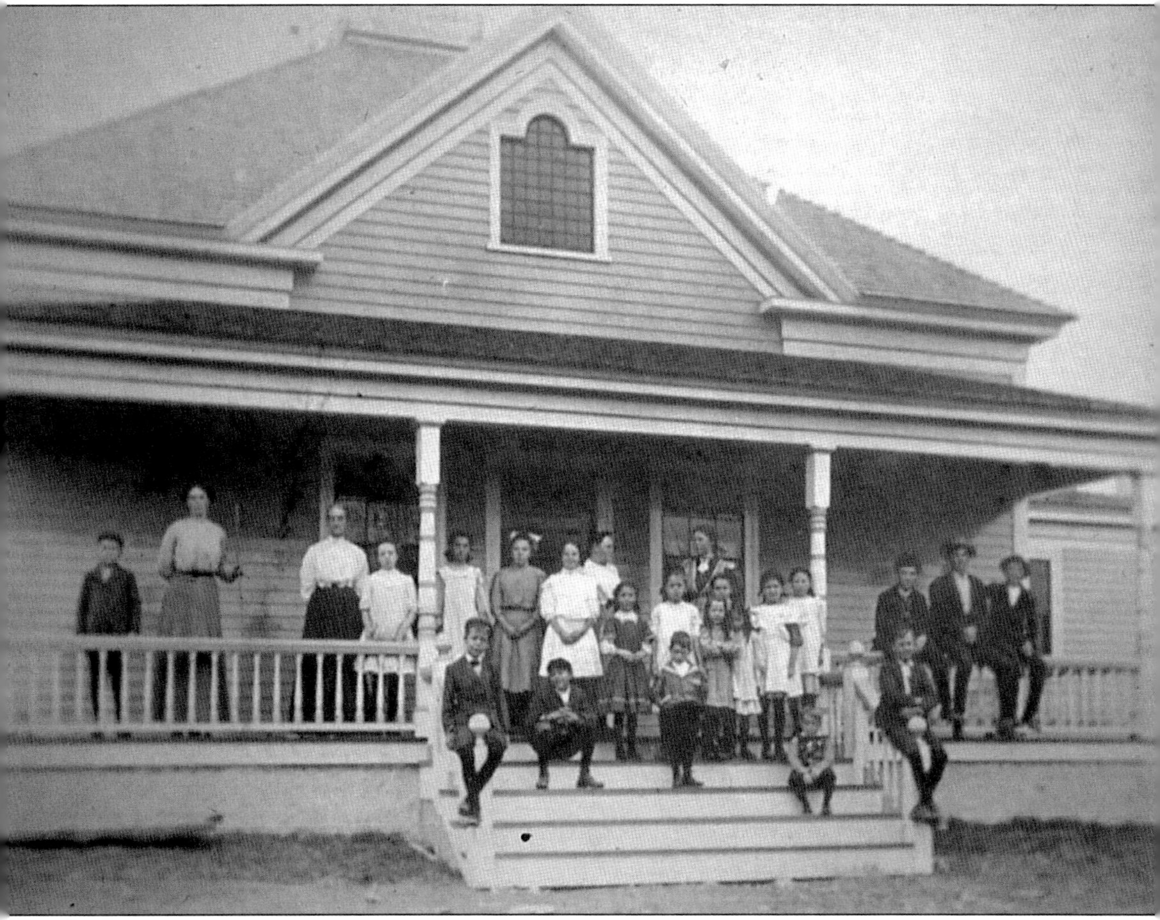

The East Raymond Schoolhouse underwent many changes before it became the Raymond Town Hall. The porch and gable were removed, the entrance was turned toward Route 85, a new entryway was put in facing the parking lot, and the office was enlarged. The multi-pane window in the gable was stored in the attic for a number of years until it was given to the Casco Raymond Historical Society on loan in 2010.

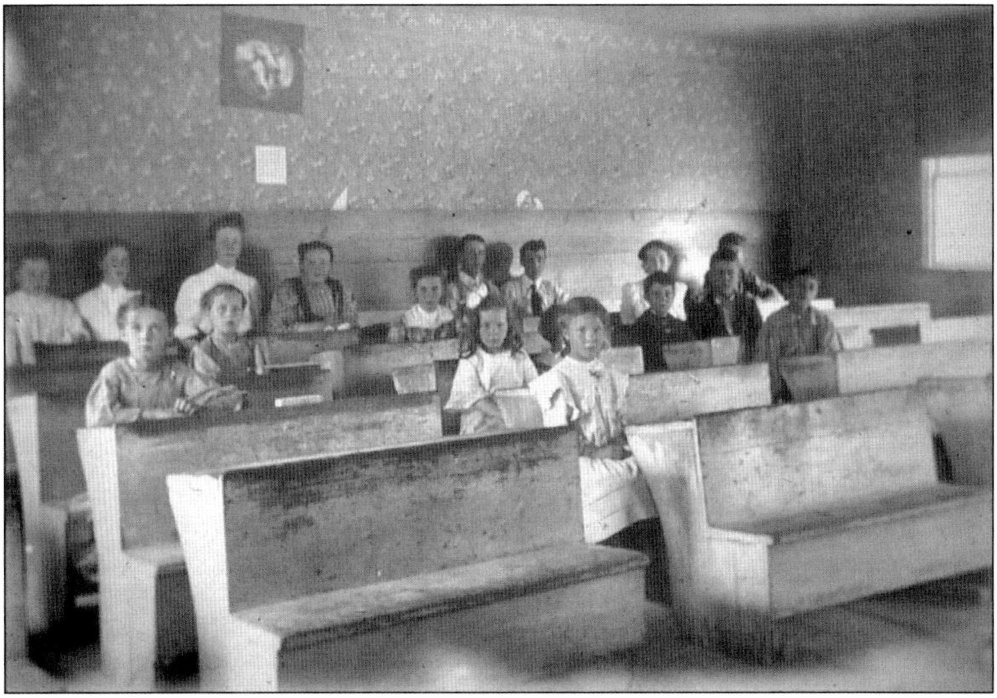

Schoolhouses consisted of a single room—large enough to hold 50 students who would be in the first through eighth grades. Inside the East Raymond School, the desks were made from wood. There was usually no lighting, and the heat would be from a wood stove, which one of the older students would maintain. With only eight- to ten-week sessions in the winter and summer, they were often ended earlier if there was no money to pay the teacher.

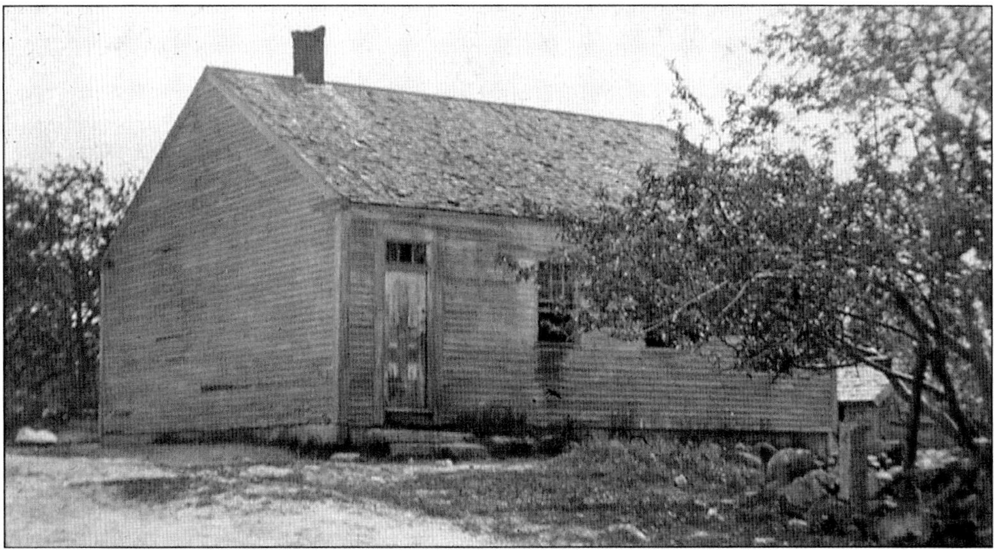

The schoolhouse of district No. 4 was across the road from the present town hall on Route 85. In the 1887 Town Report, the agent was E.C. Hall, who lived in the house across the road from the school. There were 53 students in the district, and the town appropriation was $250.62. The fall term was taught by Mary Jane Small, one of the namesakes of the present Jordan Small School, who was paid $5.50 per week with $1 for board.

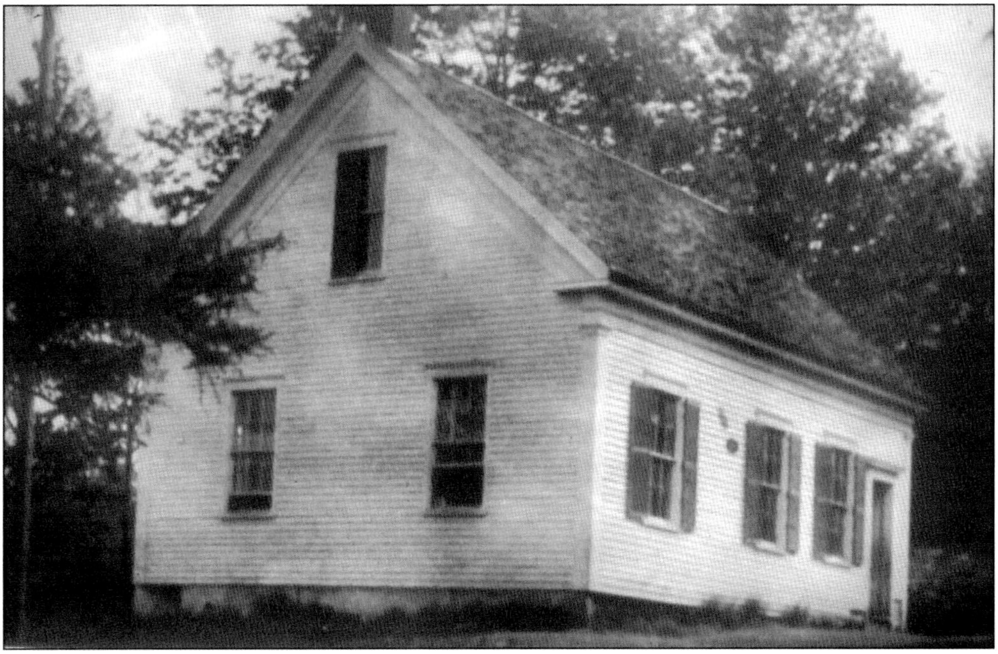

One of the 14 schools in Raymond, Mountain School was on the Mountain Road and most likely in district No. 11. Each district chose its own agent. An agent was in charge of hiring a schoolmistress or schoolmaster and arranging for their board and lodging. A schoolmaster was responsible for maintaining the schoolhouse.

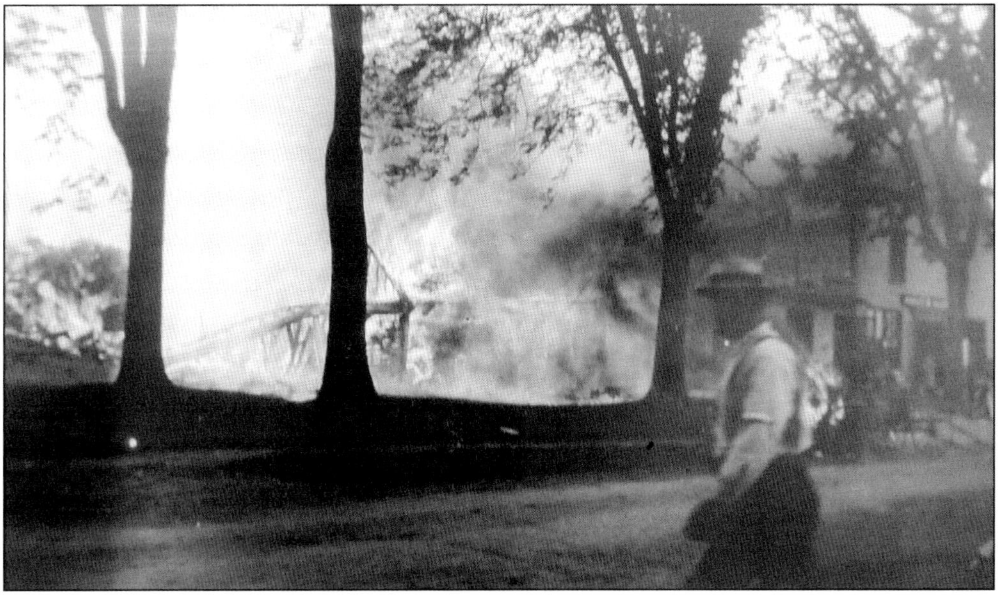

On August 1914, ashes from a kitchen stove dumped by the back door of a house on Main Street in Raymond Village started a fire that burned four houses and barns, several storage sheds, the post office, and the general store. The Raymond Fire Department had its limits back then due to rusty fire equipment, a 30 gallon pump capacity, and a lack of volunteers, but the heroes commended for their action were the boys of the Raymond baseball team, some of them being counselors at Camp Minnewawa at Panther Run.

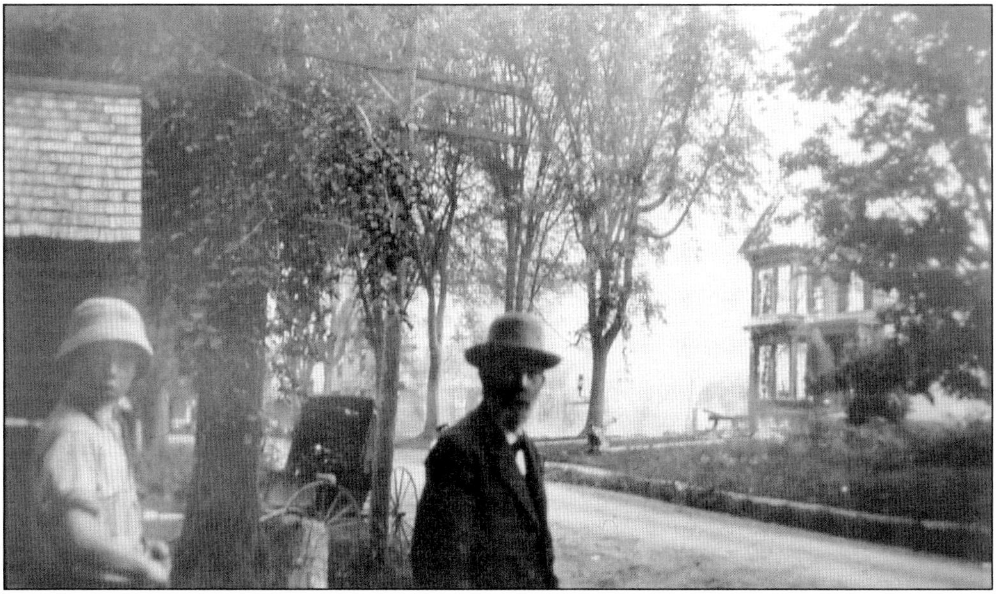

Two concerned onlookers of the 1914 fire, standing on the platform of Ed Harmon's Store, were a young Ernest H. Knight, the Raymond Casco Historical Society's founder, and Erastus Plummer, who was appointed postmaster of Raymond by President Lincoln.

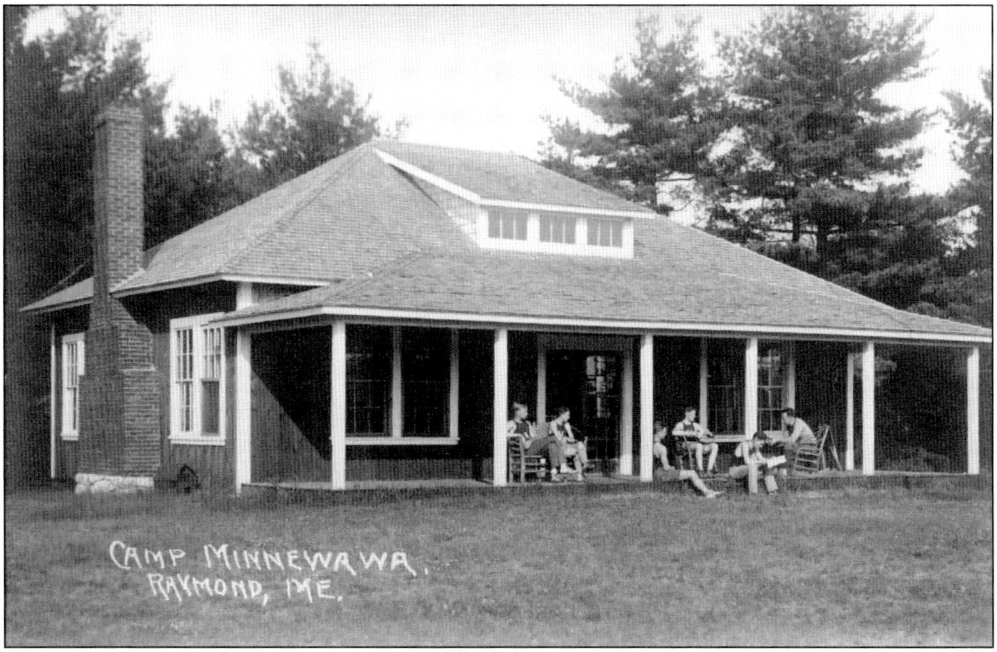

On the upper end of Panther Run, on Mill Street above the dam and stone bridge, was a boys' camp called Camp Minnewawa, founded by Guy Chipman, a successful teacher. On the flat area above their cabins reaching to Meadow Road were the athletic fields, tennis courts, and the headquarters building. The camp ended operations during World War II and was never reopened.

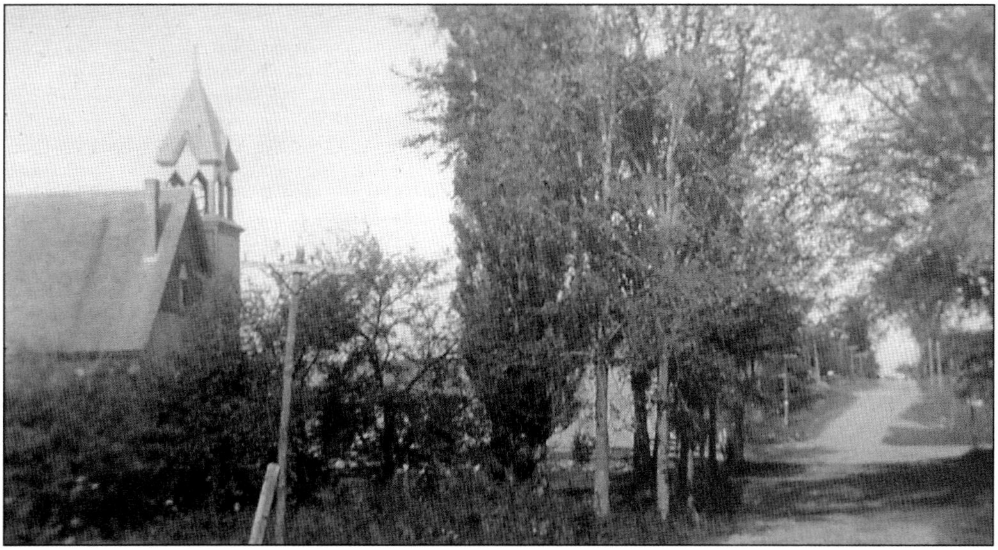

In 1888, members of the Benevolent Society of East Raymond contributed material and time for the grading of a lot on Route 85 for the building of this chapel. Citizens generously donated money, and the East Raymond Chapel was built in 1890. The East Raymond Union Chapel was added to the National Register of Historic Places in 2004.

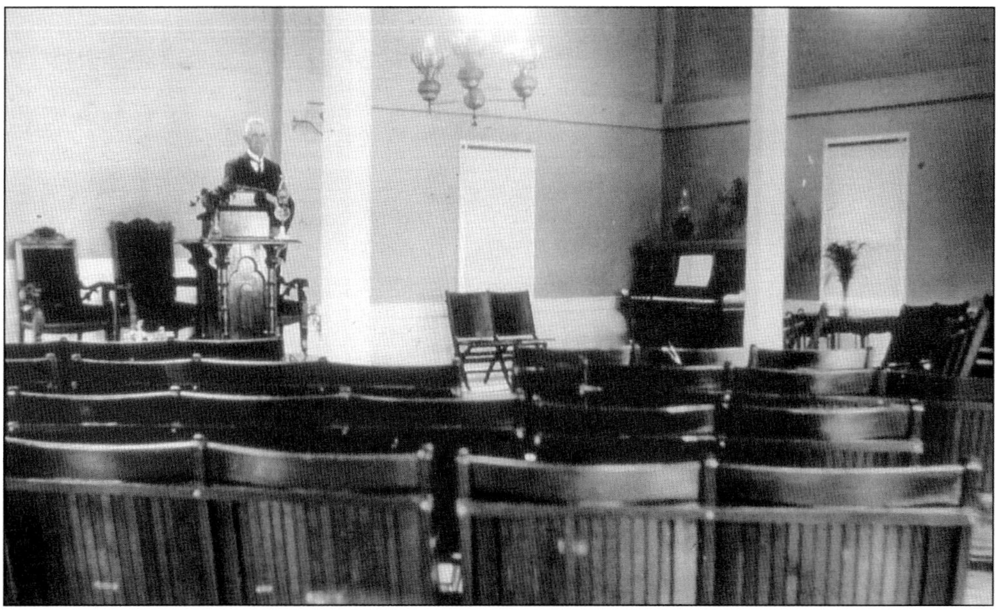

The Hawthorne House on Raymond Cape Road was originally the boyhood home of Nathaniel Hawthorne, built in 1812. Francis Radoux converted it to a church after he married Richard Manning's widow, Susan. Richard Manning's will stated that he wished to have a formal place of worship for his neighbors. The Raymond Casco Historical Society is very fortunate to have a three-seat bench from the Radoux Meetinghouse.

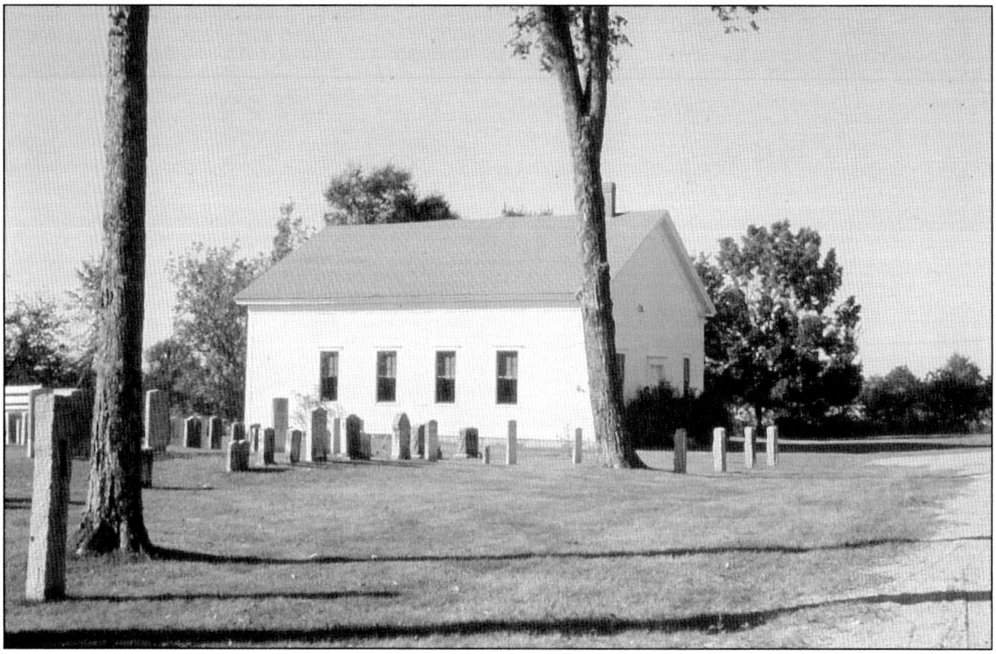

The Baptist church on Raymond Hill was one of the first two churches in Raymondtown. The land for the church was deeded by Richard Manning on March 23, 1803. The building was erected in 1834. The Reverend Leach was chosen pastor, and Deacon John Small left the sum of $500 to the church in 1855 for a parsonage.

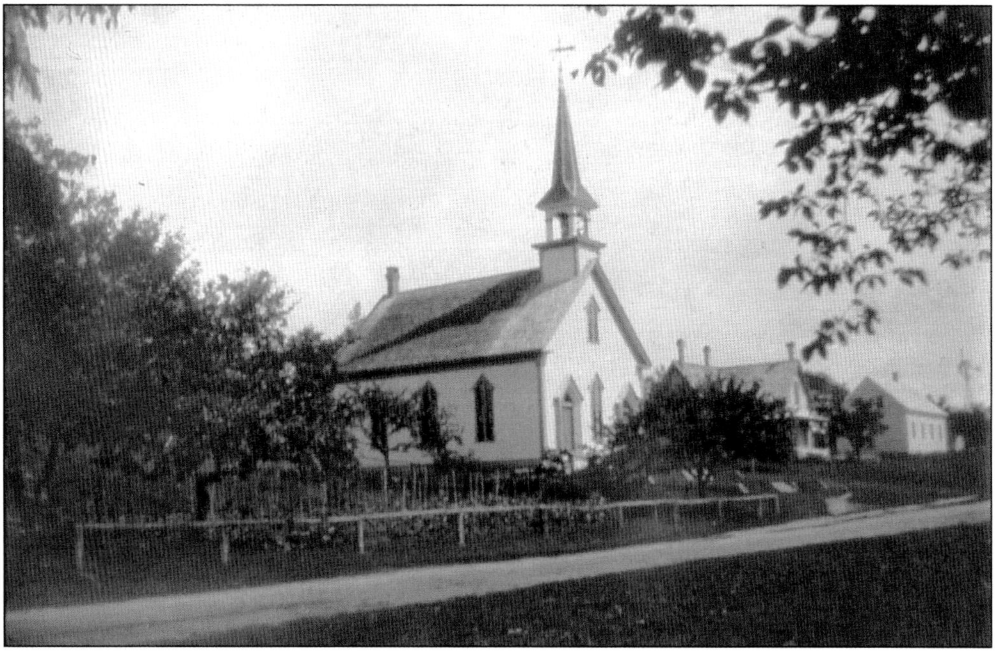

The Raymond Village Church on Main Street was built in 1879 as a Free Will Baptist Church. The Ladies Mite Society contributed $2,200 toward the building fund. The foundation consisted of split stone slabs set on the ground, and the front walk was terraced. The lighting, inside and out, was by kerosene lamps, as electricity did not come to Raymond until 1924.

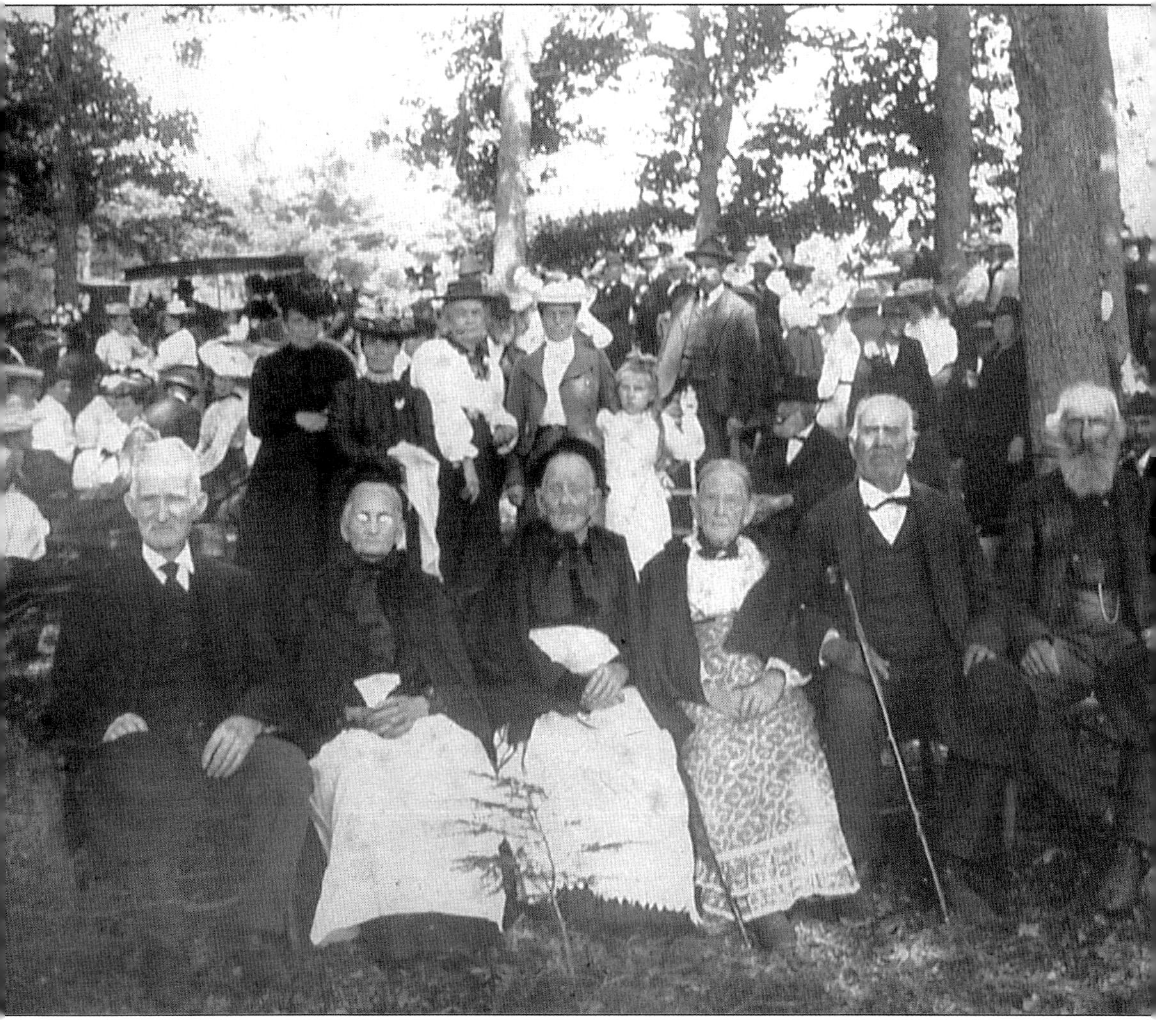

On September 12, 1902, the Strout family of Raymond held its second annual reunion. This is one of the branches of the family, comprising the descendants of Prince Strout, who came here from Cape Elizabeth and died in 1834. The crowd swelled to about 200 in this ideal setting under the shade of maples in the pasture of Daniel S. Strout.

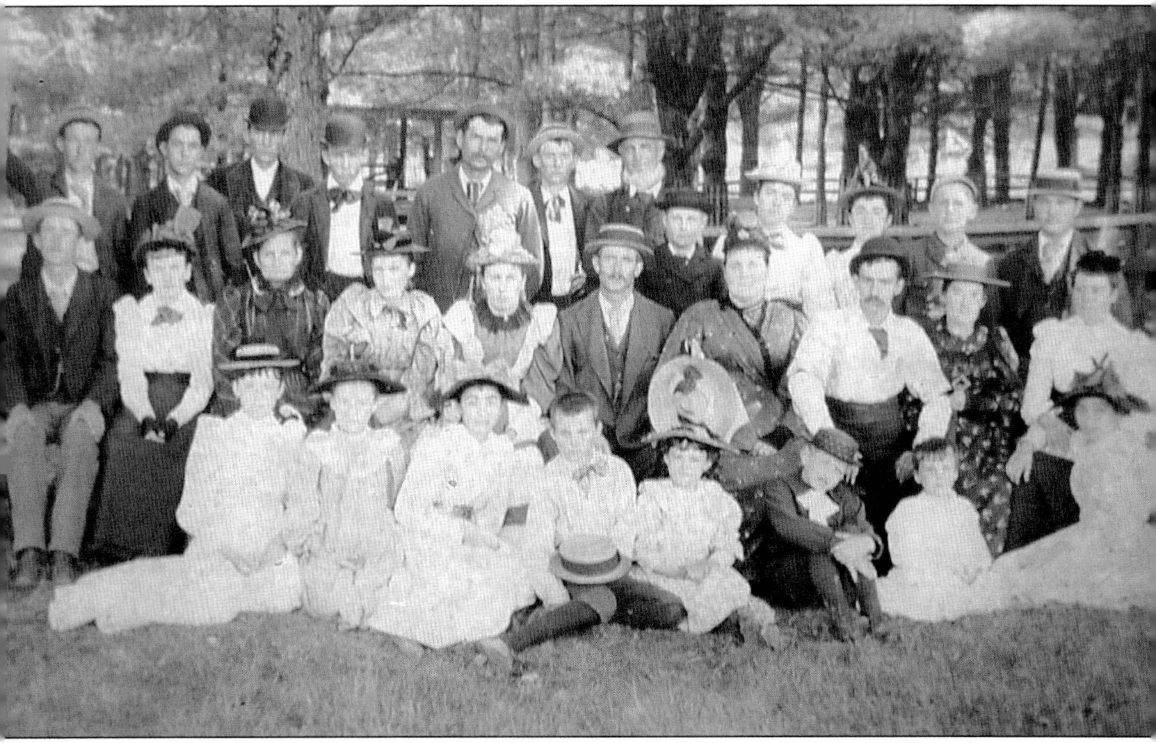

Camp Cove, now Wild Acres on Raymond Cape, was once an area for picnics and religious or revivalist camp meetings, which were popular in the mid-1800s. It had a cleared and fenced area with a small pavilion. The only way to get to Camp Cove at that time was by boat. Capt. Benjamin Knight, the man with the beard in the back row center, used his small steam engine to transport the people.

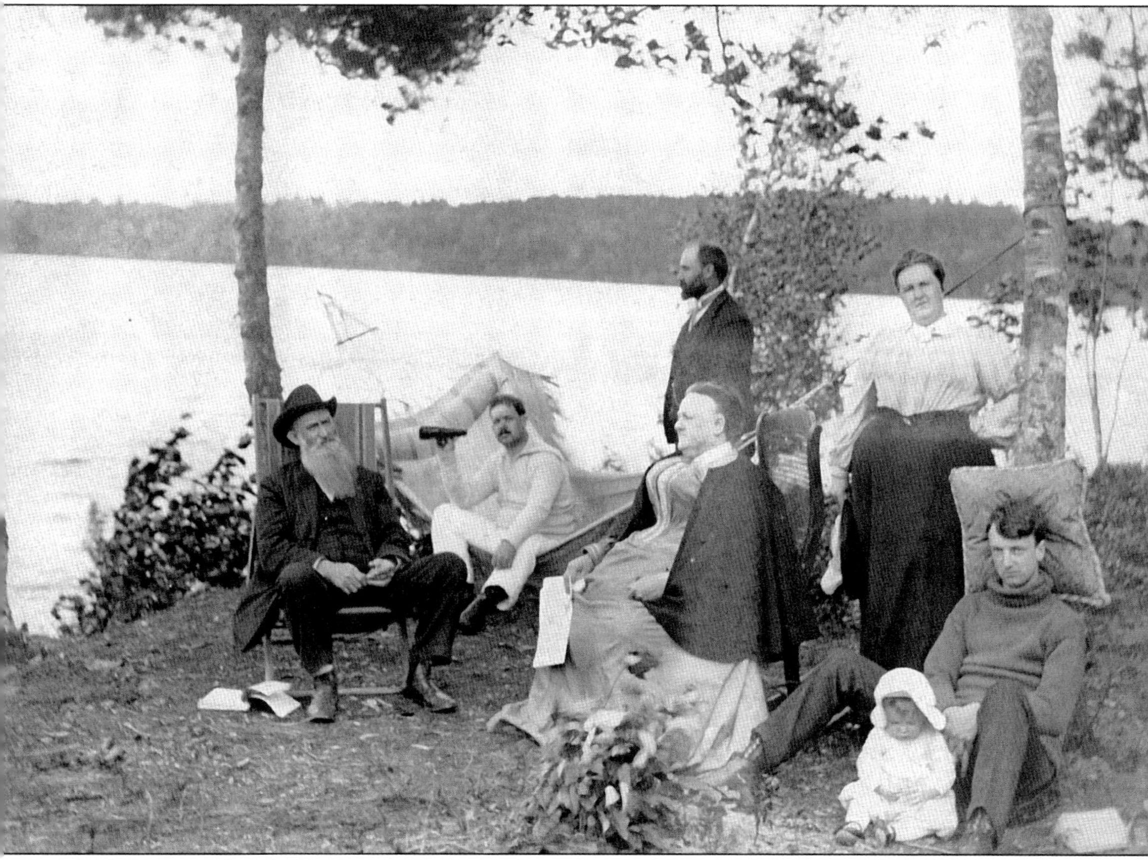

The Johnstone family lived on Crescent Lake in the early 1900s at J&R Farms. Benefactors to the town of Raymond, they gave 8.5 acres to the town on the corner of Plains Road and Webbs Mill Road (Route 85). This prominent family is enjoying a family picnic at the lake. Shown from left to right are (first row) Frank Johnstone, Mary Johnstone, and Charles Johnstone with baby; (second row) Charles Hoyt (on hammock), Will Hoyt, and Mary Hoyt. (Betty McDermott.)

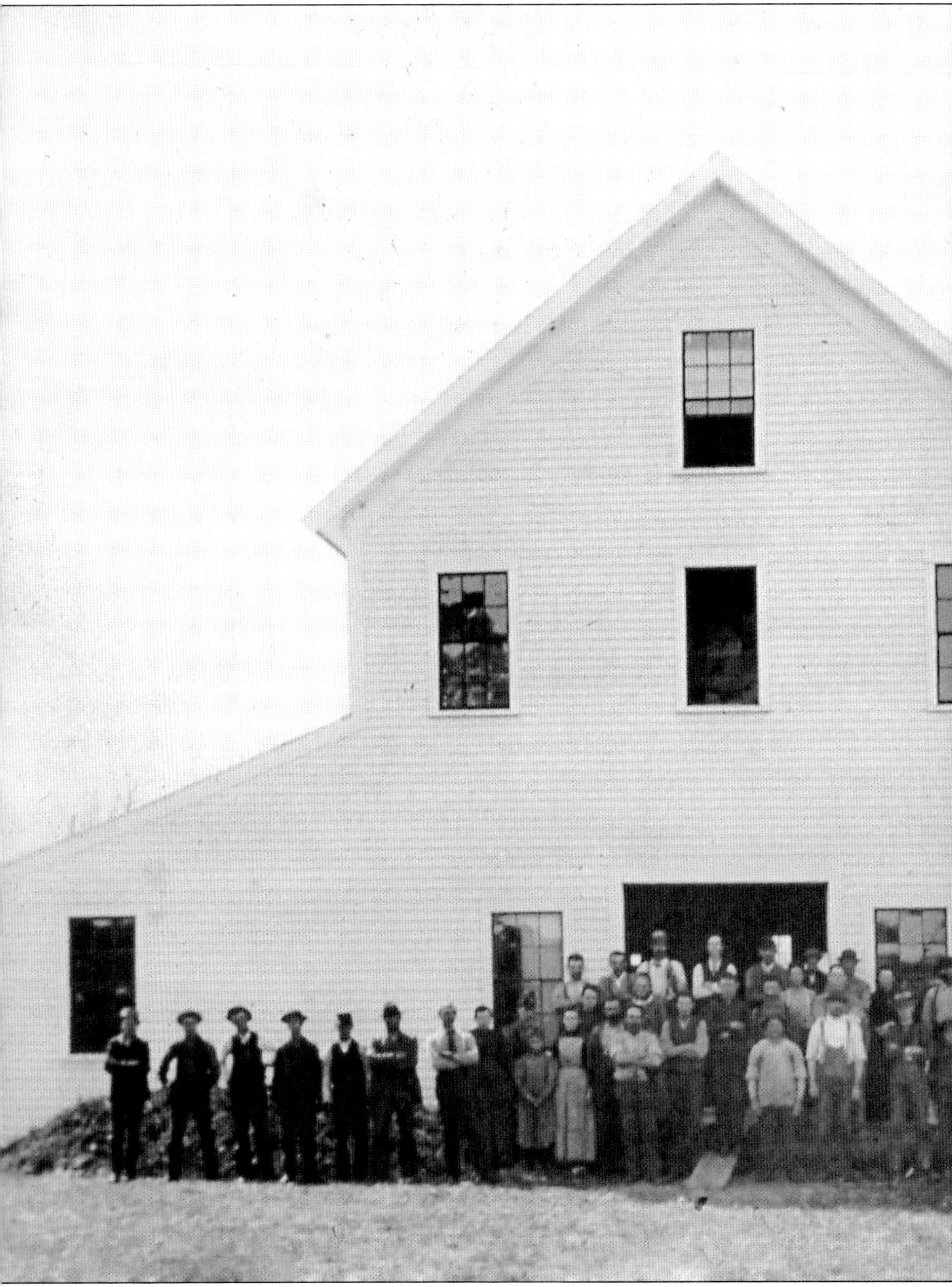

Shown here is H.L. Forham's corn-packing shop in the Lower Village of Raymond at Indian Point. At this shop, the specialties were succotash and corn, which was cooked and sealed in cans for the Portland Packing Company. This factory gave employment to men and women, with between 100 and 150 workers during the packing season. During an average packing season, 150,000 cans were shipped out.

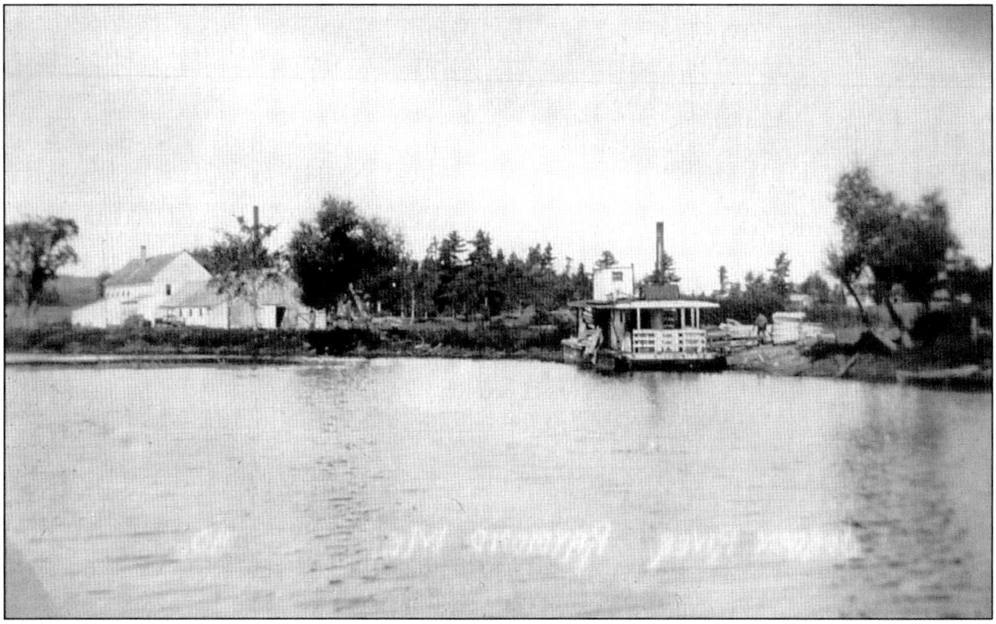

One of the many loading points for freight boats on the Jordan River was where Indian Point on Route 302 is today. This freight boat was an old steam-powered square ender that traveled between the railroad head at Sebago Lake Station and area towns, such as Raymond and Naples. This picture shows the back end of the corn shop, which was where the lids of filled cans were soldered tight.

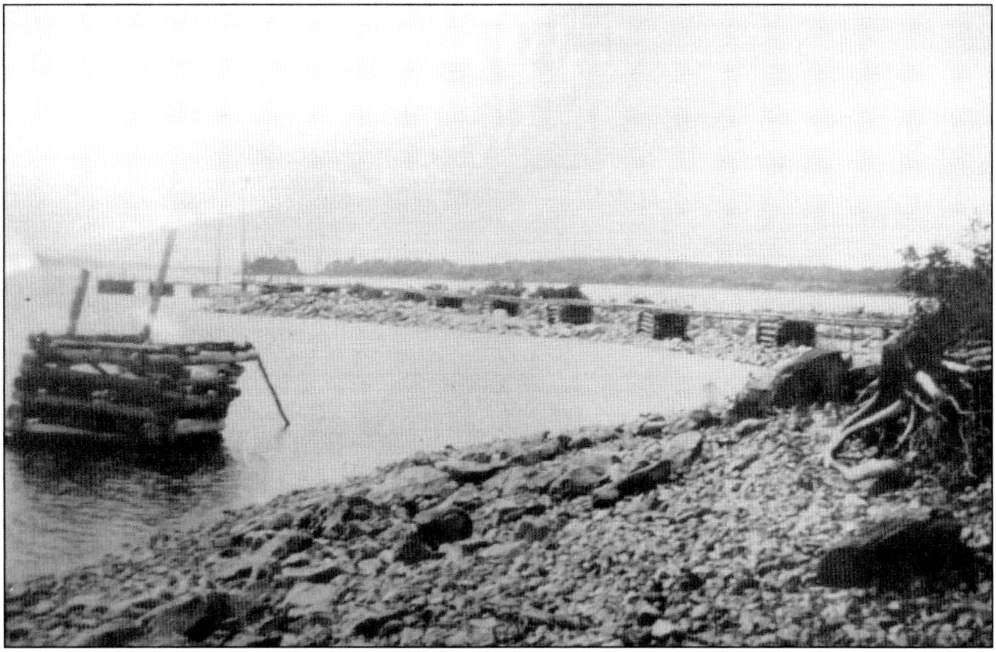

The island in front of Raymond Village on Route 302, near the Raymond Town Beach, had a rocky shore, and canal boats once used a wharf there when they could not get to the other wharfs along the Jordan River. During the steamboat days, the wharf was used for moving freight and passengers to and from Raymond Village and the railroad station at Sebago Lake Station.

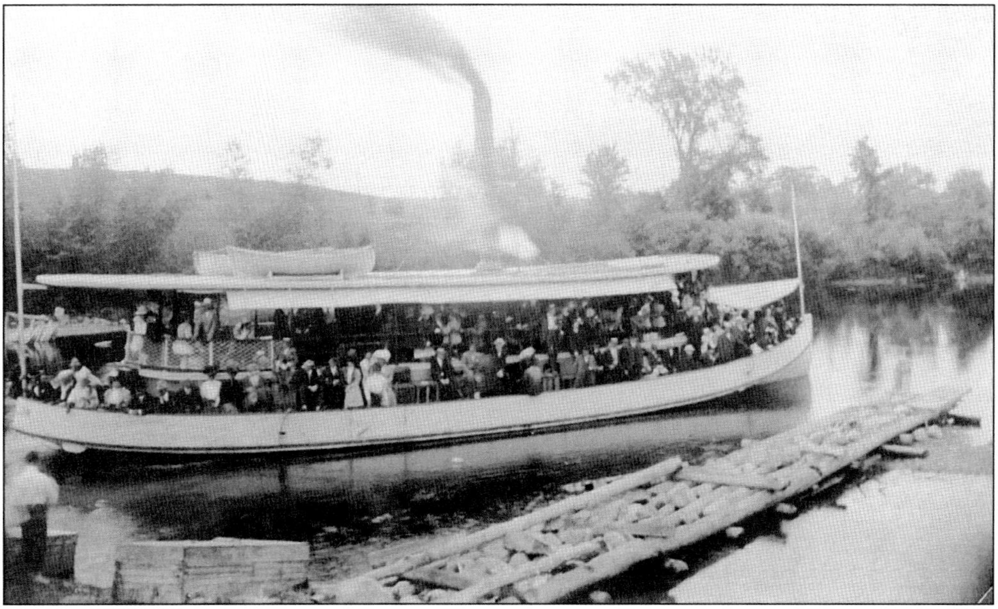

Steamboats first came to Sebago Lake in 1847 with a small side-wheeler called the *Fawn*. Canal boats were here in 1830, but steamboats were faster and more reliable. They brought visitors and tourists to the area from Sebago Lake Station to Harrison. Travel was mostly by schedule, with the larger boats making limited stops on the runs, while the smaller boats picked up passengers and cargo to transfer to the larger boats.

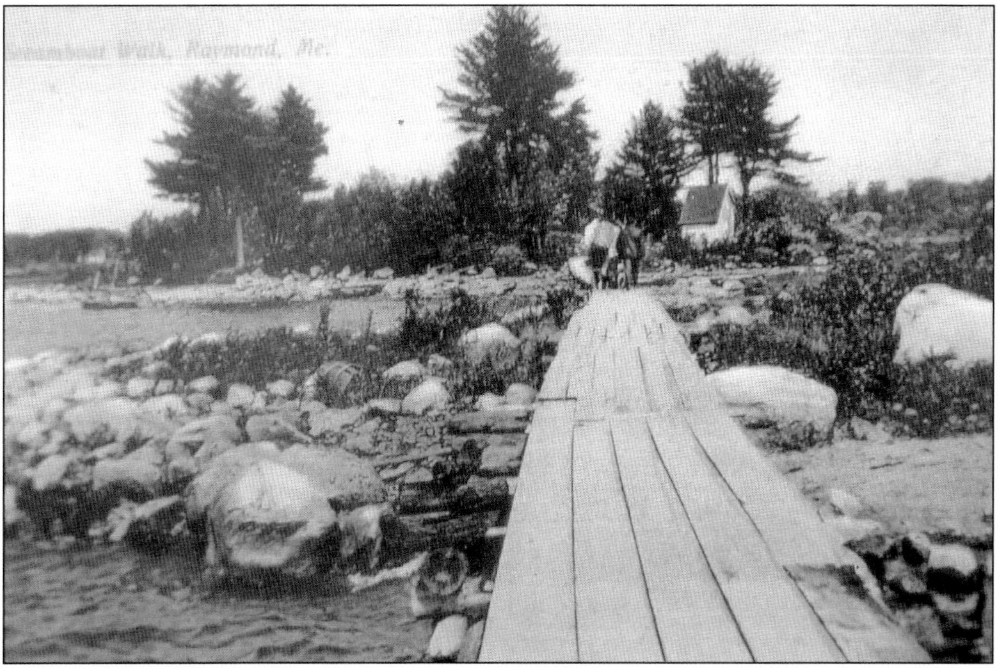

On the shores of Jordan Bay in front of Swan's Island is a rocky shoal that once supported a boardwalk, which was called Steamboat Walk. Running all the way to Main Street, the boardwalk was used by visitors or tourists coming into Raymond Village. This stretch is now called Wharf Road and runs off Route 302, near Raymond Town Beach.

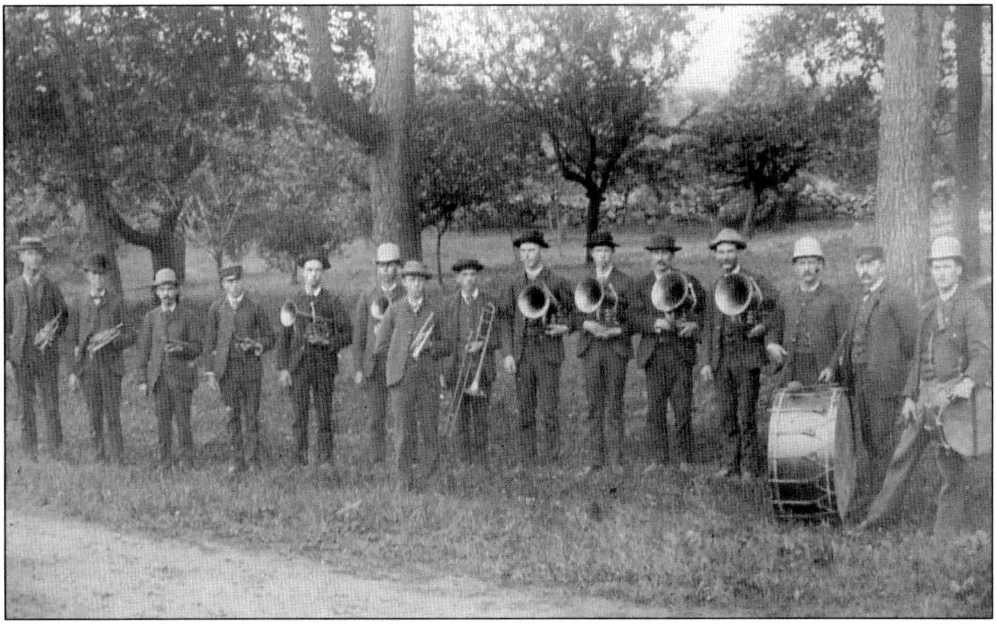

The Raymond Town Band is shown here around 1890. In simpler days, when life was hard, a little music could add both noise and joy to any celebration. Pictured are, from left to right, Rob Leach, Fred Barton, Ernest Skillings, Ham Tripp, Harry Nichols, George Burgess, Charles Barton, Scott Morton, Carl Leach, Rob Barton, George Curtis, George Leach, Win Allen, Fred Plummer, and Ed Mason.

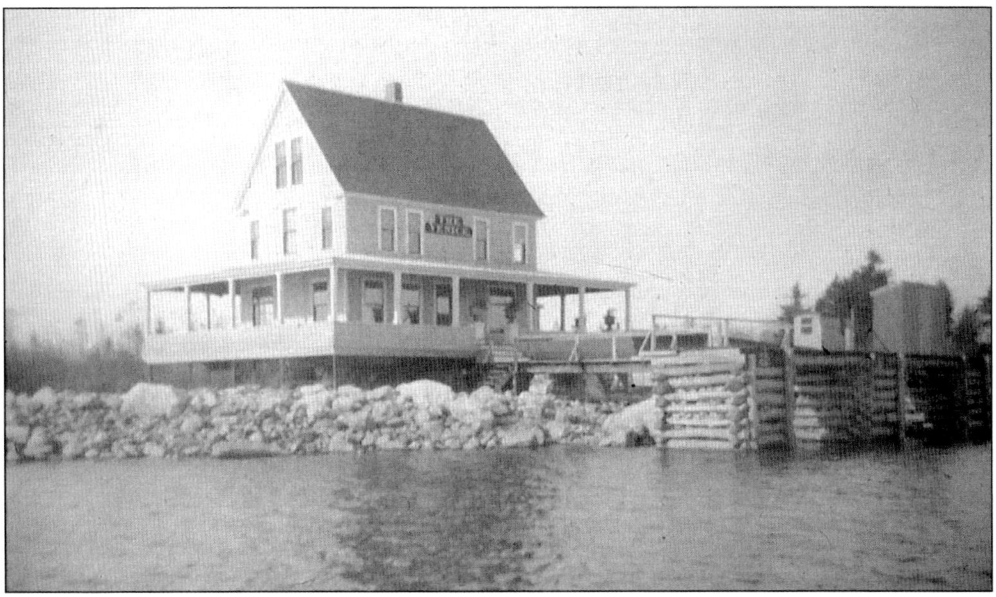

In the late 1800s, the Venice was built by Summer Plummer, of Raymond Village, as a summer school for girls. It was a beautiful building with gleaming hardwood floors, small staterooms for bedrooms with hidden drawers in the walls, and a massive colored-stone fireplace with mineral inserts along the top that spelled "Venice." It had its own steamboat landing that led up to the wide porches. It was a landmark for both vacationers and residents for many years. Falling into disrepair, it was burned in the mid-1970s.

The walk bridge, or what could be called a xylophone bridge, over Jordan River was an old plank bridge near what is now the Good Life Market on the corner of Route 302 and Route 85. The bridge was sheltered by a large tree, into which a circular platform with seats was made in the spreading trunk. It became a popular resting spot for locals and tourists alike.

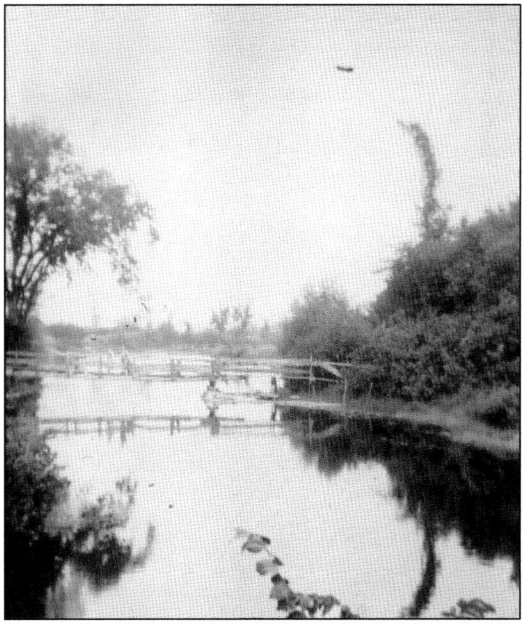

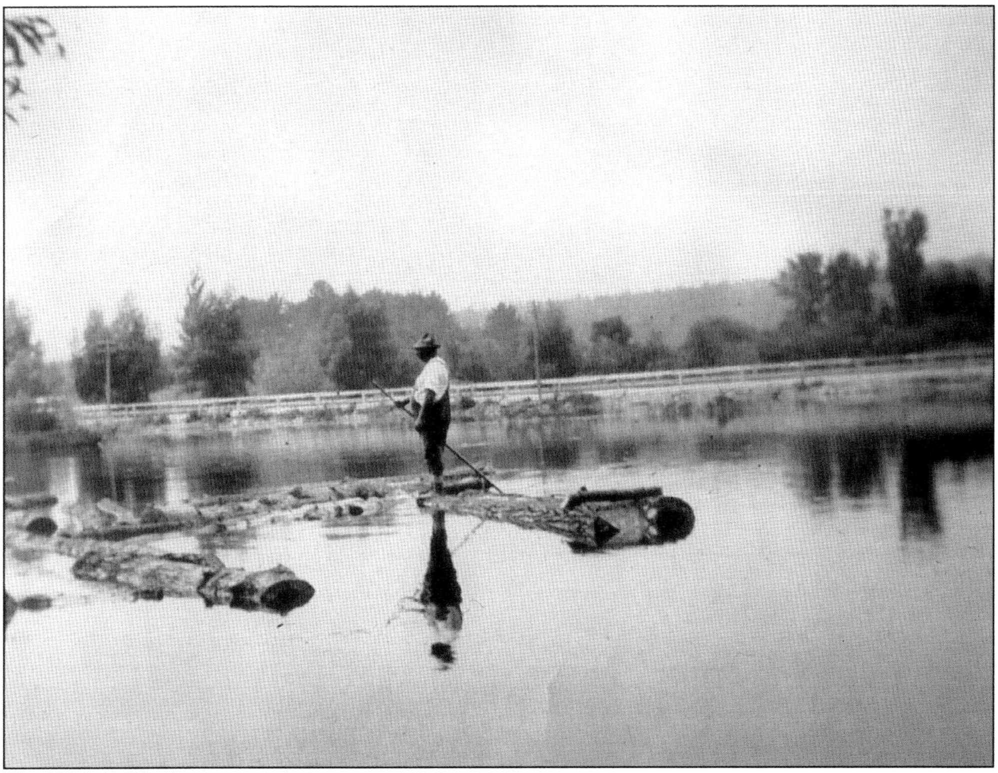

There was a time when log drives on the Jordan River were an annual event. Timber cut near Rattlesnake Pond (now Crescent Lake) and Panther Pond was floated down Panther to the dam at Mill Street, sluiced through the spillway into Jordan River, rafted into Jordan Bay with boom logs, and towed to the sawmills on Sebago Lake. This picture shows a log drive on the Jordan River. The man shown here is John Berry, who lived on the Plains Road.

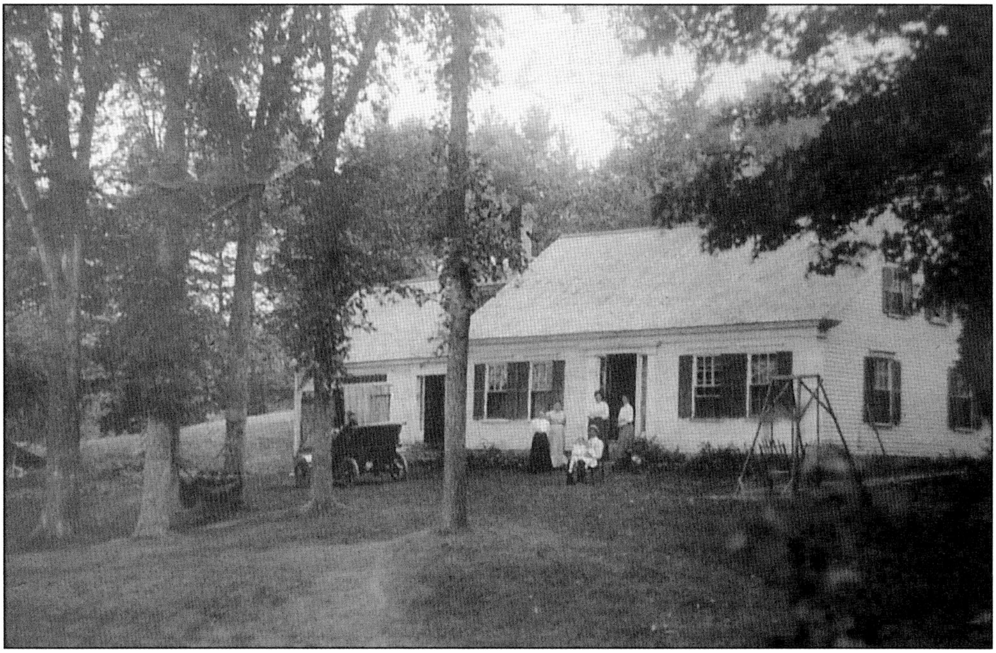

The home of Reginald and Helen Brown on Main Street was called Bay View Farms because of the outstanding views of Sebago Lake, which were not inhibited by trees. Reginald Brown worked with his brother Doc Brown at Dielectric as general manager. This house has seen many changes through the years. Joel Mason is shown here with his family.

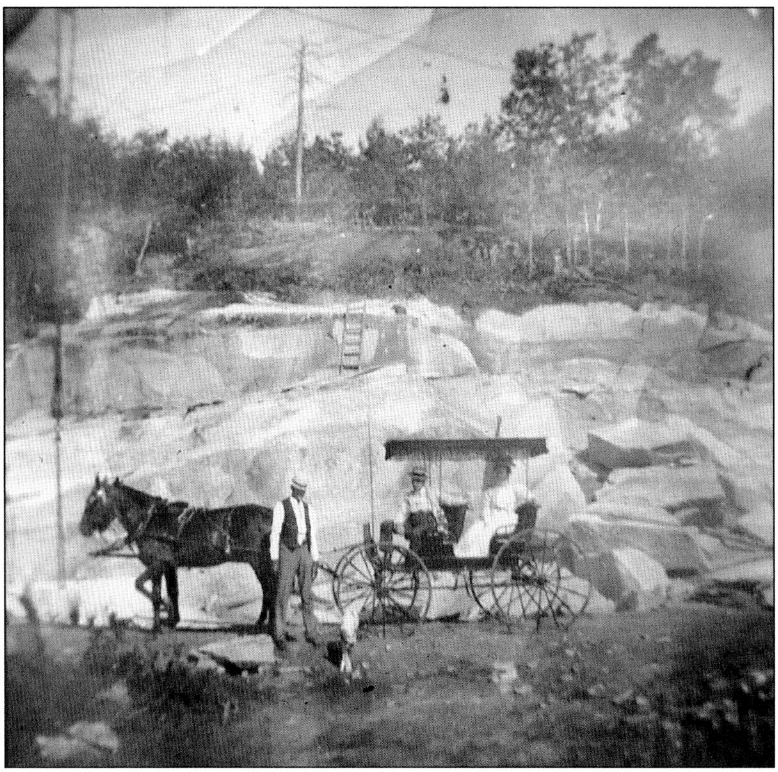

Located behind Reginald and Helen Brown's home was this quarry. The gin pole and cables seen in this picture were used to work the quarry. The rocks from here were used to build Roosevelt Trail (Route 302) in the 1950s, thus eliminating Main Street, which was known then as Route 302. Charles Knight is standing by the horse in this picture.

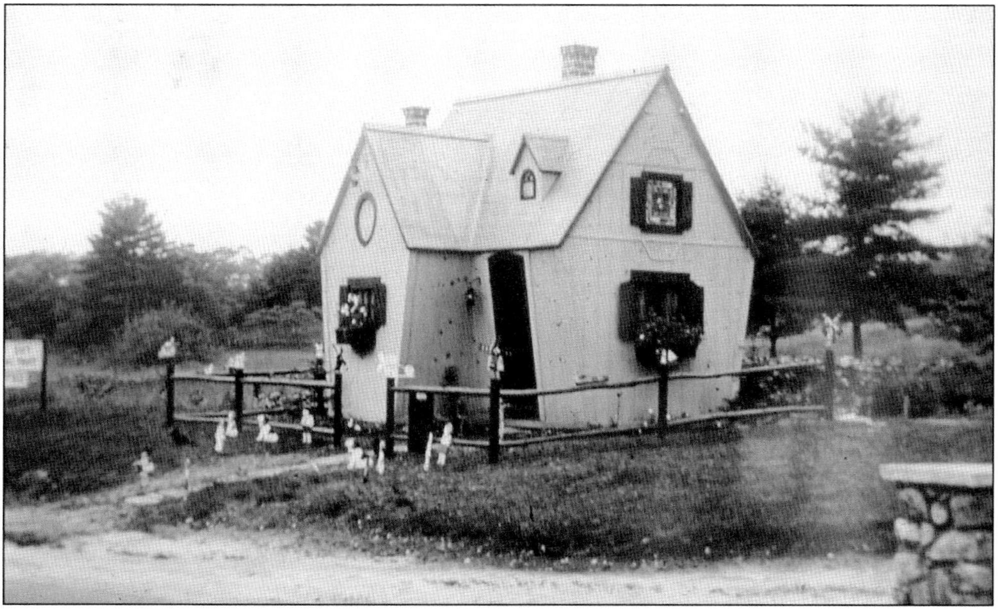

A landmark for people traveling through Raymond when Main Street was Route 302 was the "House that Jack Built." Based on a storybook picture, Will Foster and his son Donald were the original builders of this angular structure; other additions were included over the years—the restaurant was the last part to be added. With Will's wife, Pearl, and daughter-in-law Lucy, they developed a loyal clientele over the years for whom annual visits were a must.

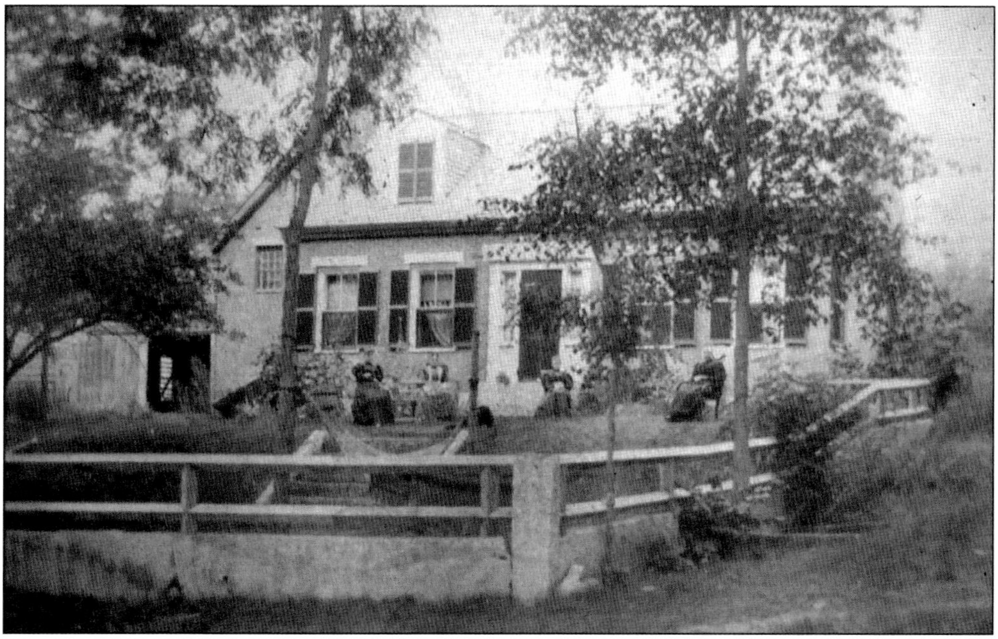

The original Isaiah Gould home on Main Street was a one-story brick house that was later raised to two stories with a wooden second floor. Behind the home was an icehouse, a necessity for families before electricity. This house was destroyed by fire but rebuilt on the same foundation. The barn, made of brick, has survived through all of these changes. Isaiah was the grandson of Obadiah Gould, an early settler on Quaker Ridge.

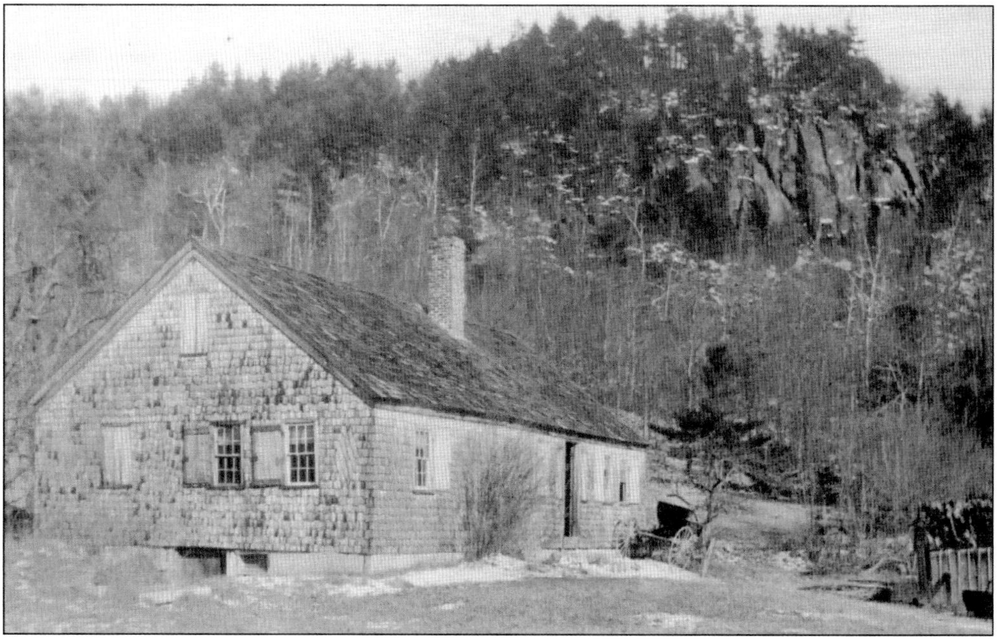

John Spiller married Rebecca Day, daughter of Thomas and Elizabeth (Manning) Day. Elizabeth Manning Day was the half-sister of Richard Manning, one of the land proprietors in Raymond Town. In 1789, John built his home on the Conesca Road under the ledges of Rattlesnake Mountain, and it was that home where he and his wife, Rebecca, raised their family of 10 children.

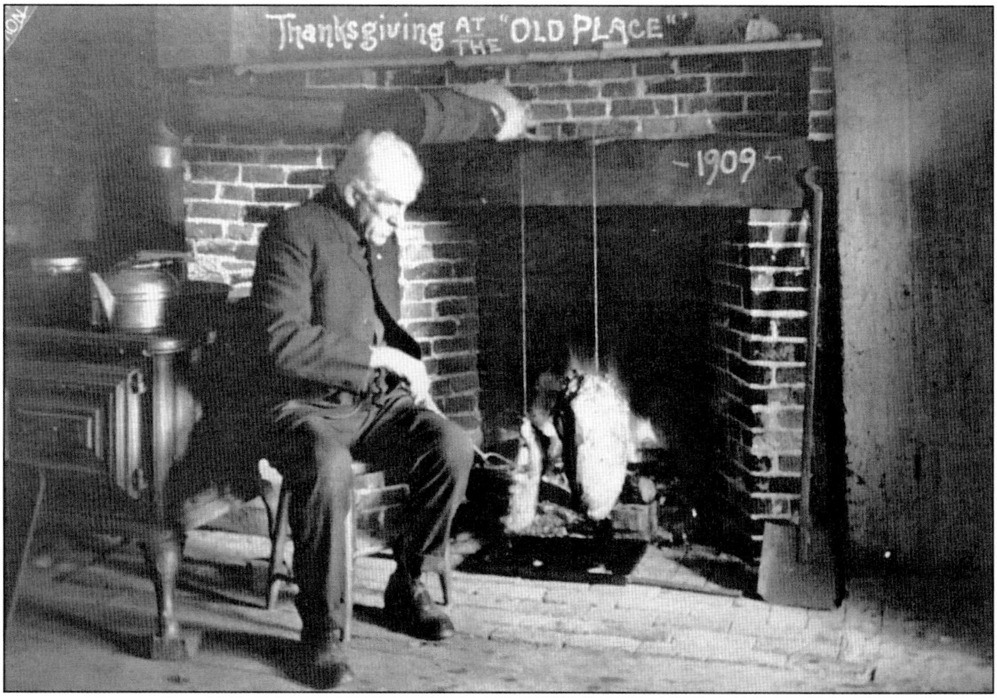

Hamden Spiller was one of the grandchildren of John and Rebecca Spiller. In 1909, as an elderly man, he came back to the old home place, where he had lived with his family on the Conesta Road, to cook Thanksgiving dinner in the fireplace just as his mother had done so many times.

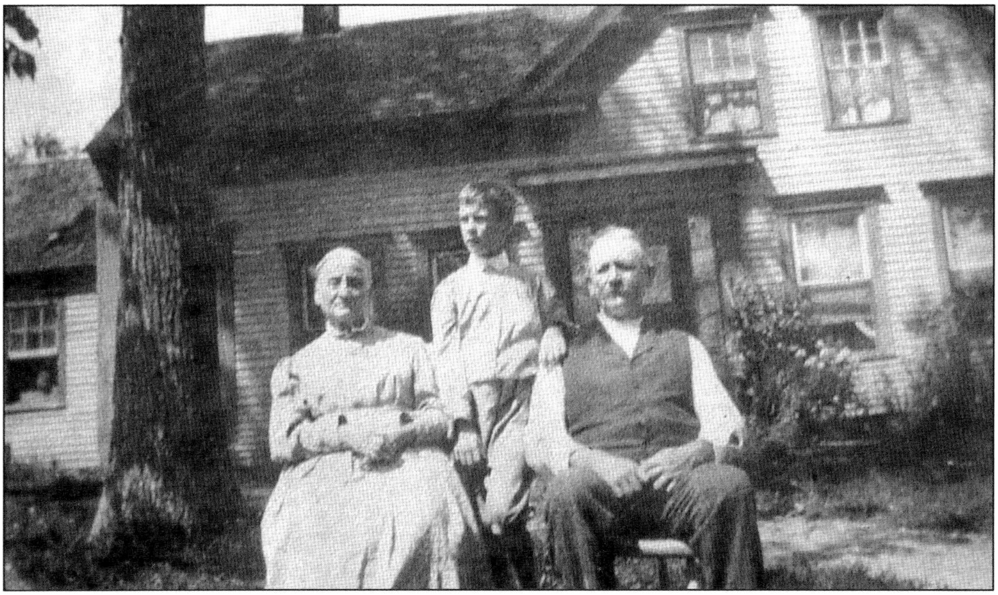

Mary Wilson Files is pictured with her son Erastus A. Files and her grandson Raymond Files. Mary's nephews built the Wilson Spring House in North Raymond. The Files family home was at the bottom of Spiller Hill in Raymond.

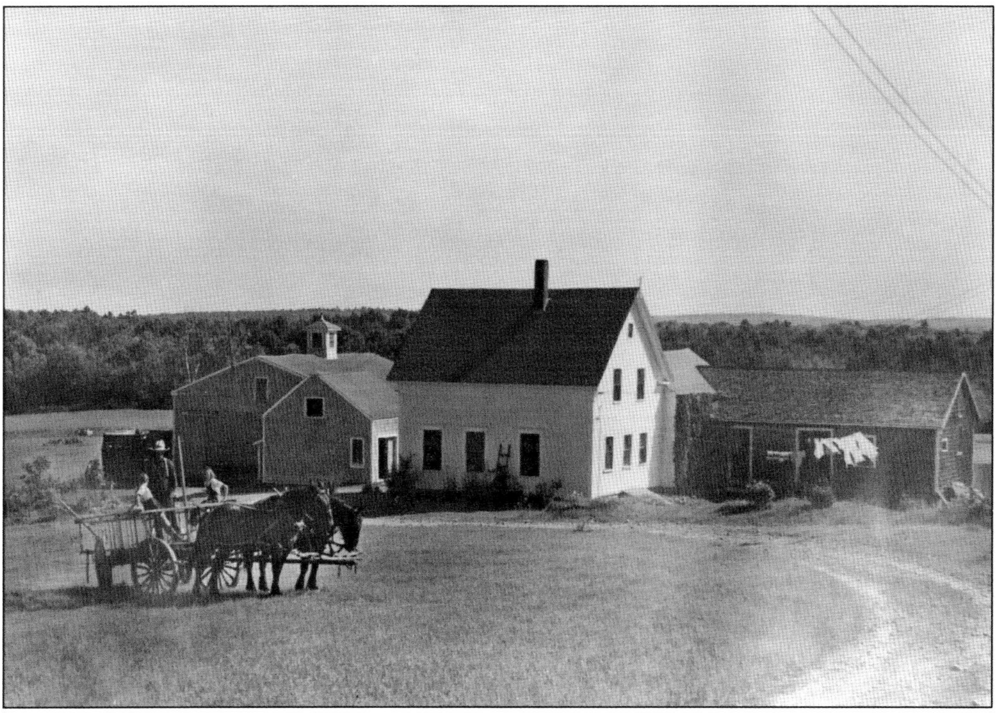

Enoch Shaw, farmer and chair maker, built the Shaw Farm on Raymond Cape in the mid-1880s. Dan Shaw operated the farm, along with his wife, Cora, who was a champion cow caller for many years. Starting with their own vehicle to transport students to school in 1957, Dan and Cora were school bus drivers for over 35 years. Dan and Cora's descendents still live on the family's property today.

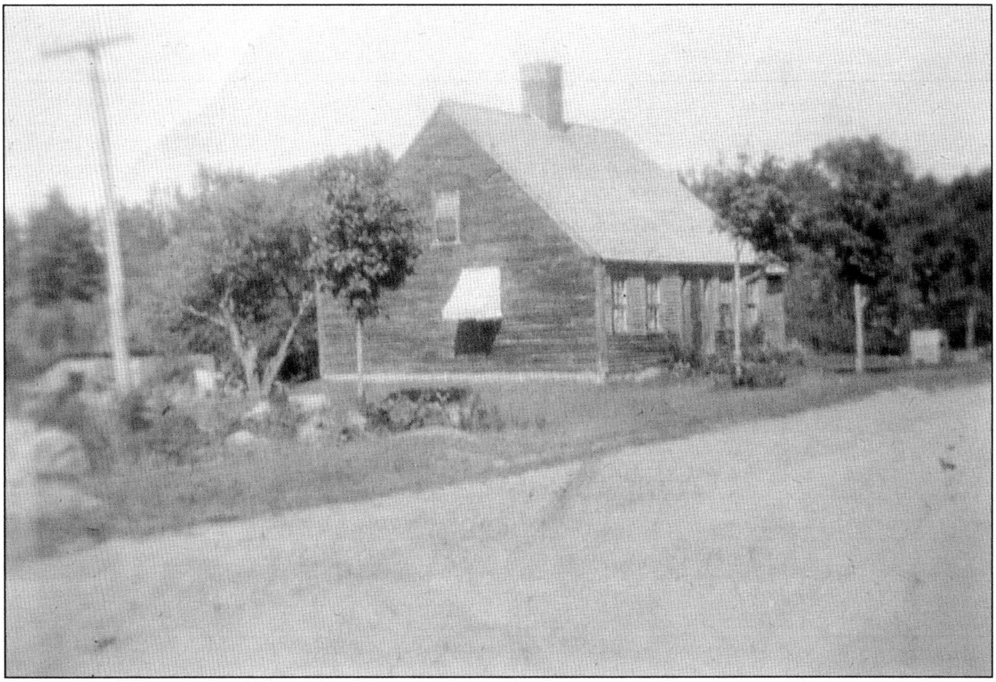

The Davis and Brown families built one of the older homes in Raymondtown in 1780 on Route 85. For years, it was called "the old house," but now, the name is "ye olde house." Over the years, it has been used for various things; many additions and modification have been made to the building.

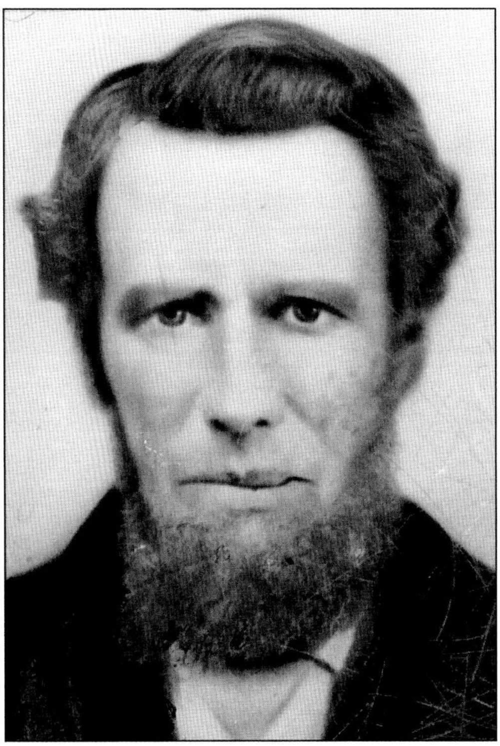

Tom Brown ran the mill at Jordan River and lived in "the old house," built in 1780. He owned a substantial amount of land in Raymond and is buried in Village Cemetery. Grace Watkins went to live with Tom and his wife, Myra, when she was a young girl.

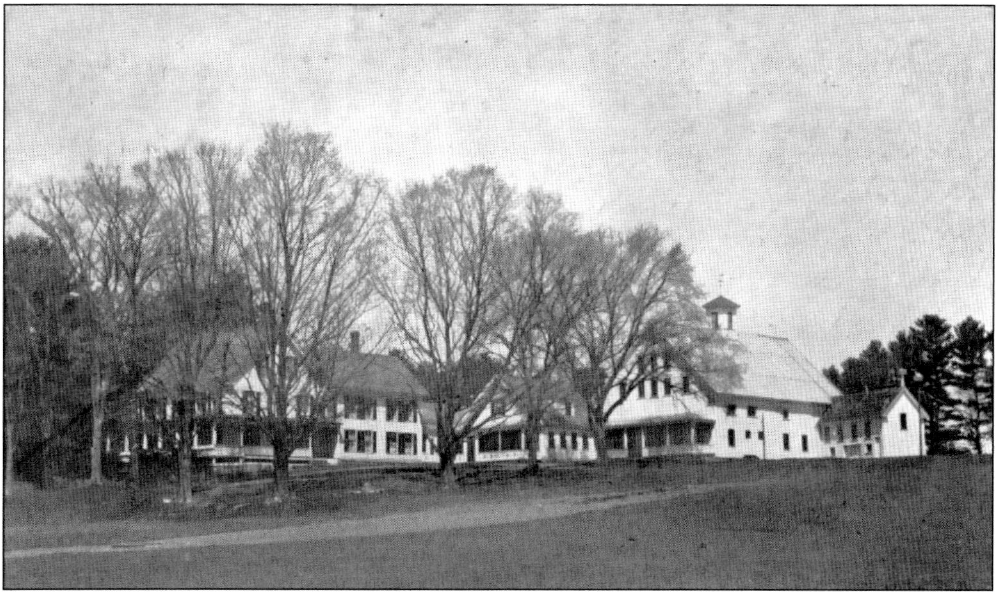

One of the more successful farm homesteads converted to a summer boarder business at the turn of the century was Pine Grove Farm. Starting in the late 1800s, this popular summer resort was owned and operated by several generations of the Hayden family, John, Irving, and Gardner. Sadly, the house was torn down, and only the original barn is left. The barn is used as a recreational building and is now known as King's Grant.

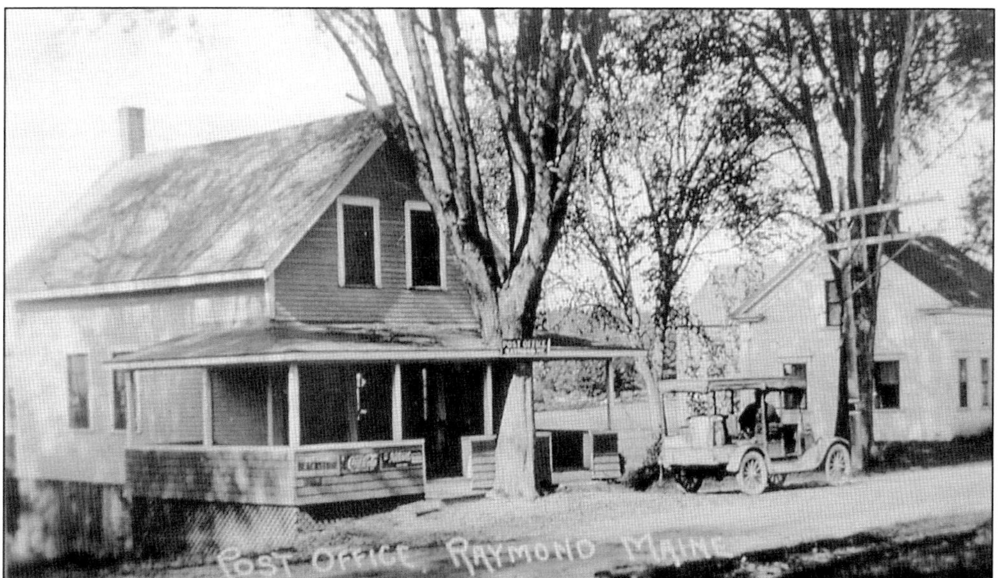

After the fire of 1914, the Raymond Post Office was moved to the building that was once Skilling's Harness Shop. While waiting for the stage to deliver the mail, many of the local folks would socialize in the ice cream parlor where they could also get penny candy and peanuts.

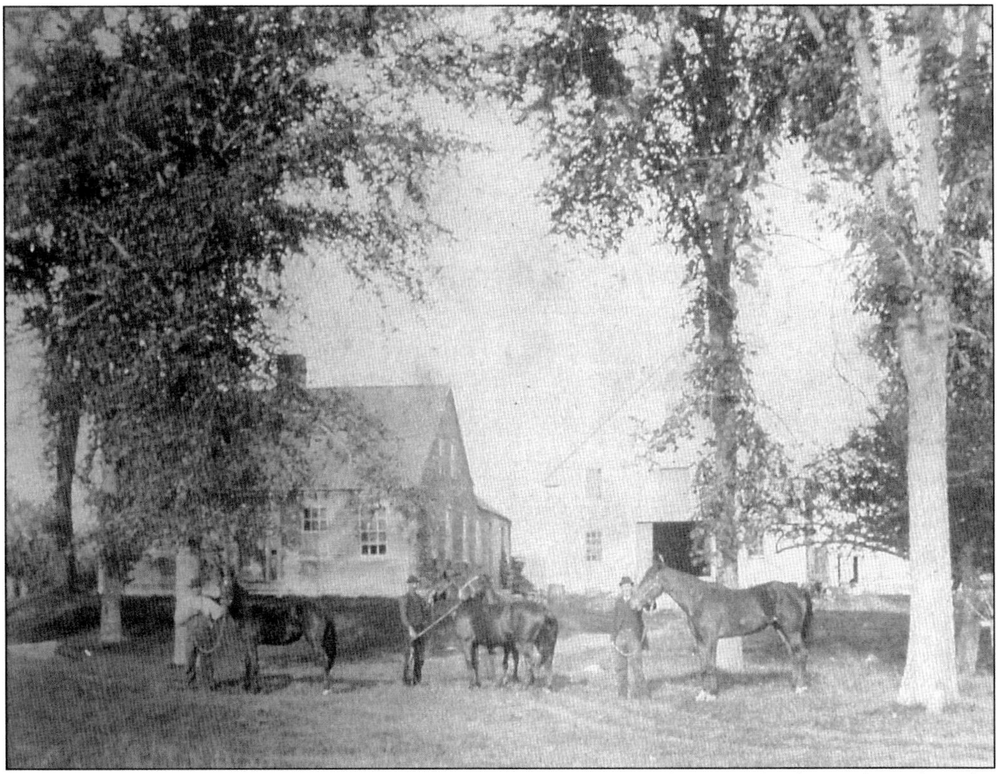

David McLellan's farm, on which Edgar Welch worked, was on the easterly slope of Rattlesnake Mountain on Route 85. Observing that the sun set much earlier here than at the farms to the north or south, Edgar worked for many years off and on, day or night, to correct this by rolling boulders down from the top of the mountain in the hopes of gaining more hours of daylight for his legally blind boss. There is an expanse of rock halfway down the mountain testifying to the determination of this man.

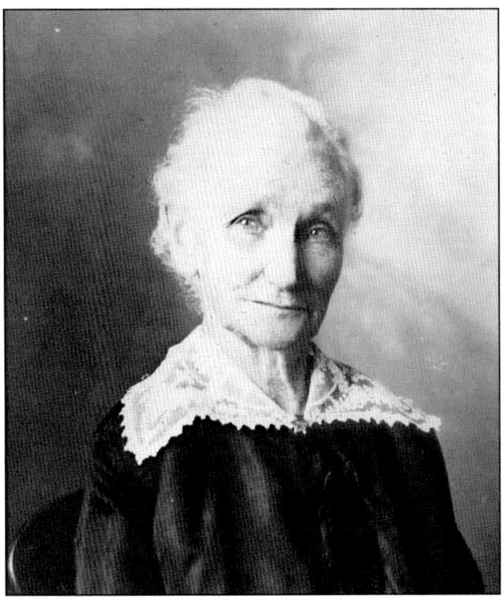

David McLellan's wife, Carrie, was a woman of small stature but large determination. After her husband became incapacitated by rheumatism, in order to save the family farm, she planted and harvested garden crops, tended to the animals, took in boarders, cooked, sewed for neighbors, did piecework for the coat factory, and played the melodeon for the neighborhood hymn singings.

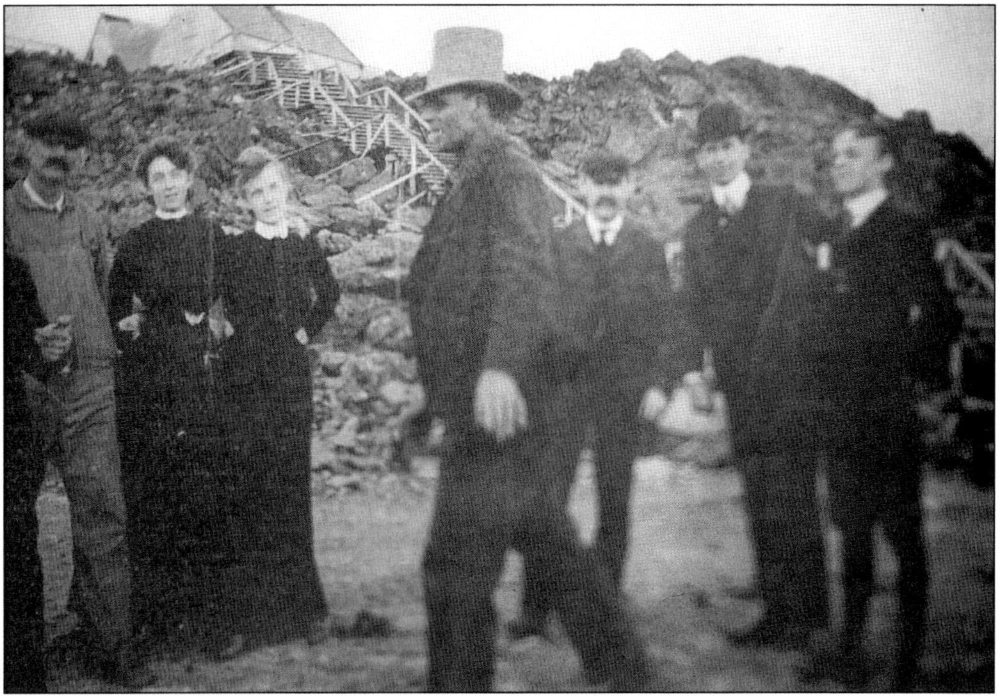

Edgar Welch was born in 1849. He was a hard worker and running was his pastime. Dropping whatever he was doing, be it summer or winter, he would be off running barefoot. For many years, he would run from his home in Raymond to the top of Mount Washington and back home again. A man with a team of horses once challenged Edgar Welch to race him to Portland. Starting from Raymond Village, the team left him far behind, but when the man and his team got to Congress Street, Edgar was there waiting for them!

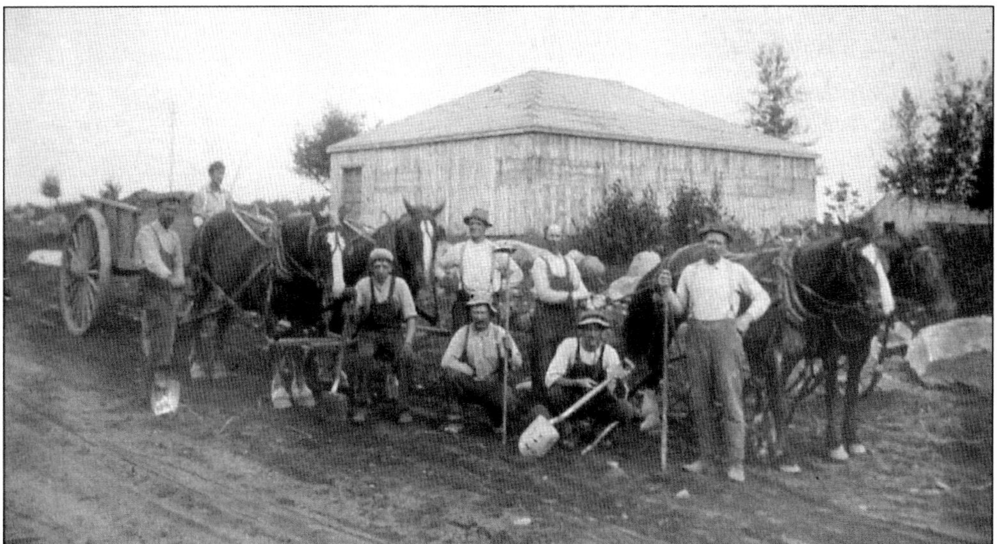

As the turn of the century began to draw near, roads in Raymond and Casco began to connect neighbors and areas of the towns. There were road crews everywhere, and one of those crews used the horses of David McLellan. They were known as the "Topsy Road Crew."

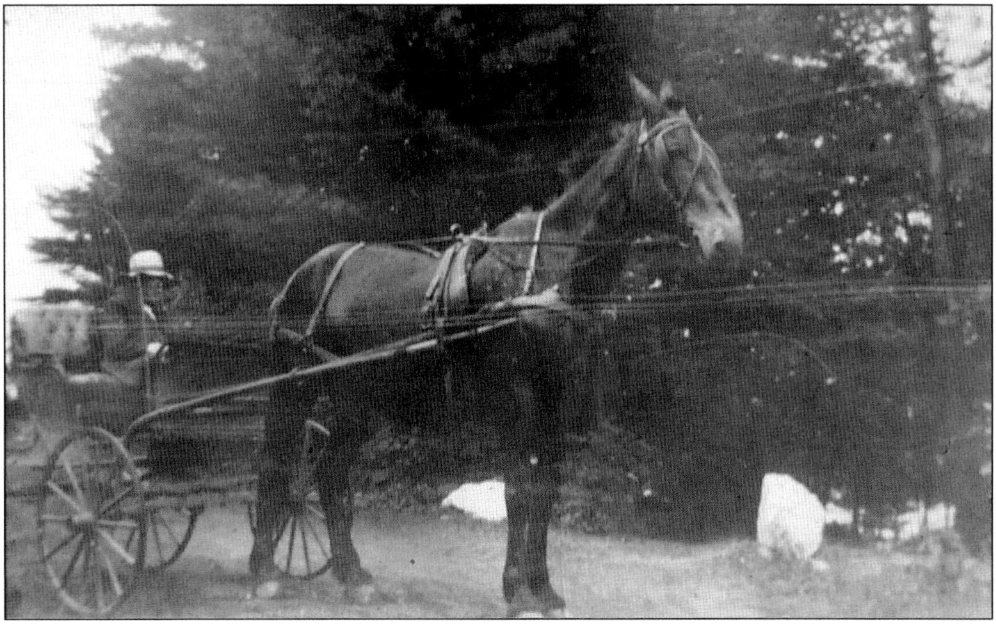

This picture shows Sam B. Brown and his horse Dixie. Brown was a traveling Baptist preacher in the early 1900s, performing many marriages on his journeys. He preached at the Radoux Meetinghouse, which was Nathaniel Hawthorne's boyhood home at one time. He was also a well-known musician. For many years, he was a familiar face and a welcomed sight to many local people. His home was where the WGAN tower is now located.

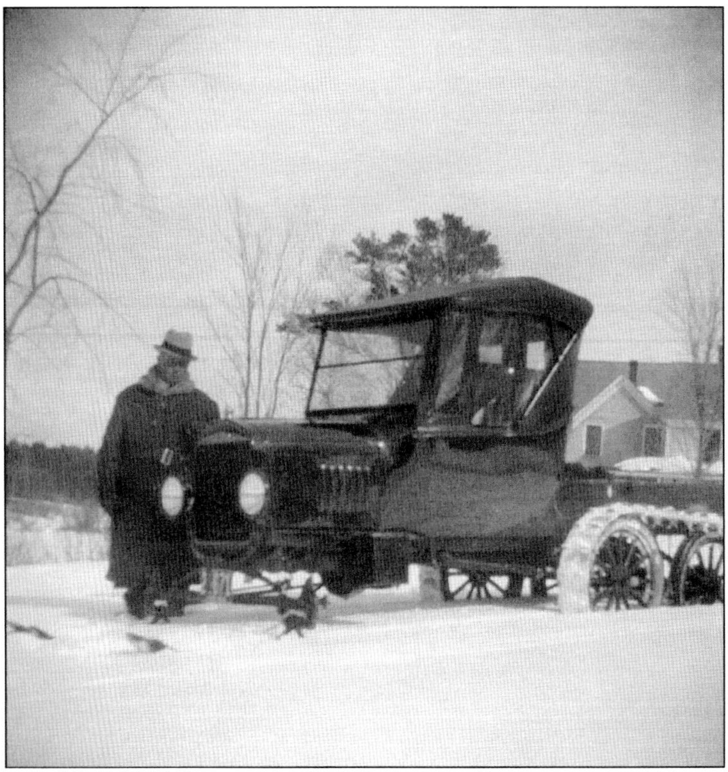

In the mid-1920s, "snow vehicles" were novelties that were used for winter travel, as they required no specific trails or roads and automobiles were unable to be used in deep snow. The front wheels of a snow vehicle were taken off and replaced with skis, and a set of tracks with two wheels was attached to the rear wheels. At one time these were popular for rural mail delivery.

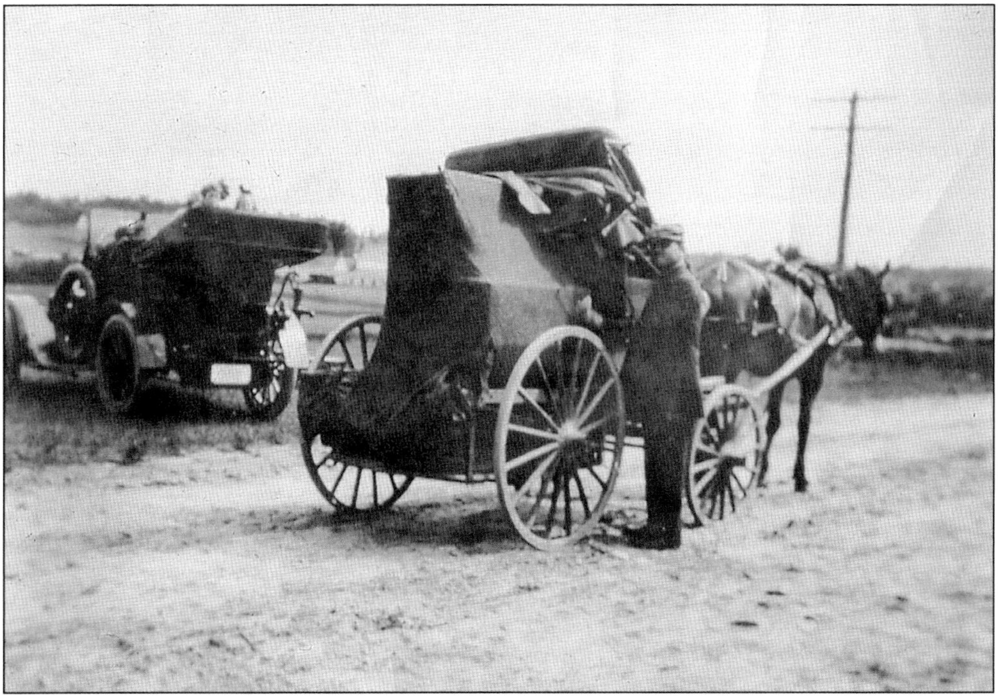

In simpler days, during the easy summer months, there was the itinerant music vendor who visited towns on his meandering circuits, carrying hand instruments in his bags or, as shown here, traveling with a horse-drawn Hurdy-Gurdy. Listening to his music was free, but a coin for a meal for himself or his beast or repair services on his wagon was appreciated.

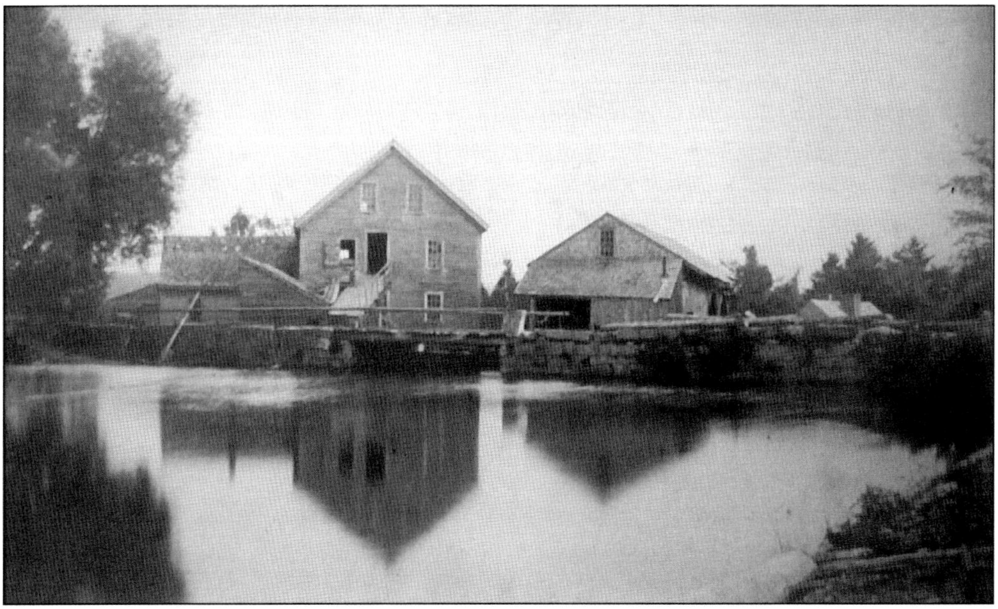

The buildings seen here were located above the old fish hatchery on Mill Street. Nehemia Mitchell operated a tannery, and "Mill" Jesse Plummer ran the sawmill. All the buildings shared common water rights. The logs floated from Panther Pond into Panther Run to the sawmill, where they were then drawn up the ramp to be sawed. These buildings burned down in the mid-1800s.

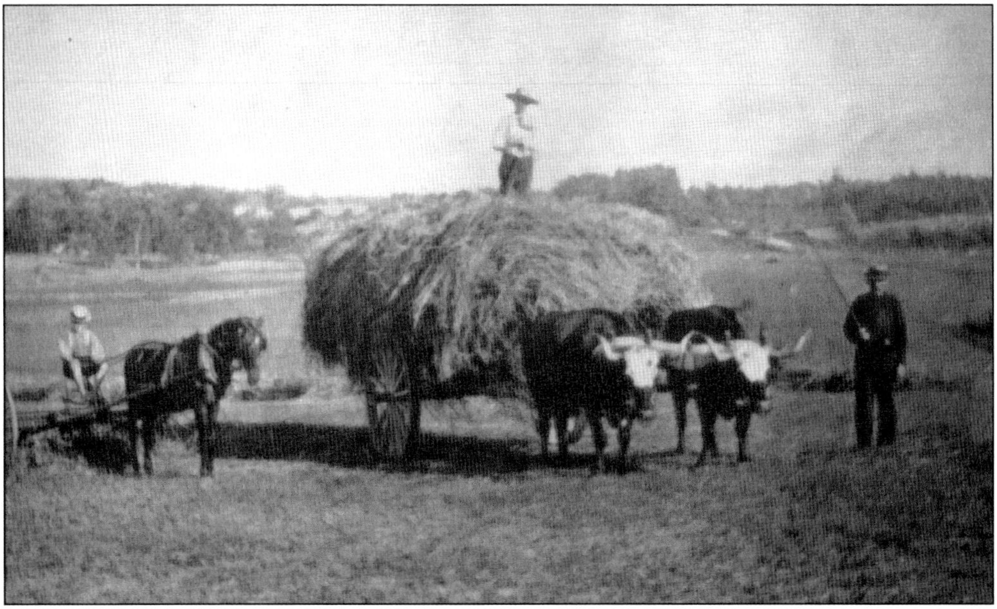

The golf course at King's Grant, once Pine Grove Farm, was a hayfield with generations of Haydens farming it. Oxen were used for most of the farm work, and this picture shows the drag rake used to gather the scatterings after the windrows had been loaded on the hayrack.

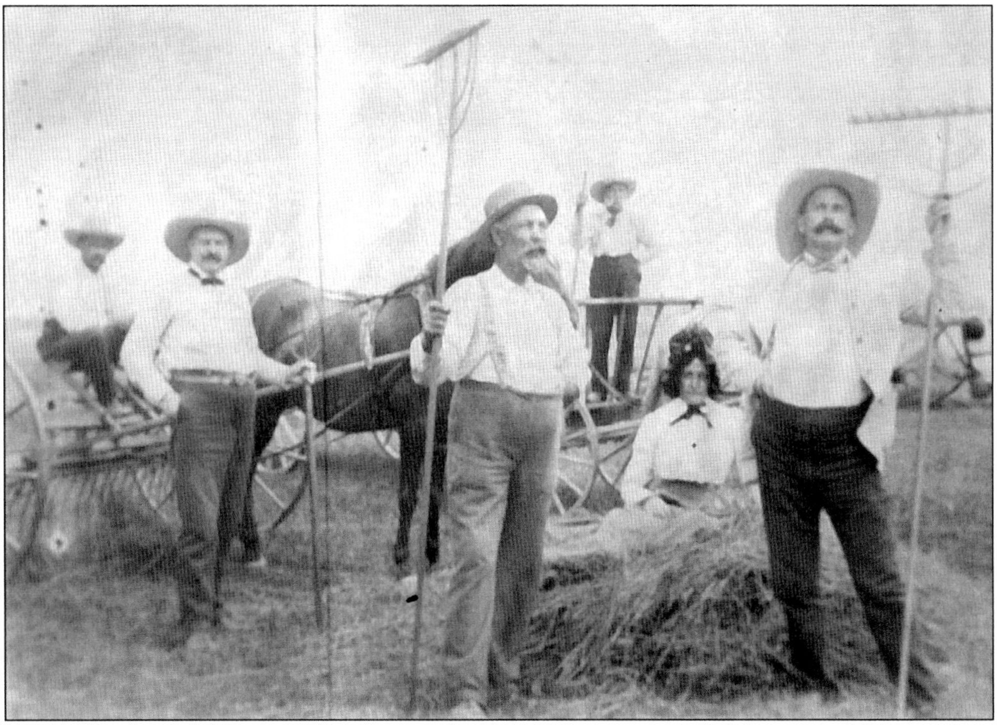

Henry Harmon lived in the Crockett House, located behind what is now Key Bank on Route 302, from about 1880 until 1900. Henry was an enterprising farmer, with his fields extending all the way to the Windham town line. This picture shows his visitors in the field; whether to work or pose is not known.

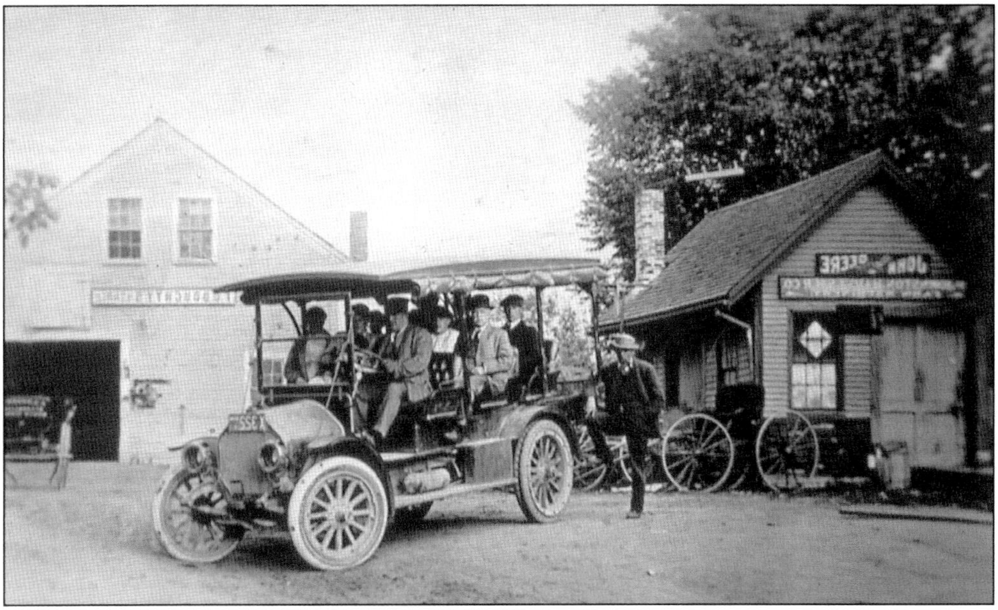

In 1921, the Motorized Stage went from Windham to Raymond to South Casco. Many travelers came for two weeks or more, vacationing at one of the many small inns or boarding houses. The stage was such a novelty that children stopped their play to run out and watch it go by. If they were not blinded or choked by the dust it stirred up, they saw it whiz past at 15 or 20 miles per hour.

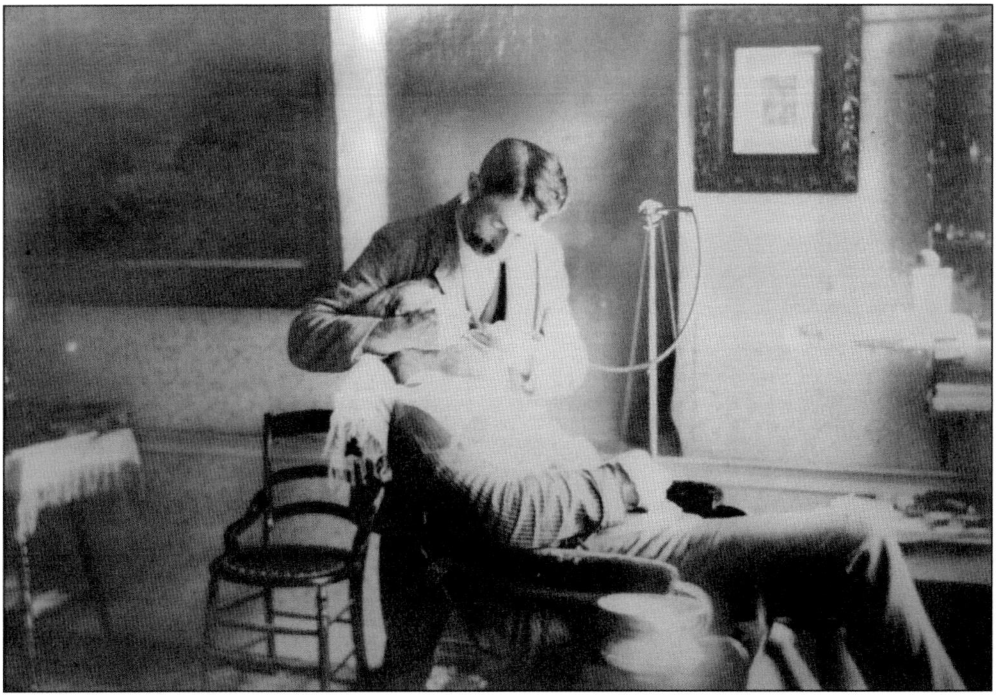

A dentist by profession and a proprietor by choice, Dr. Lloy once owned the Elm Tree Inn. His home was on Route 85, and he operated a guest hotel out of it in the summer, with his dentist office being in the front room. At a time when there was only a foot-powered drill, Summer Plummer is having a tooth repaired in this photograph.

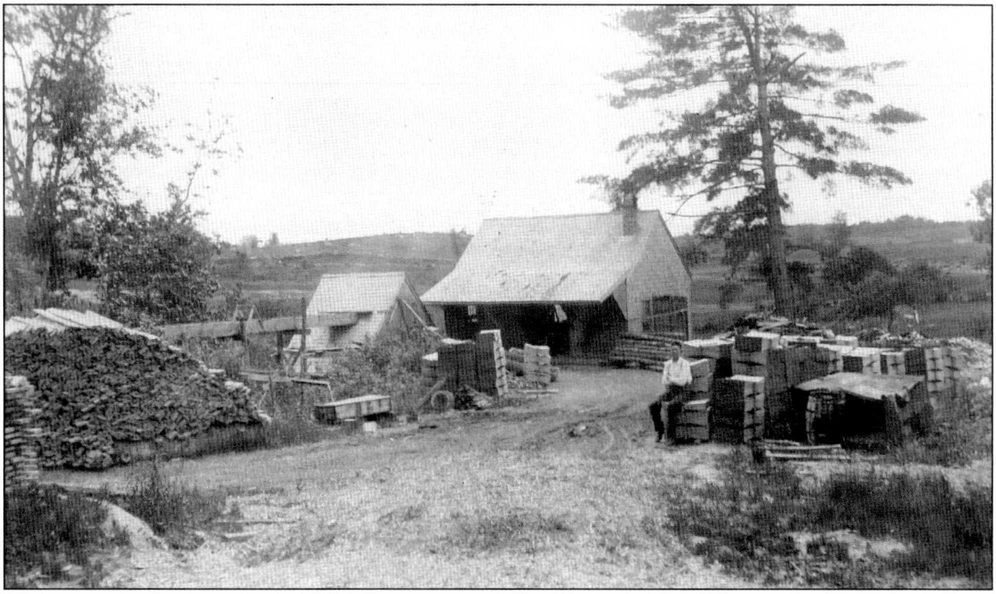

One of the early mills in Raymond was behind "the old house" on Route 85. William Nason operated it for the milling of short stock for staves and shingles. It then became the cooper shop of Robert and Carl Leach, who made barrel staves, mainly of the size used for shipment of molasses from Cuba.

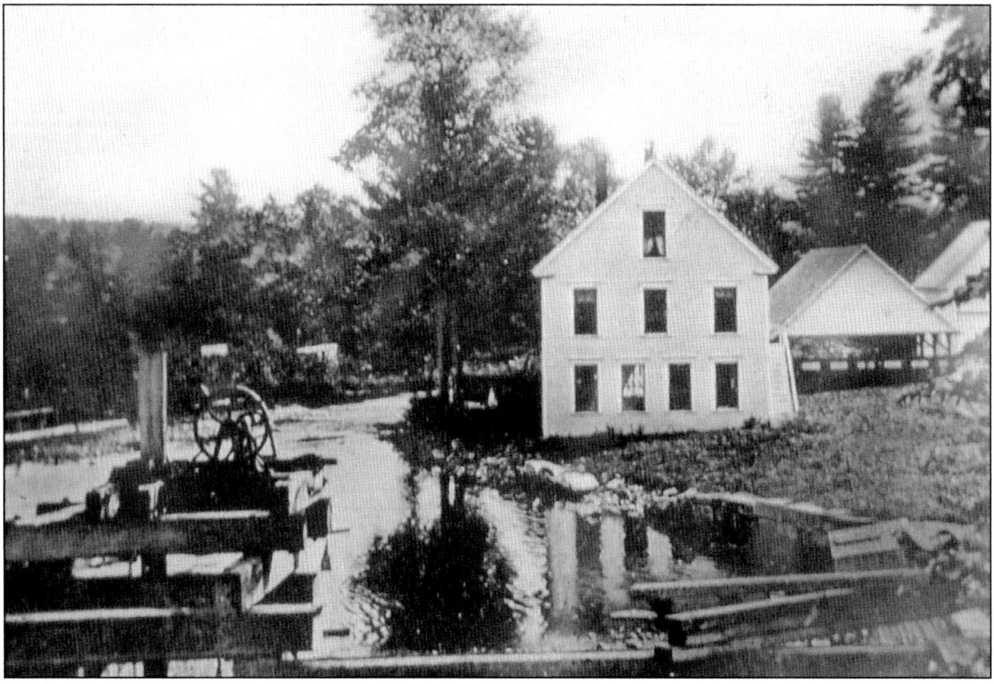

Raymond Fish Hatchery's buildings consisted of the main building, which had living quarters on the second floor for the George Libby family, and the hatching troughs on the ground floor. Behind it were the covered rearing pens and a house for the coal that was used in the steam boiler for heating the main building and the hatching troughs. Maine State Fishing Hatchery operated from 1901 until it closed in the 1950s. The buildings were demolished around 1975.

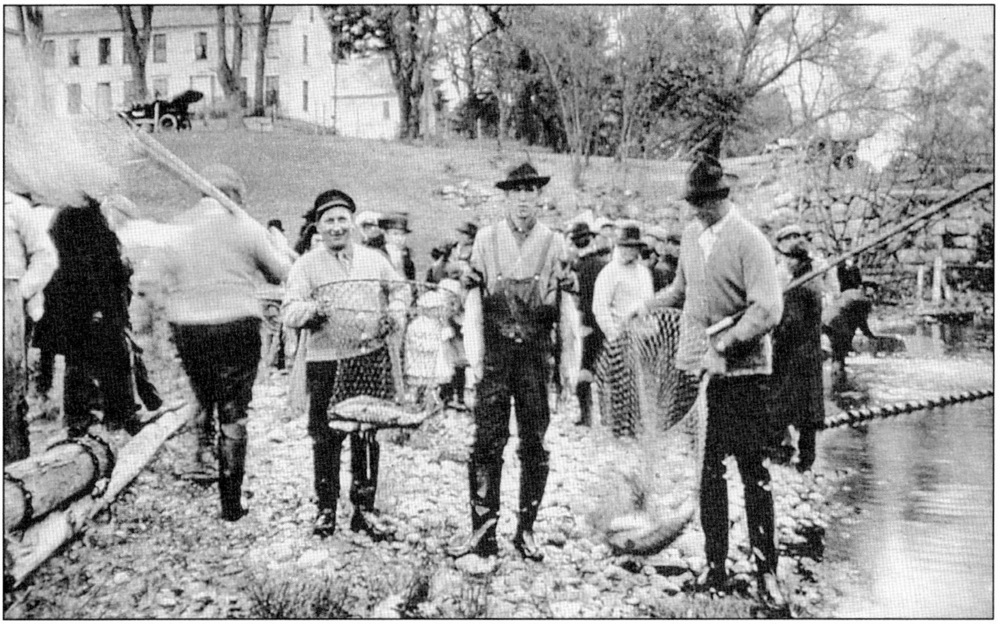

The big salmon have always attracted visitors when spawning fish came up the Jordan River. Albert Plummer (center), superintendent of State Fish Hatchery No. 1, holds up two beauties. The netting of salmon at spawning time was an annual event that drew large numbers of sightseers and notable visitors, one of them being Hiram Ricker, of Poland Spring fame. At one time, there were 2,500 or more fish to strip, some weighing up to 35 pounds or more.

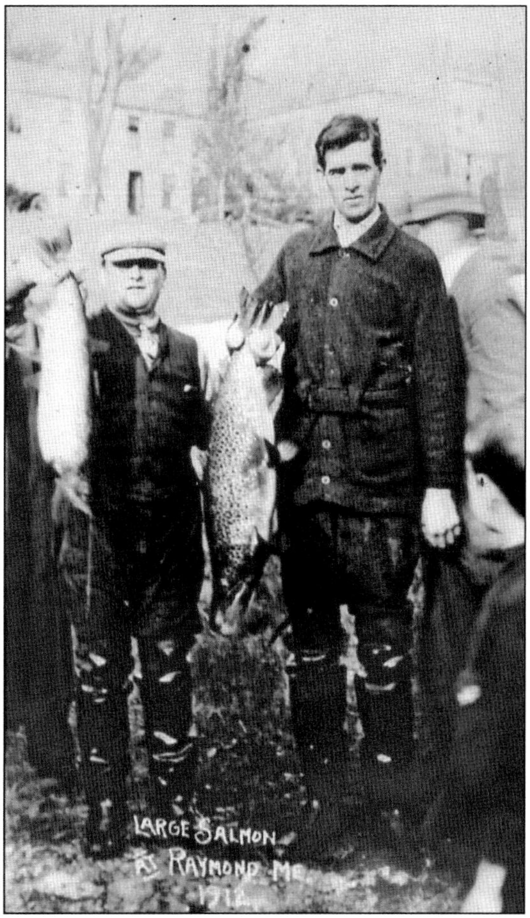

Samples of the larger salmon taken from the pool area are being held here by George Libby (left) and Albert Plummer (right). Records of State Fish Hatchery No. 1 from 1901 to 1930 show that, in 1919, 1,250,000 eggs were stripped from the female salmon. Netting, holding, and stripping salmon in those days would have been hard work.

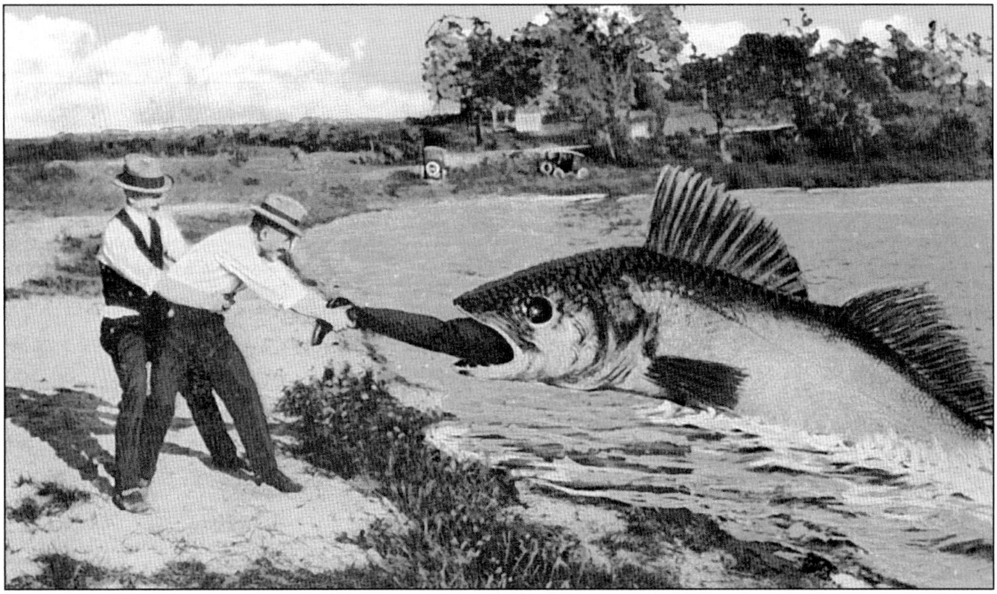

Legends are known of the salmon in Maine, and with a big fish like this waiting to be caught, it is no wonder sportsmen from all over the world beat a path to the shores of Sebago Lake. It was often said around these parts that if you could not catch a fish in Sebago, they would catch you.

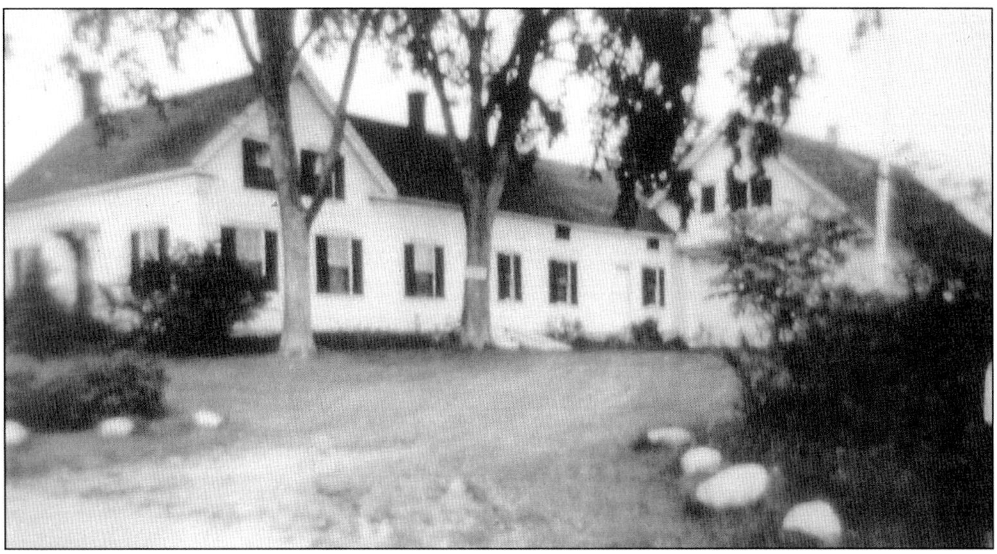

In 1924, William Gladstone bought his home sight unseen. More than 135 years old, this eight-room house looked out on Raymond Lake and the While Mountains. Born in 1882, Gladstone, as a young teen, ran away from home and went on to become a vaudeville star. He did shows all over the country, many of them at US Army camps during World War I. One of his biggest achievements as an entertainer was reciting *Gunga Din* for Pres. Theodore Roosevelt and Pres. Warren G. Harding.

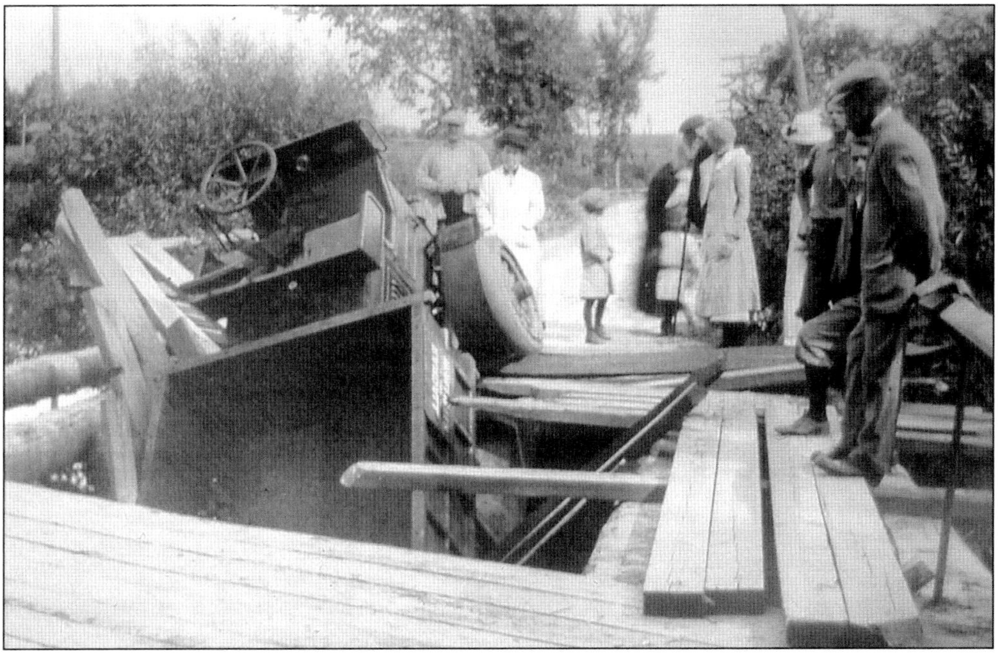

Around 1915, the old bridge at the junction of Route 85 and Route 302, where the roadside turnout is now, was covered with planks that groaned and rumbled when a vehicle passed over it, sending a shower of sand down on an unlucky rowboat that might be under it. As there was no way to call a tow truck at the time, maybe a neighbor's ox team pulled this truck out.

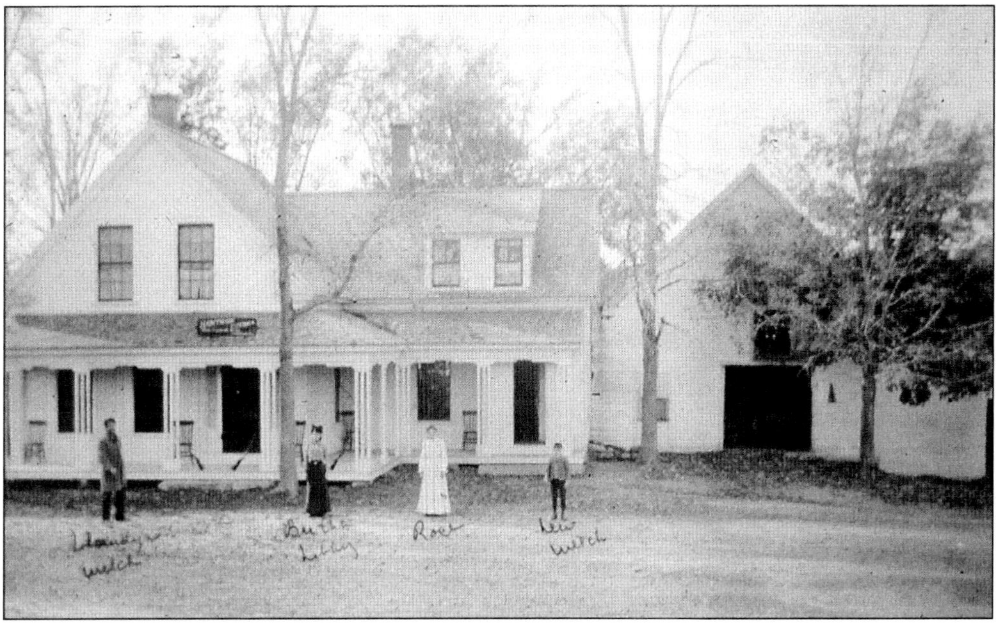

This is a picture of the Llewelen Welch place across the street from the Hawthorn House on Raymond Cape Road. At one time, it took in boarders and was called Hawthorne's Cottage. "Judge" Llewelen Welch served as a trial justice for this area for many years. He also operated a general store across the road. This picture shows, from left to right, Llewelen Welch, Bertha Libby, and Rose and Lew Welch.

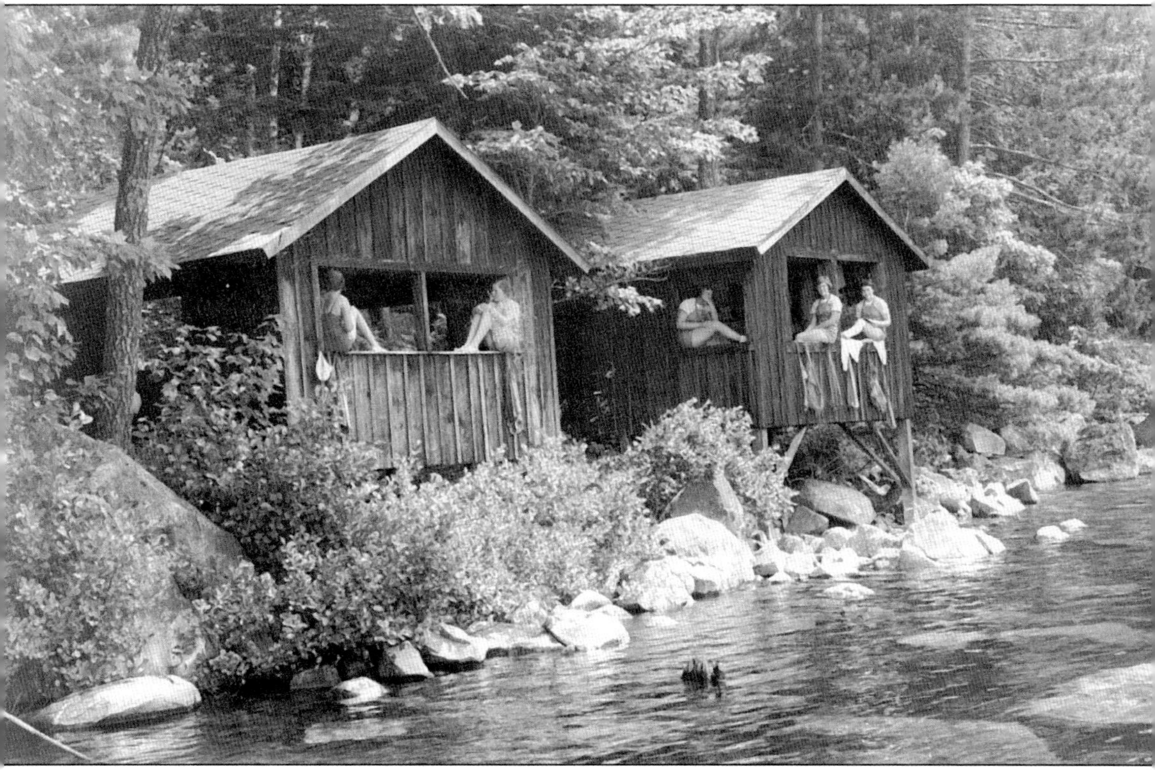

The Luther Gulick Camps were founded by Dr. Luther Halsey Gulick and his wife Charlotte in 1907 and are still in operation today as one of the most outstanding summer camps in the world. Pictured here are two of their cabins, Bent Nail and Twisted Screw, on the shores of beautiful Sebago Lake. Doctor Gulick was a founding father of Camp Fire Girls, one of the very first camps for girls in the United States. Wohelo was designed to let girls experience wildlife in a safe and controlled atmosphere.

More than 50 years ago, Dielectric founder Dr. Charles "Doc" Brown was involved with research that resulted in materials used for the transmission lines for early radar systems that were used during World War II. After the war, technology was applied to the new field of television, and they supplied equipment for NBC, CBS, and ABC. Dielectric was incorporated in 1942 by Doc Brown, and following one of his fondest dreams, he moved the company to his home town of Raymond in 1954. Today, their equipment is sold all over the world.

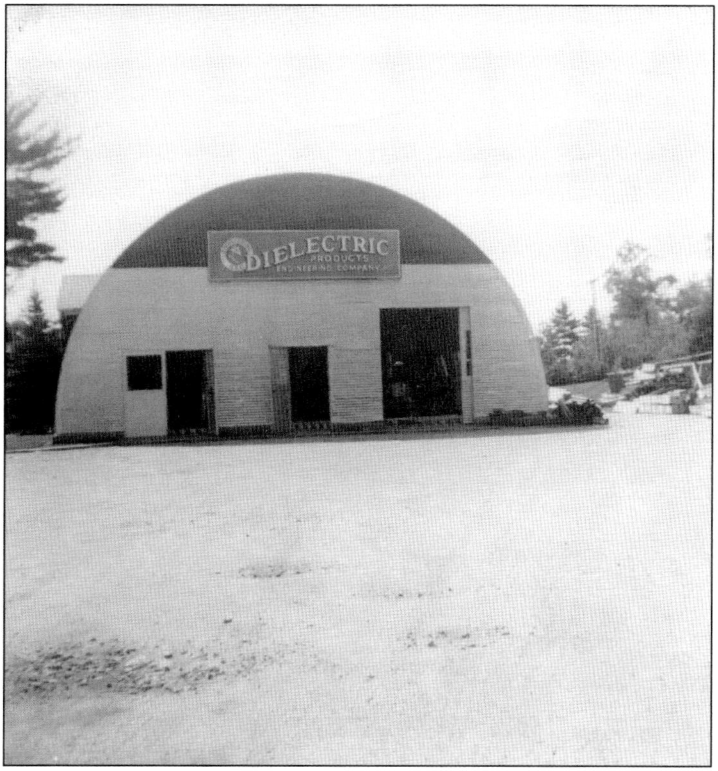

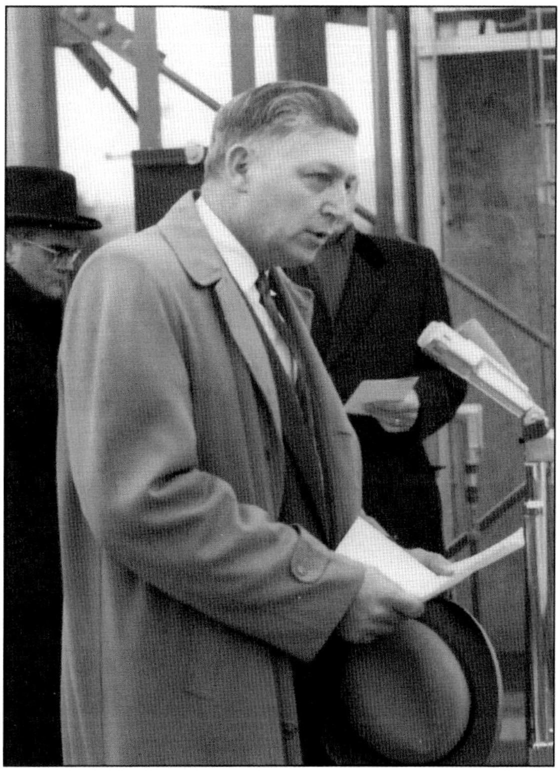

Carlton E. Edwards (1909–1991) lived all his life on the family dairy farm in North Raymond. Carlton served in the Maine House of Representatives for six terms during the 1950s and even served as a house minority leader. He also was a selectman in Raymond for 53 years, a state record, following in his father's footsteps.

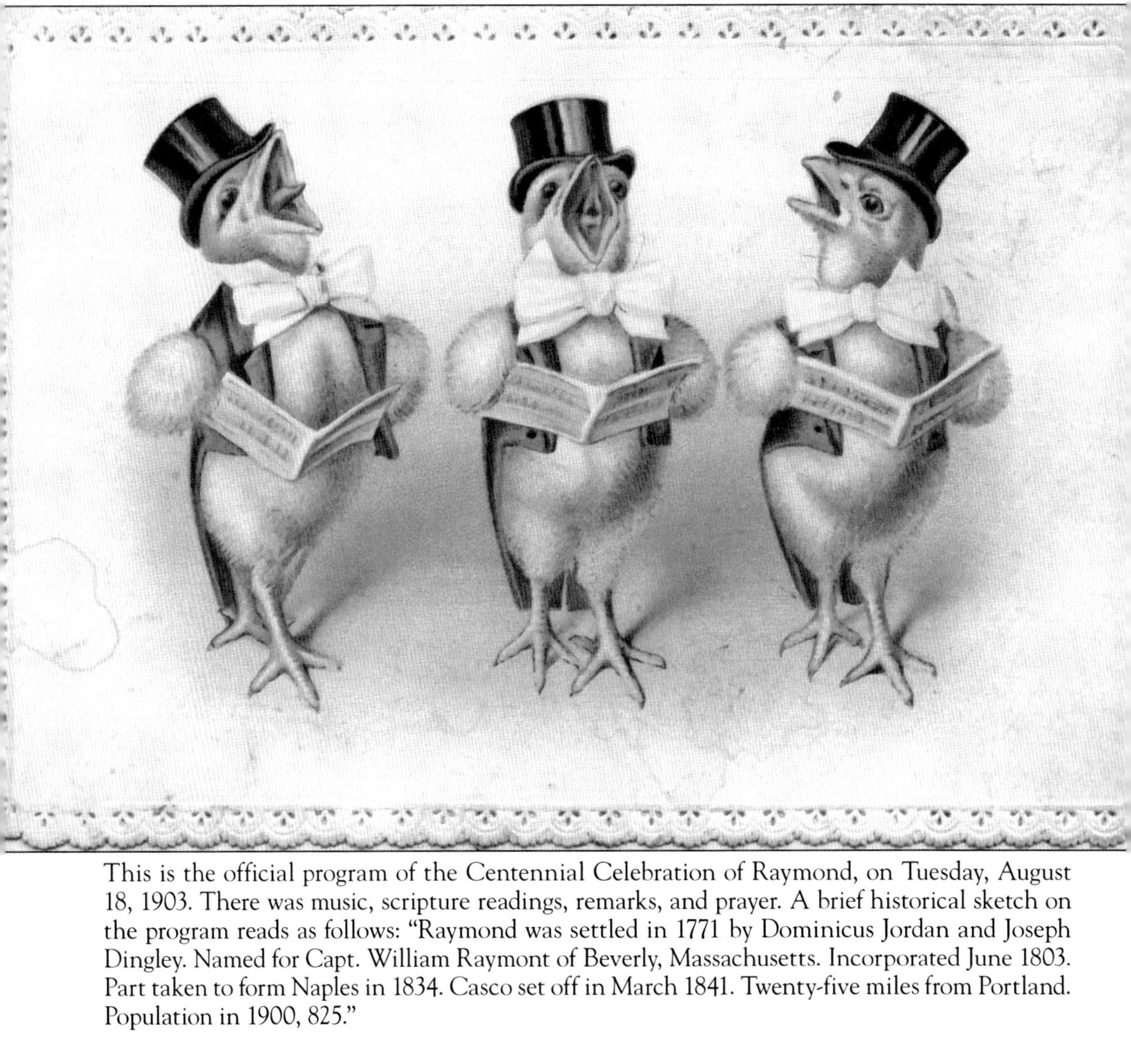

This is the official program of the Centennial Celebration of Raymond, on Tuesday, August 18, 1903. There was music, scripture readings, remarks, and prayer. A brief historical sketch on the program reads as follows: "Raymond was settled in 1771 by Dominicus Jordan and Joseph Dingley. Named for Capt. William Raymont of Beverly, Massachusetts. Incorporated June 1803. Part taken to form Naples in 1834. Casco set off in March 1841. Twenty-five miles from Portland. Population in 1900, 825."

Three

CASCO

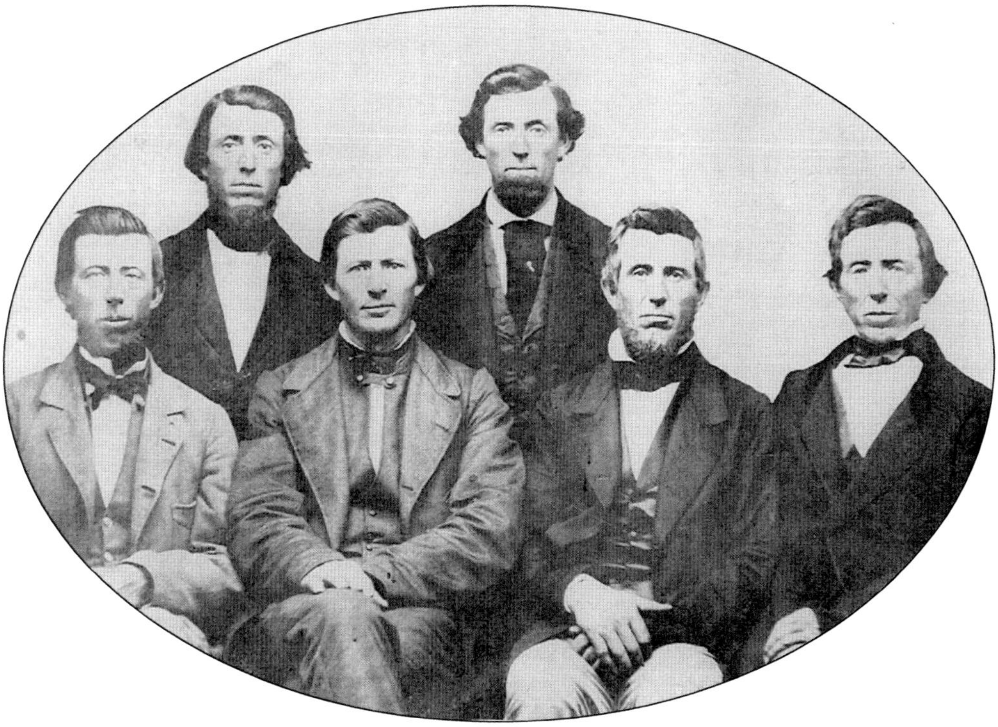

The sons of Richard and Mary (Mayberry) Cook shown here are Benjamin, Richard, William, Silas, Oliver, and Daniel. In the mid-1800s, they ran the mills in Cooks Mills. They operated a lumber mill and made boxes, barrels, shook, and spool strips. Oliver ran a gristmill and sawmill called Oliver M. Cook and Company. William ran a shingle mill called William M. Cook and Company.

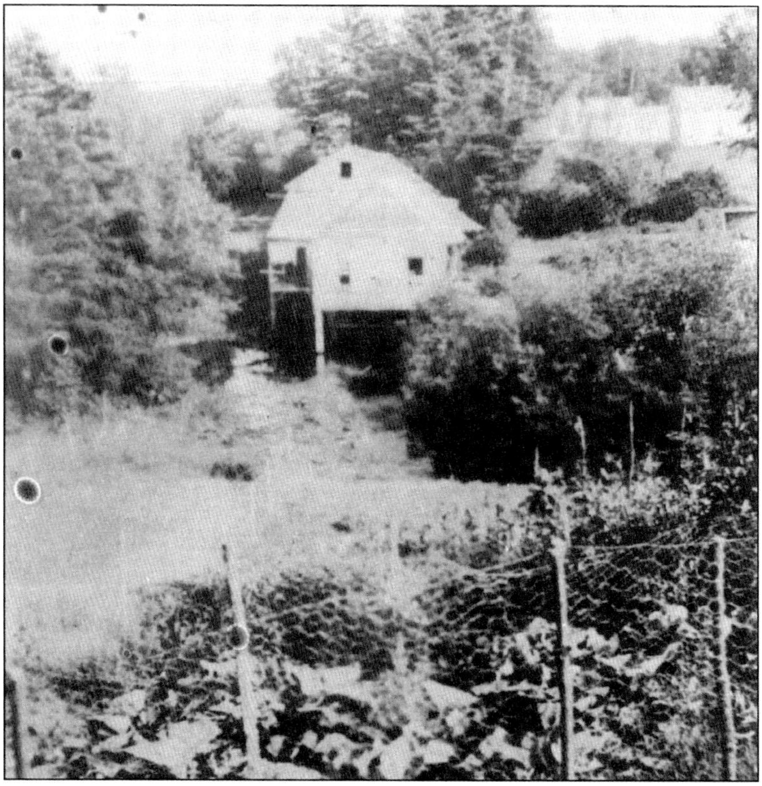

Shown here is one of the mills started in the mid-1800s in Cooks Mills. It was located at the brook on the right side of the Cooks Mills Road going toward Naples. They made boxes and shook. Shook is barrel staves broken down and baled together. They were then taken by wagon to the Portland wharfs and shipped all over the world.

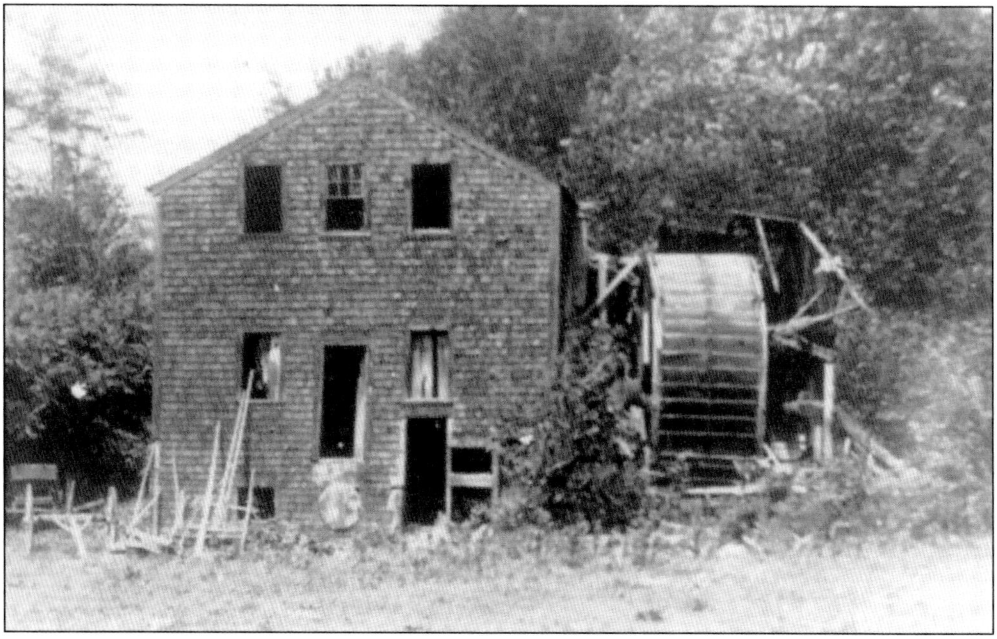

Built in 1856, the Hog Meadow sawmill was about a half mile north from Route 85 on the right side of Route 11. The pond was held by a natural stone barrier, through the top of which was cut a gap to pass water through a flume to the water wheel. The name, Hog Meadow, came after domestic hogs had been allowed to run loose and overtake the area.

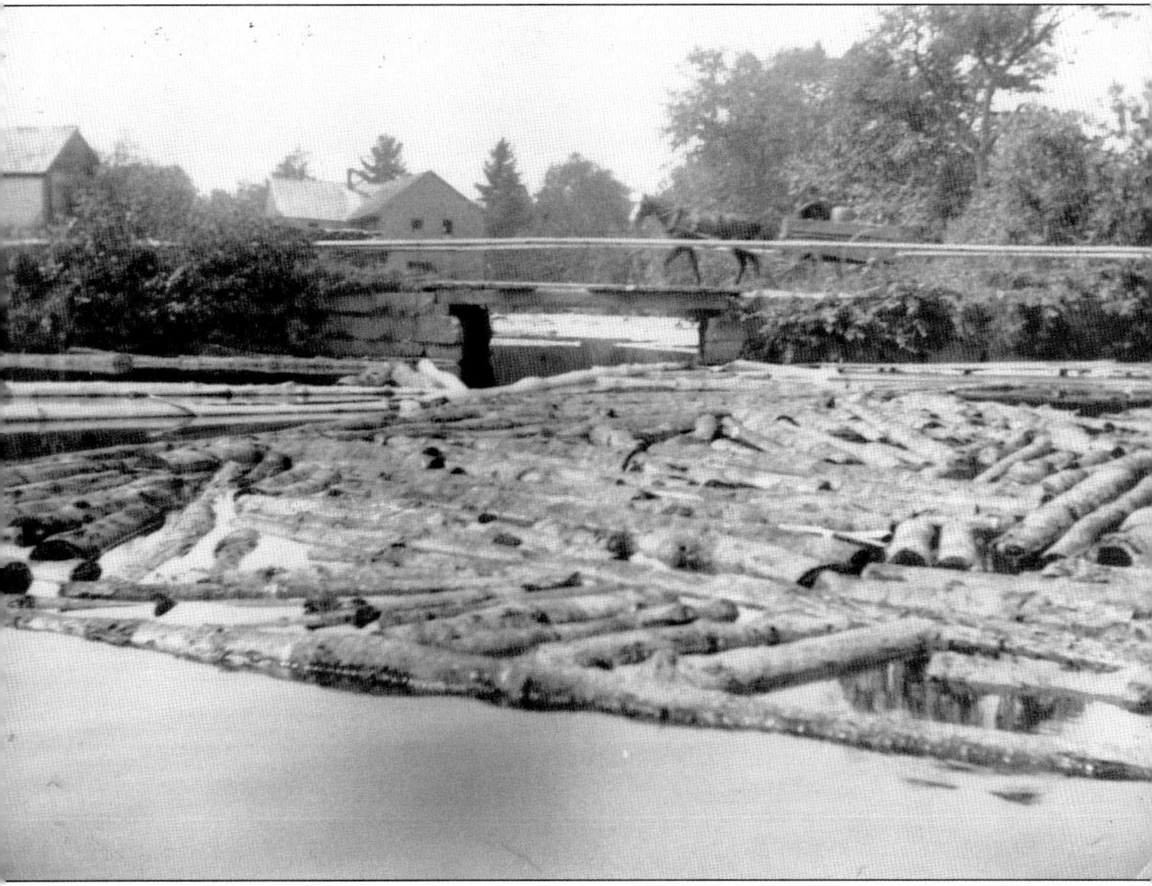

Casco has always been a lumbering community. In 1837, John Holden built a sawmill and a gristmill at the outlet of Pleasant Lake. Deacon Richard Mayberry purchased the mills in 1871 and added a shook and shingle mill. Eventually, Sumner O. Hancock purchased this mill site from Nathan Decker. This mill burned in 1931 but was immediately rebuilt. Today, this is the site of the well-known operation Hancock Lumber, which has flourished under the outstanding leadership of the Hancock family.

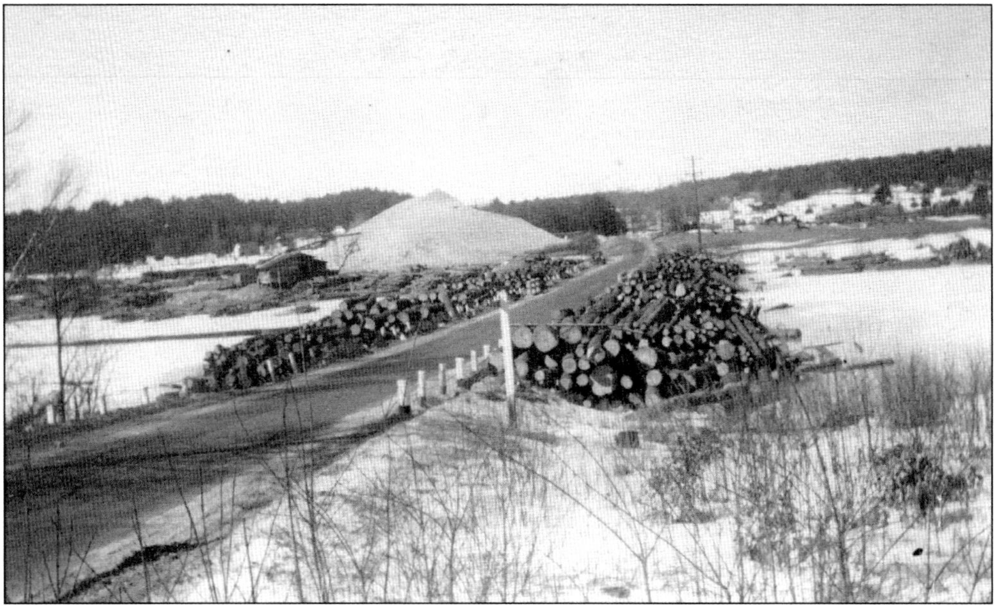

Willard Libby built a sawmill on Route 302 near the Raymond Casco town line in the 1940s. Large piles of logs lined both sides of the dirt road, and a large sawdust pile was once a landmark on entering the village of South Casco. He produced long lumber, one million board feet in 1952, and also made box ends that were shipped to S.D. Warren in Westbrook for packing of their paper.

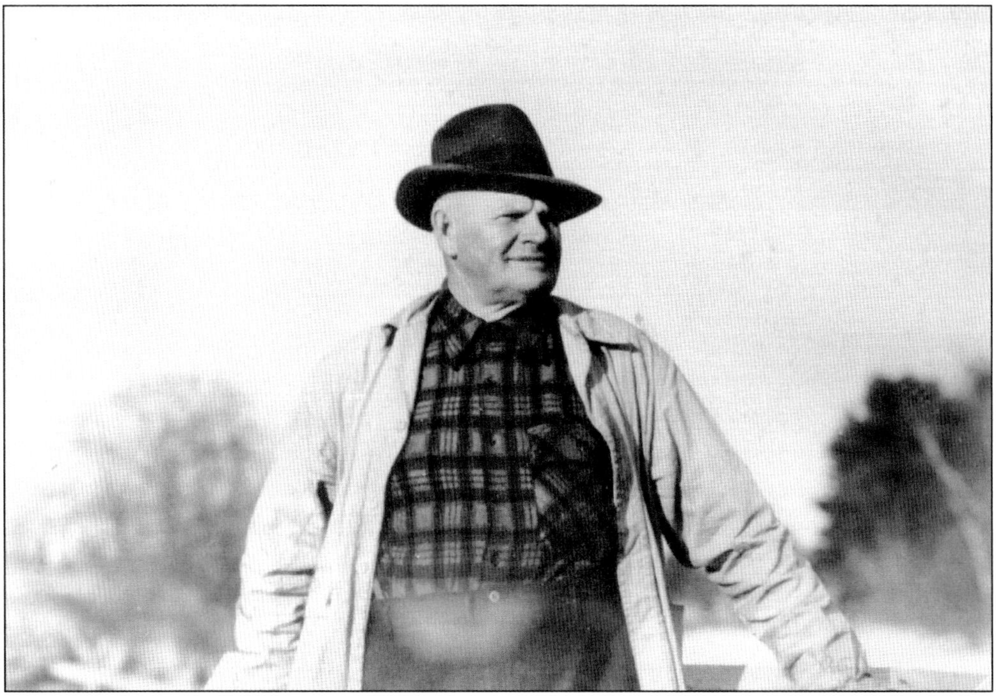

Born in 1882, Willard Libby was the son of William H. Libby and Callie (Watkins) Libby. He was a well-liked and successful businessman with many sawmills in the area. For easier access to one of his mills on the road once called Crossroads, located off Quaker Ridge Road, he paid for this road to be built, thereby earning a new name for the road, Libby Road.

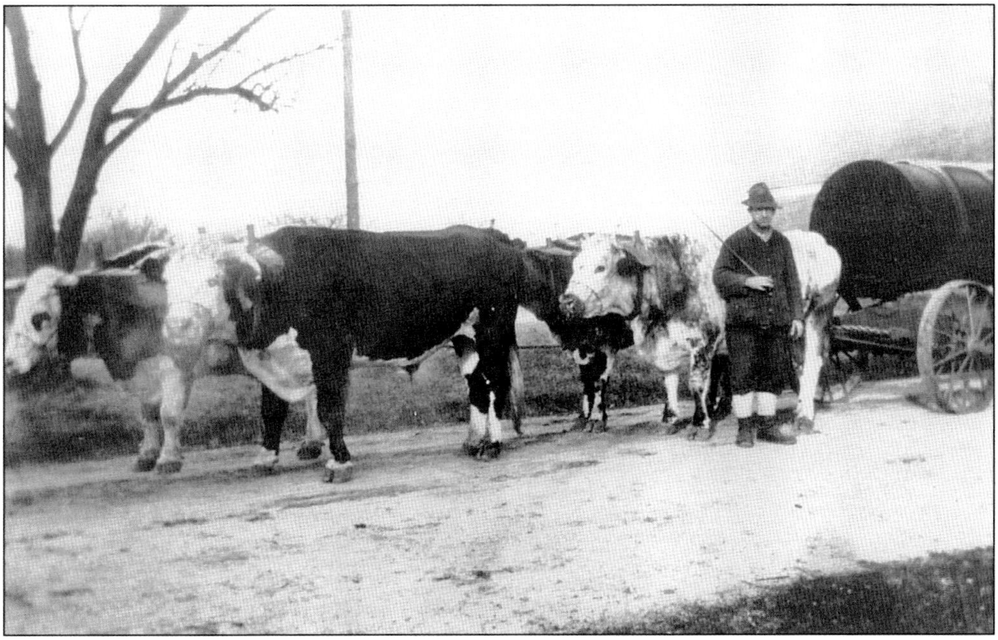

Before the days of easy hauling by trucks, logs were milled into lumber as close as possible to where they were cut. The logs were taken to temporary mills that had to be set up and dismantled; this process could take up to two weeks. Walking all over Casco and nearby towns, Perley McAllister is shown here with his team of oxen taking his steam boiler to a temporary mill.

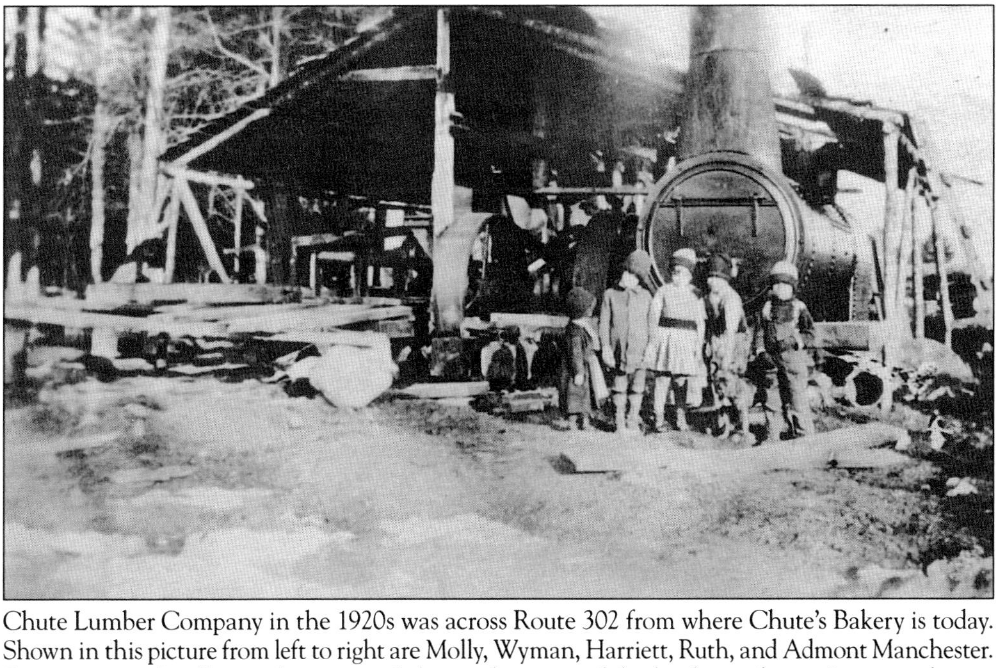

Chute Lumber Company in the 1920s was across Route 302 from where Chute's Bakery is today. Shown in this picture from left to right are Molly, Wyman, Harriett, Ruth, and Admont Manchester. Steam-powered mills greatly increased the productivity of the lumber industry. It was no longer necessary to set up near a river or waterway.

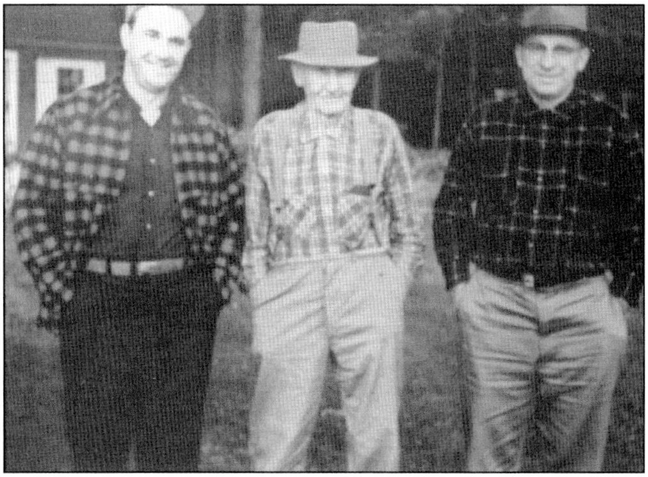

One sawmill in South Casco, started about 1916 by Willard Chute, was the Chute Lumber Company. Operated by steam, the mill was portable. In 1939, the mill was destroyed by fire and was rebuilt as Lake Region Lumber Company by Willard's sons Leander and Robert. The mill continued operations with Leander and his sons and son-in-laws until the mid-1980s. Shown here are, from left to right, Leander, Willard, and Louis Chute.

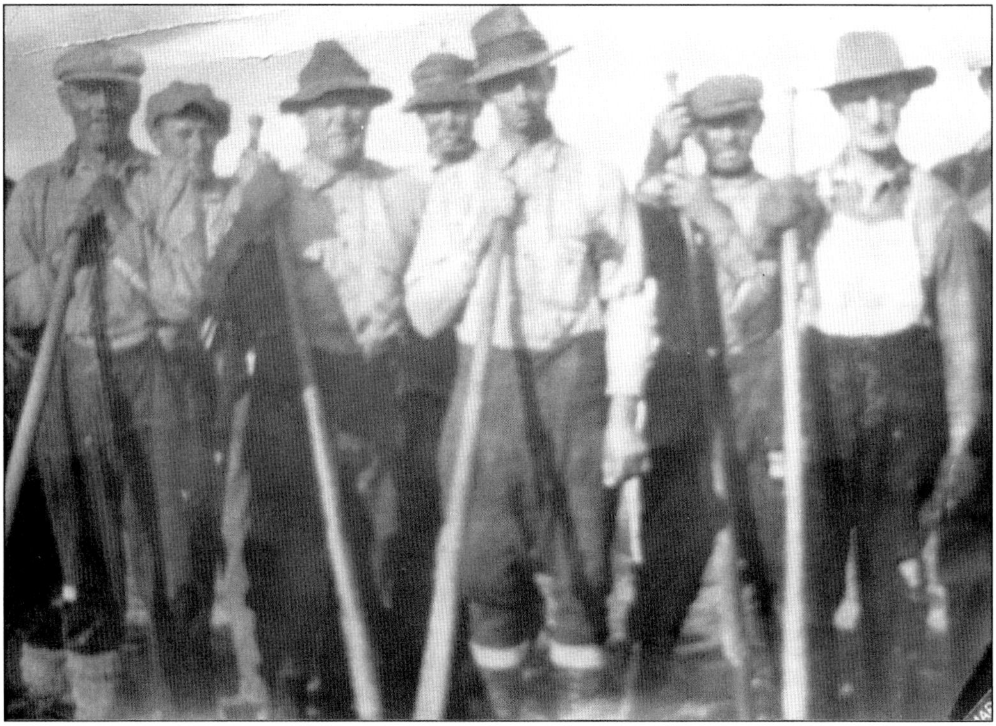

Born in 1887, Leroy G. Tenney, with his wife, Myrtie, and their family, lived on the Fred Tenney farm on Tenney Hill. Leroy was a farmer and worked in the lumber business. Logs were cut in the Jugtown area by the DuPont Company and were then floated down Crooked River into Songo River. These were then boomed down Sebago Lake and into the Presumpscott River. In 1926, at the age of 39, Leroy Tenney lost his life running a log drive. Shown here are, from left to right, Harry Milliken, Ernest Milliken, Harris Knight, John Edson, Leroy Tenney, Warren Flagg, Sid Perkam, and Everett Merrill.

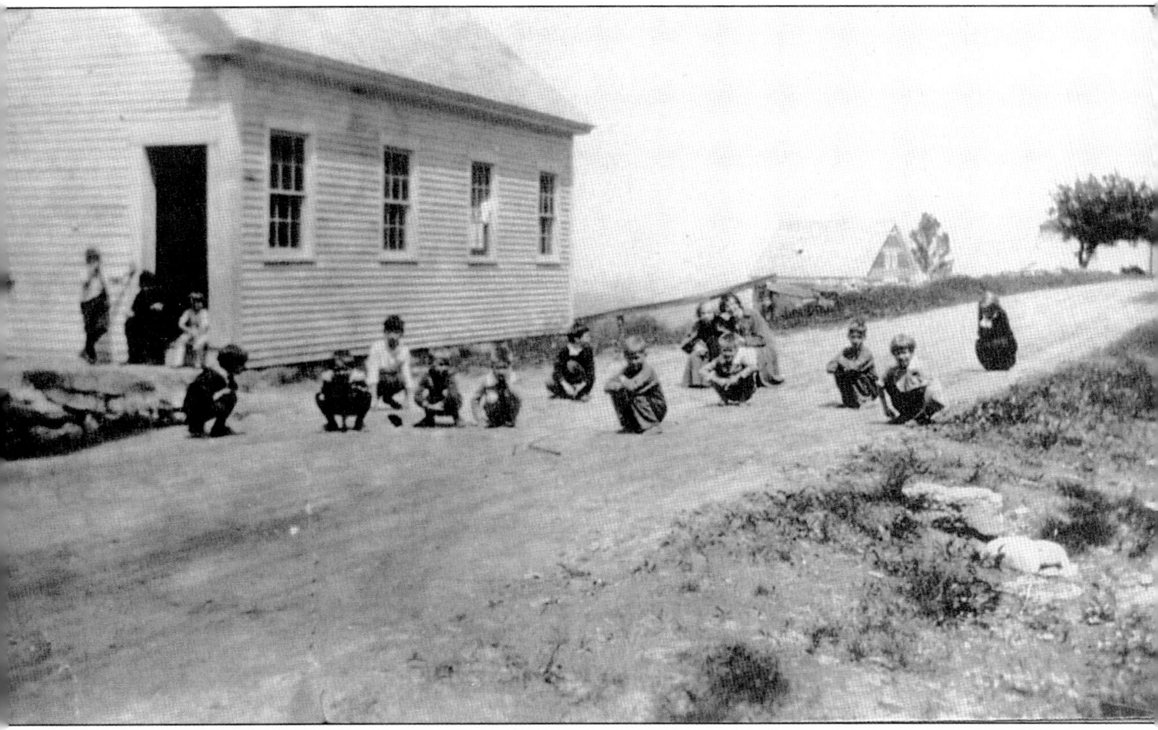

Quaker Ridge School in district No. 4 was built in 1849. This school was on property owned by William Hall and Isaiah Gould. They did not ask for a deed or money; it was a gift in support of education for the children of their town. In 1923, "Scooch Tag" was played right in the middle of Quaker Ridge Road because that was the only area available for their playground.

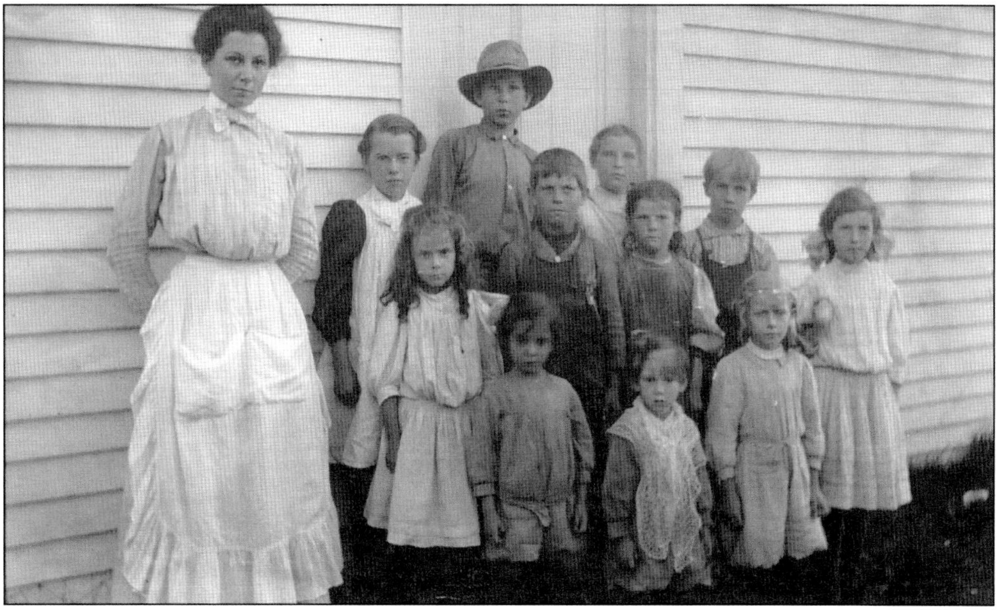

Children of district No. 5 were served by the Shadigee School. Located on Route 11, about two miles east of Route 121, the school burned in the mid-1940s. Shown here in 1910 are, from left to right, Maude Burgess the teacher, and students Hazel Thompson, George Burgess, Sadie Small, Avis Meseve, George and Lucy Small (Watkins), Charles Edwards, twins Harriet and Catherine Burgess, and Helen and Alice Cook.

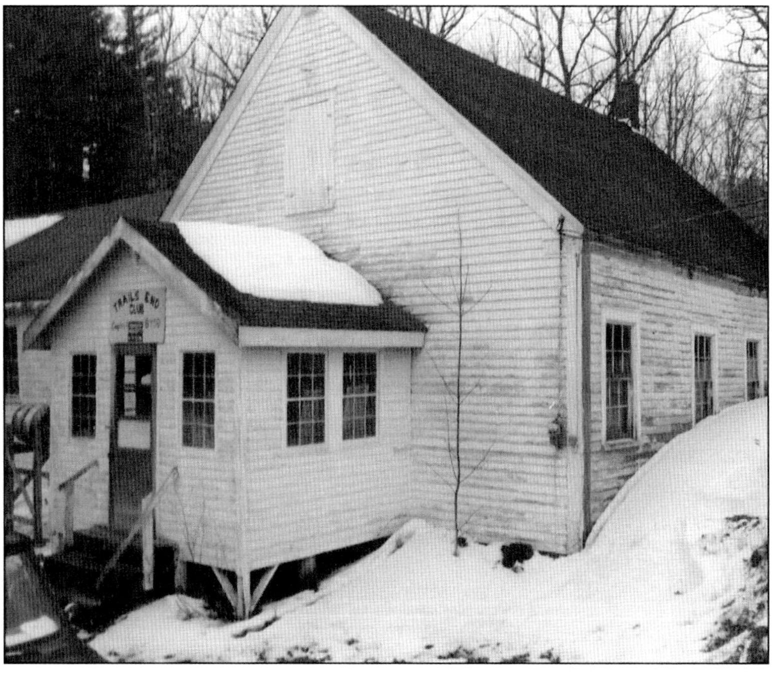

In 1851, the South Casco School in district No. 1 was built on Quaker Ridge Road, near the junction of Libby Road. In the late 1940s, Dr. Bischoffberger, a beloved local doctor for many years, would travel down from Naples and give children their shots for school. After the school was closed, the building became the American Legion Hall. It was destroyed by fire in 1979.

The Webbs Mills School, located on Route 11 and in district No. 9, had a large number of students and was the first to need two teachers. There were two doors in the front, one for boys and one for girls. Inside, there was one large classroom, with heat from a wood-burning stove in the center of the room. The school closed in 1946; today, the building is owned by the Sunshine Club and is used as the Webbs Mills Community Center.

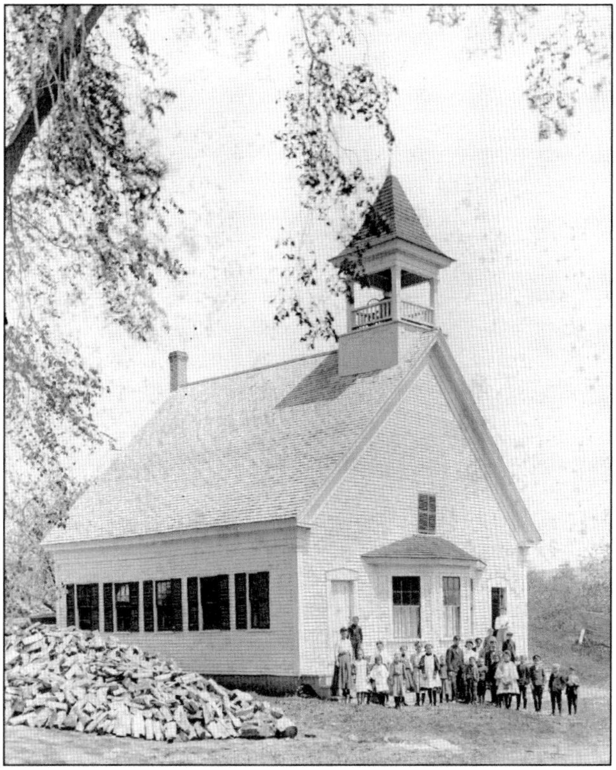

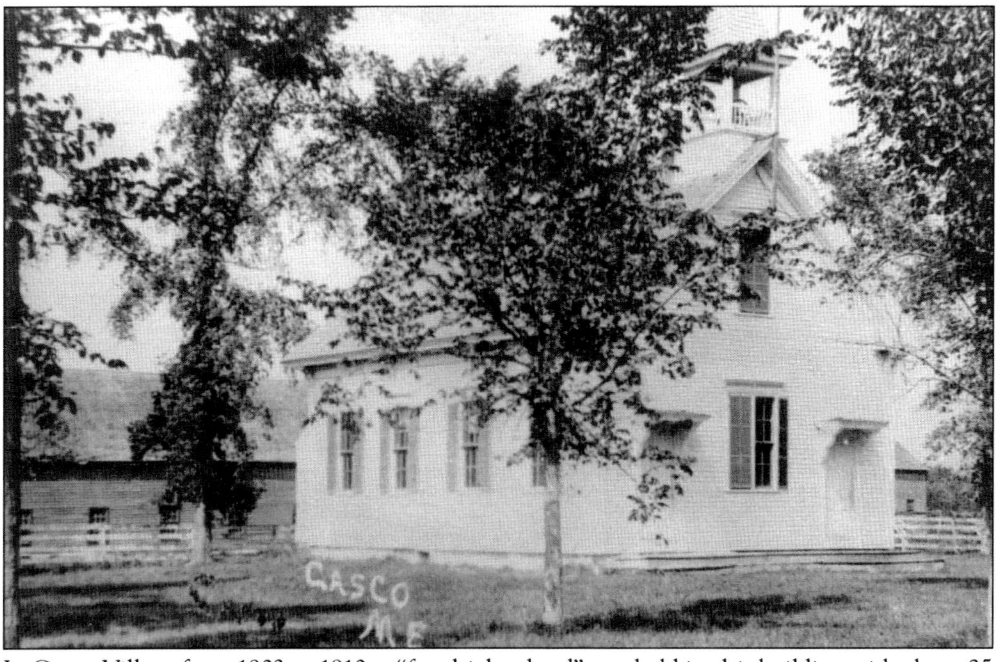

In Casco Village from 1903 to 1910, a "free high school" was held in this building with about 25 to 30 students in attendance. The building burned down in 1911, and classes were held in the hall over Holden and Gay's store until a new school could be built. In 1912, a new school was built on the same site that would become Casco High School.

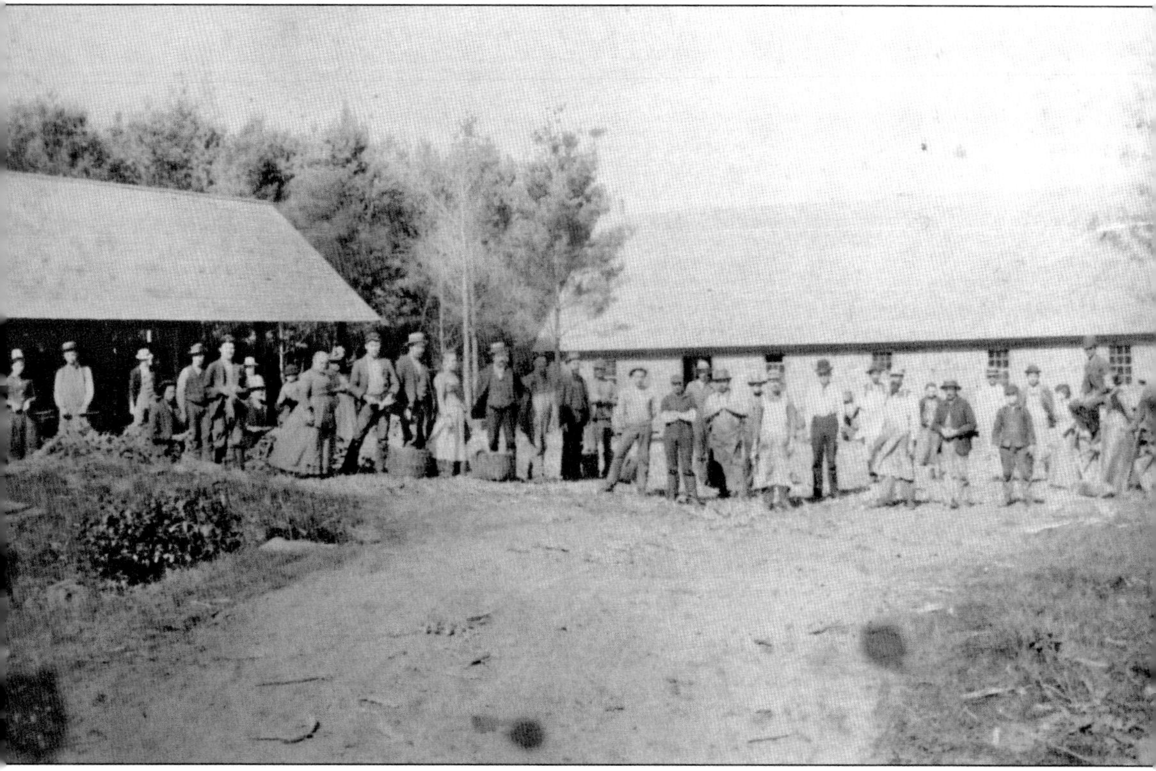

By the turn of the century, Casco had one corn shop, J.N. Eastman and Company. James learned the trade while employed at Burnham and Morrell Company and operated his canning business through the 1920s. Brands of sweet corn canned by J.N. Eastman and Company included Casco Poppy and Casco Pride.

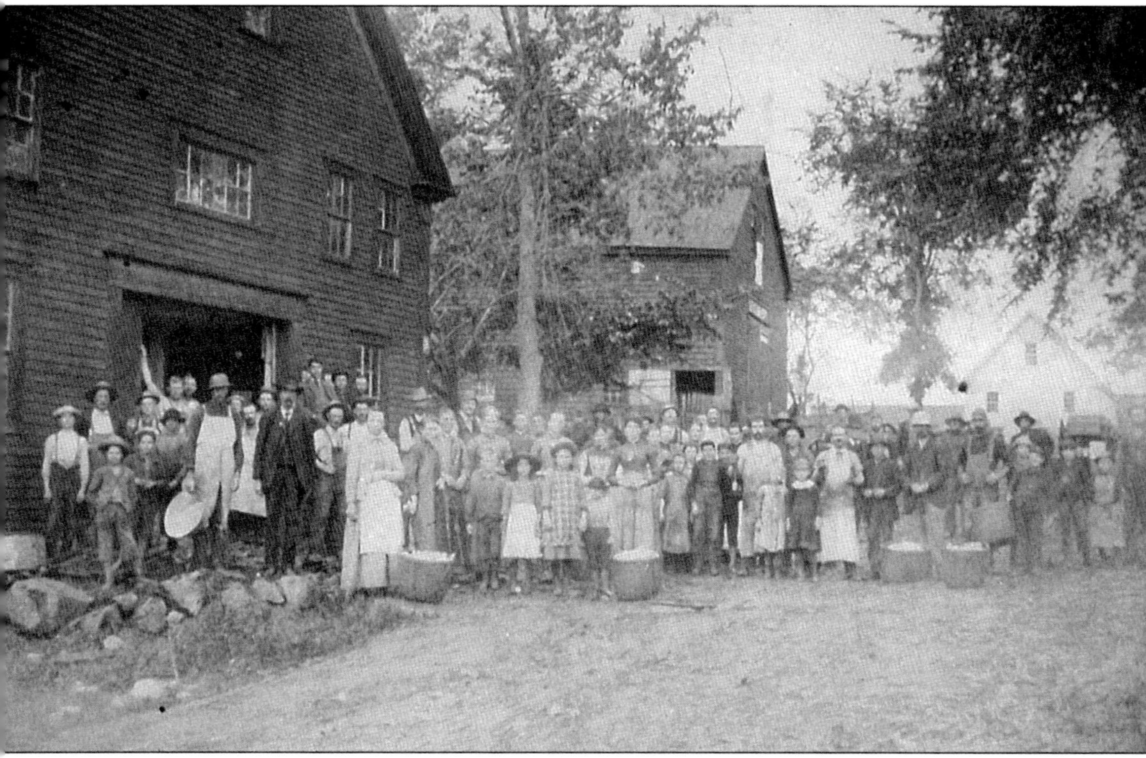

The first locally run corn shop was established in Webbs Mills by John McLellan, of Raymond, in the late 1870s. John McLellan and Company had two corn shops, one in Casco and the other in South Windham. They canned corn and beans in Casco until about 1899.

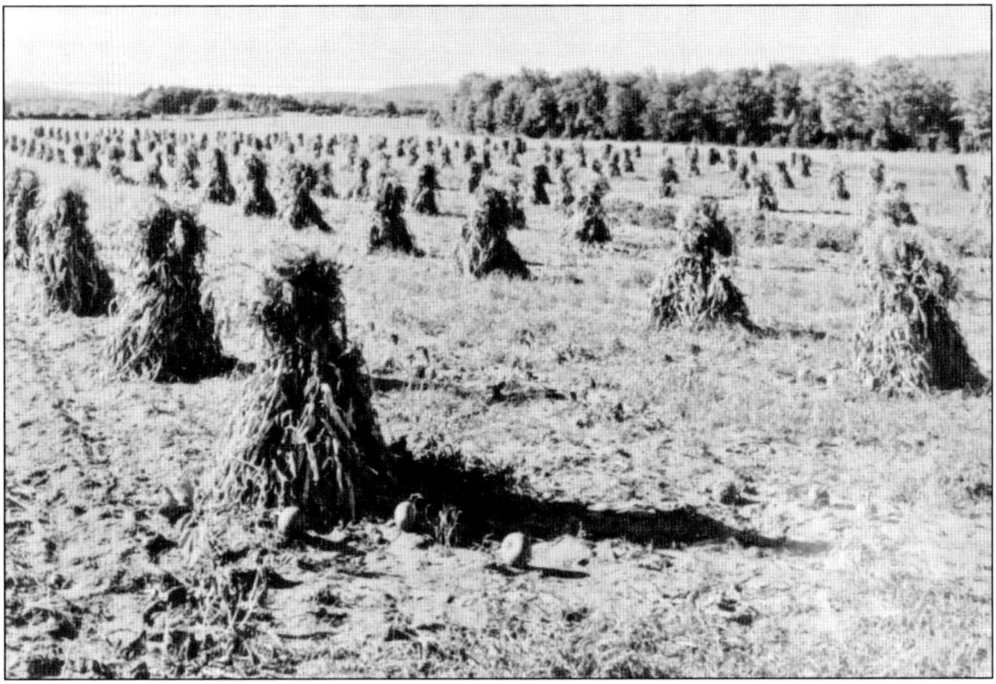

Many farmers raised fields of corn for the local corn shops. The average corn shop would need about 75 acres of corn annually for a good production. After the ears were picked from the corn stalks, many farmers would arrange the stalks, as shown above, for easier removal from the fields.

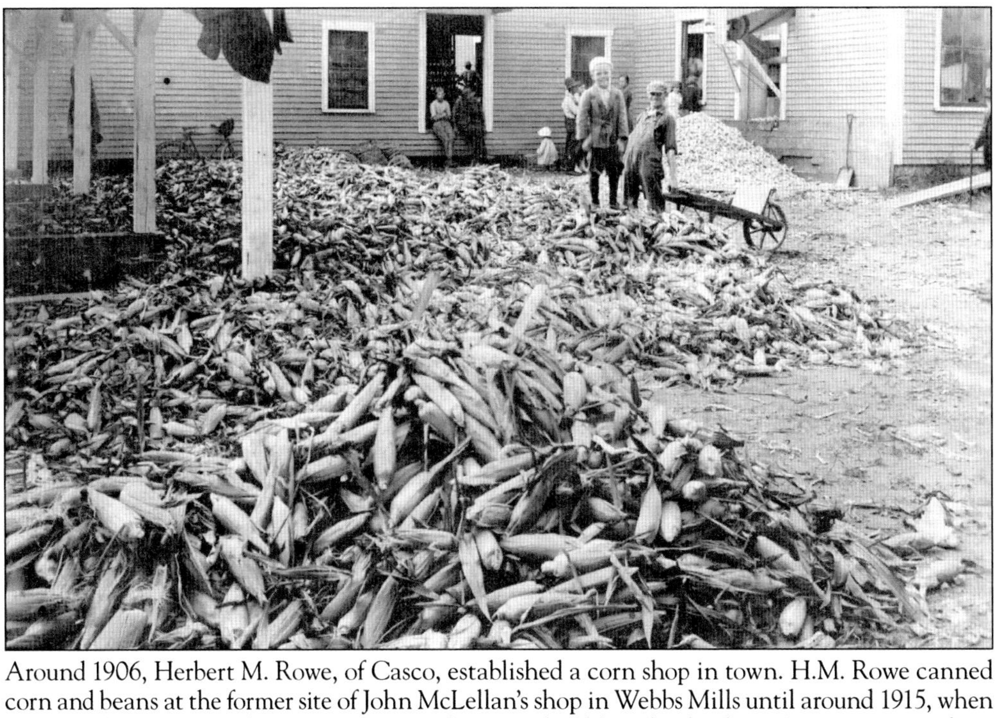

Around 1906, Herbert M. Rowe, of Casco, established a corn shop in town. H.M. Rowe canned corn and beans at the former site of John McLellan's shop in Webbs Mills until around 1915, when the Fernald, Keene, and Trust Company of West Poland bought the firm. As one can see from this photograph, many corn shops employed men, women, and children to do the husking.

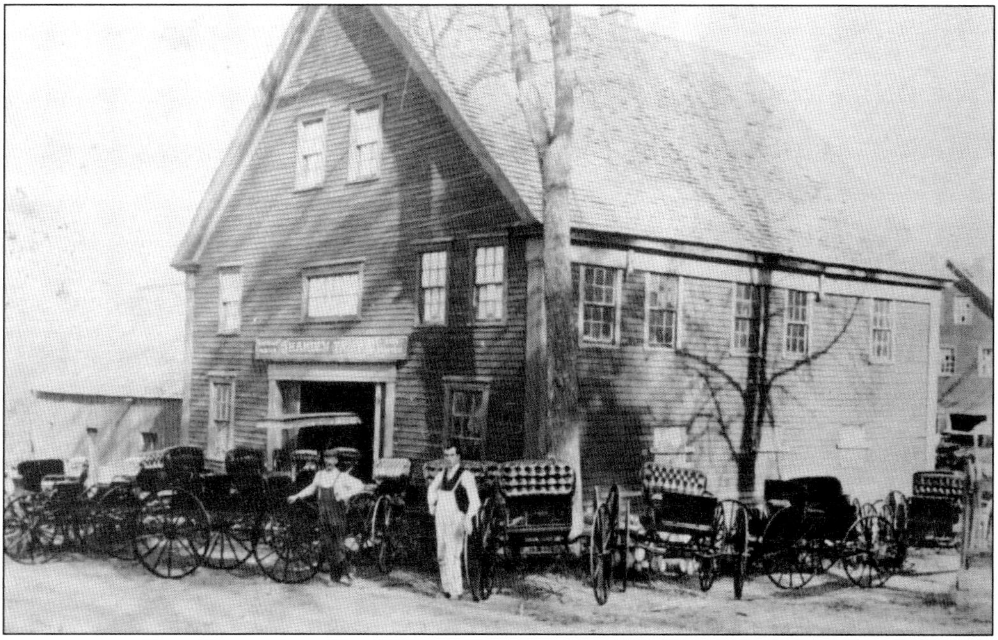

The carriage shop of Hamden Tripp, at one time Richard M. Webb's, was across the street from the present Community Hall in Webbs Mills. Hamden was a well-liked photographer of Casco, as well as a carriage maker. This picture shows Hamden, in the apron, in front of the carriage shop proudly showing his beautifully finished products. This building burned down in the 1930s.

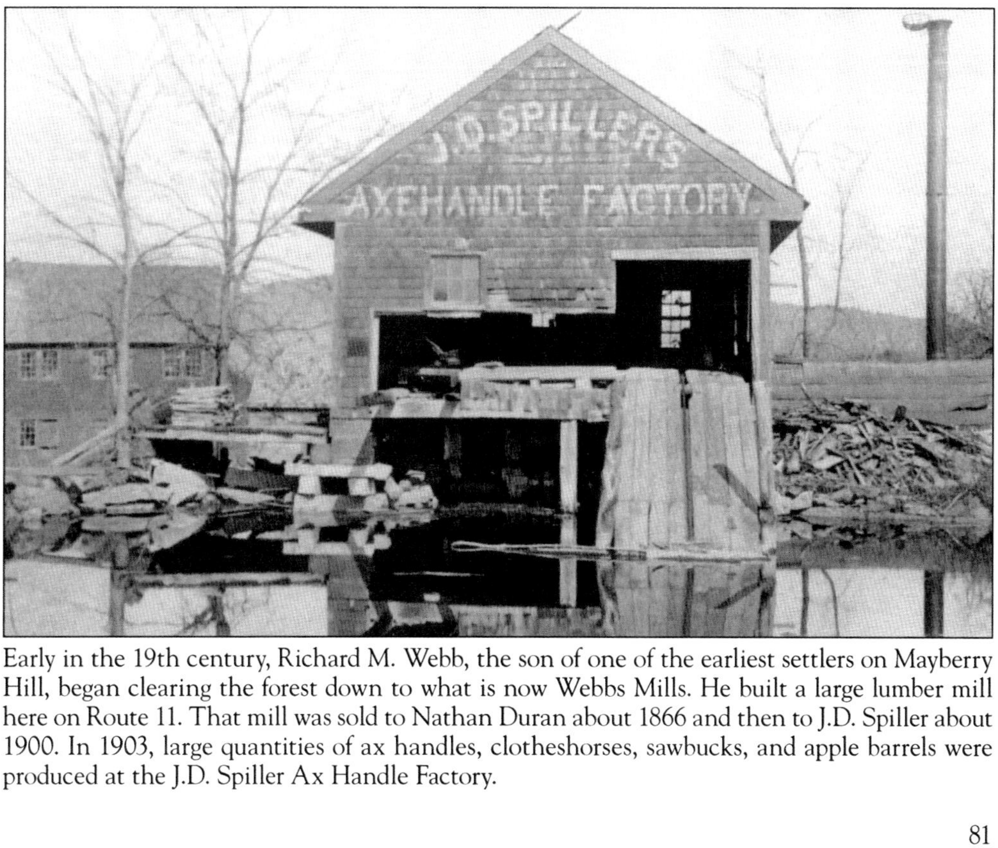

Early in the 19th century, Richard M. Webb, the son of one of the earliest settlers on Mayberry Hill, began clearing the forest down to what is now Webbs Mills. He built a large lumber mill here on Route 11. That mill was sold to Nathan Duran about 1866 and then to J.D. Spiller about 1900. In 1903, large quantities of ax handles, clotheshorses, sawbucks, and apple barrels were produced at the J.D. Spiller Ax Handle Factory.

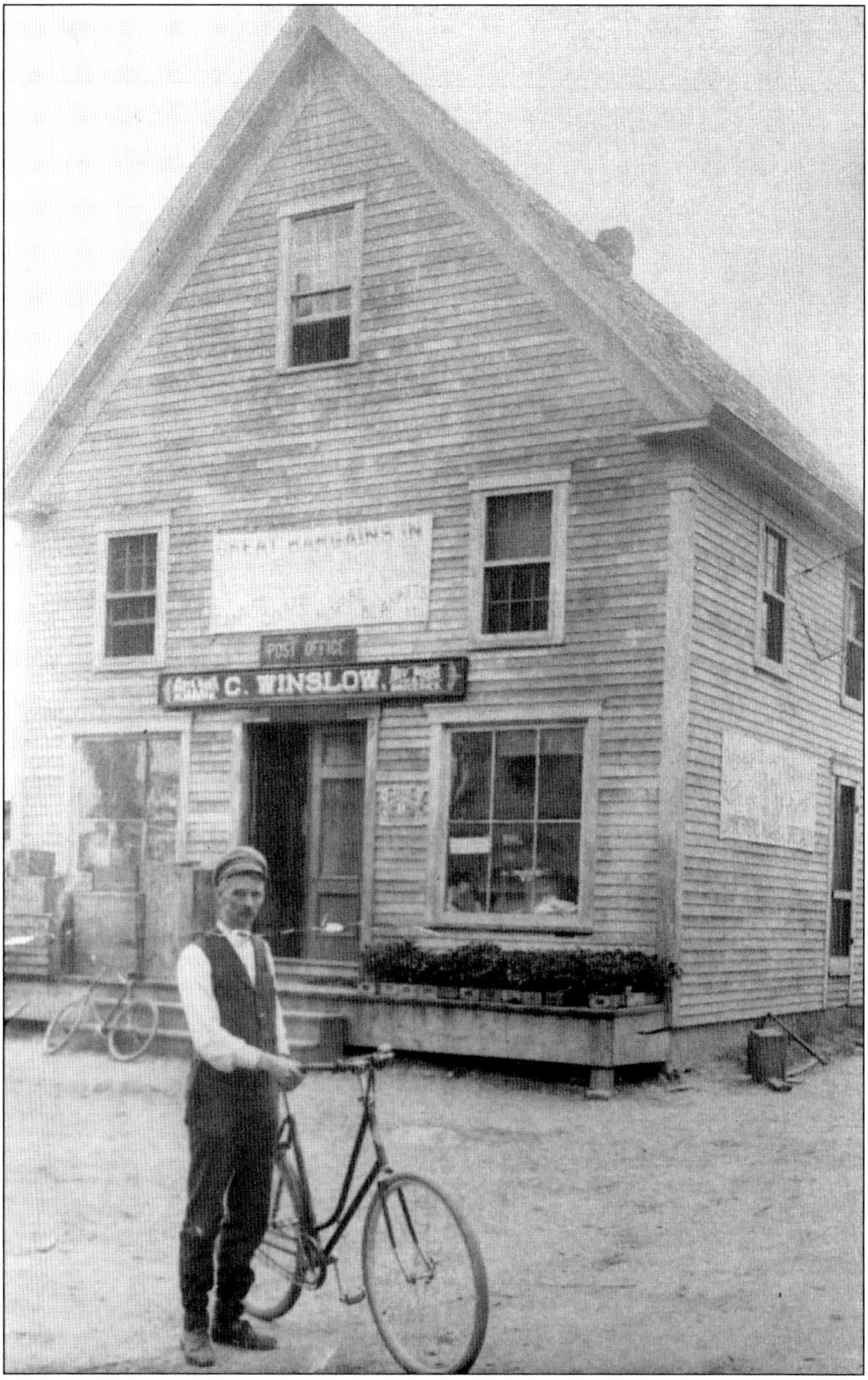

Around 1900, Cad Winslow's store and post office were considered the center of the Webbs Mills area of Casco. This store was well stocked with all the staples and necessities that customers could not raise on their own. Two large wood-burning stoves circled with chairs made a great spot for playing checkers or passing time on cold winter nights for many local folks. Cad never drove a car but rode his bicycle everywhere he went.

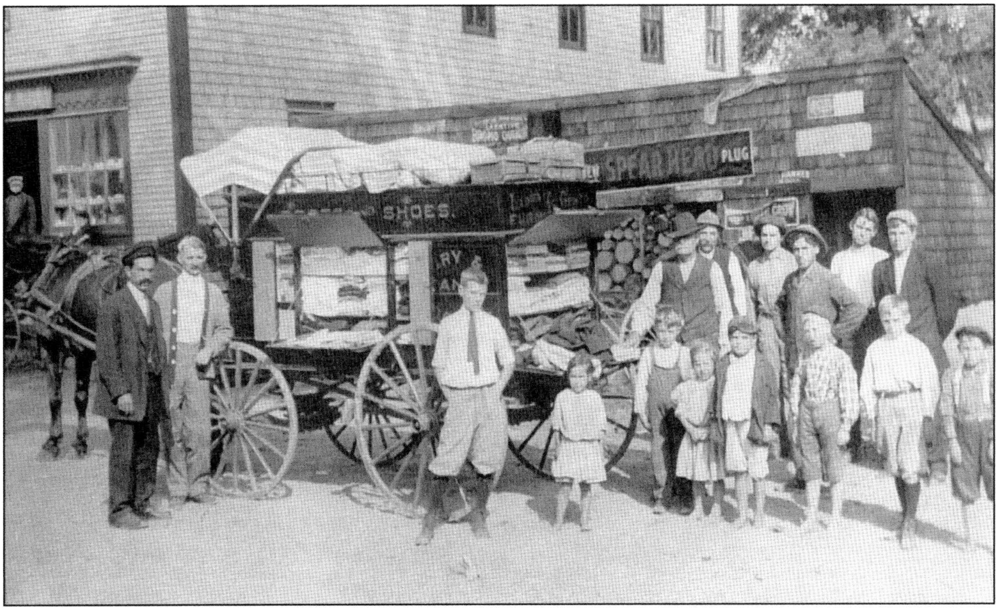

Everyone loved to gather around the traveling peddler's wagon to see what he had, which was usually anything from patent medicine to shoes or furniture. Shown in this picture, taken in front of Cad Winslow's store around 1913, from left to right, are Ray Files, Velma Small, Kenneth and Rita Bartlett, Charles Small, Murray Tenney, Clarence Files Cyrus Winslow, "Pick" Small, and Cad Winslow. (Paul Edes.)

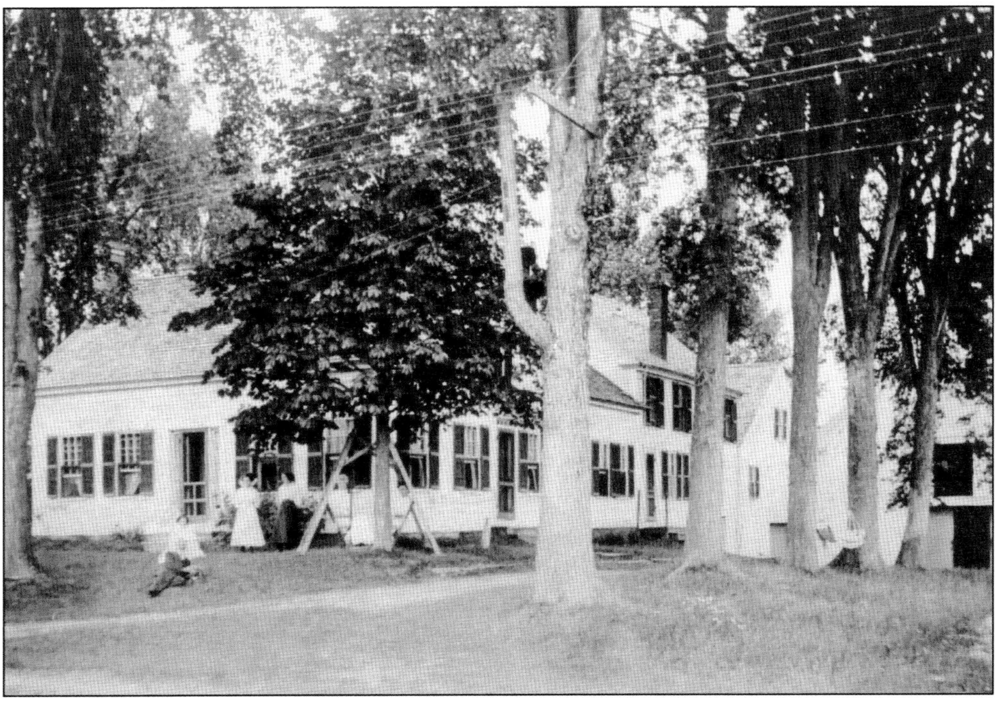

Richard M. Webb, the first settler in Webbs Mills Village, built this home. Cad Winslow lived here with his family in the late 1900s. The house was at one time a very large set of buildings, but fire destroyed the barn and outbuildings right up to the back door.

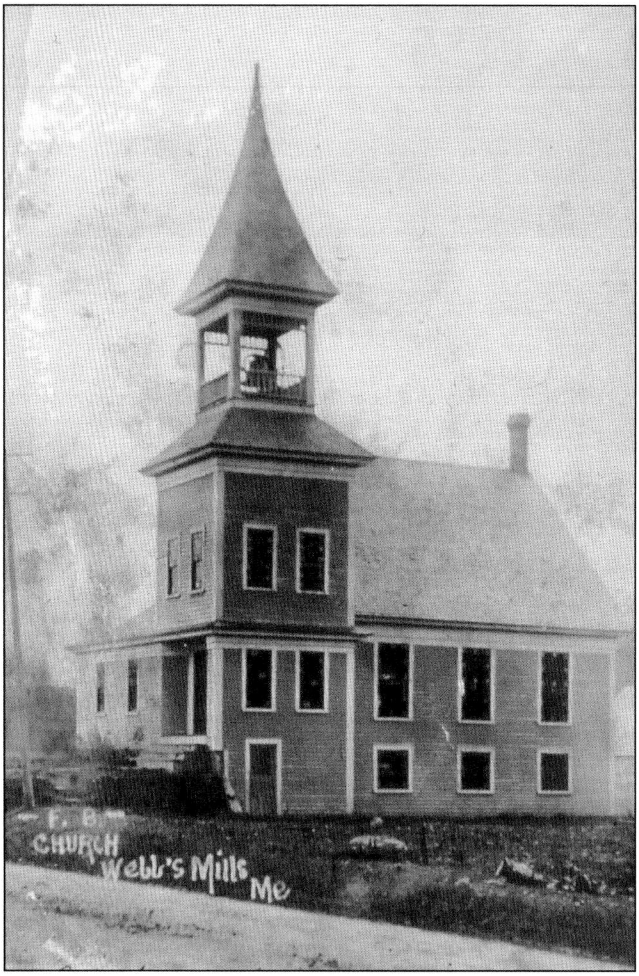

Before the current church in Webbs Mills was built, a group of Methodist Episcopalians formed in Raymond in 1844 and met for services at the schoolhouse in Webbs Mills; however, this group was not large enough and could not continue. In 1876, a group of Free Baptists congregated until their services ended in 1902. A Parish Society was then formed, and the pretty Webbs Mills Free Baptist Church was built next to the millpond on Route 85 in 1903.

Dr. Leland Poor, MD, came to Casco in 1893 after graduating from Bowdoin Medical School. For 40 years, he and his wife, Mary, lived on Route 85 in the only brick house in Casco. No records exist as to who built this house or how old it is, but some elements of the structure indicate it could be 160 years old.

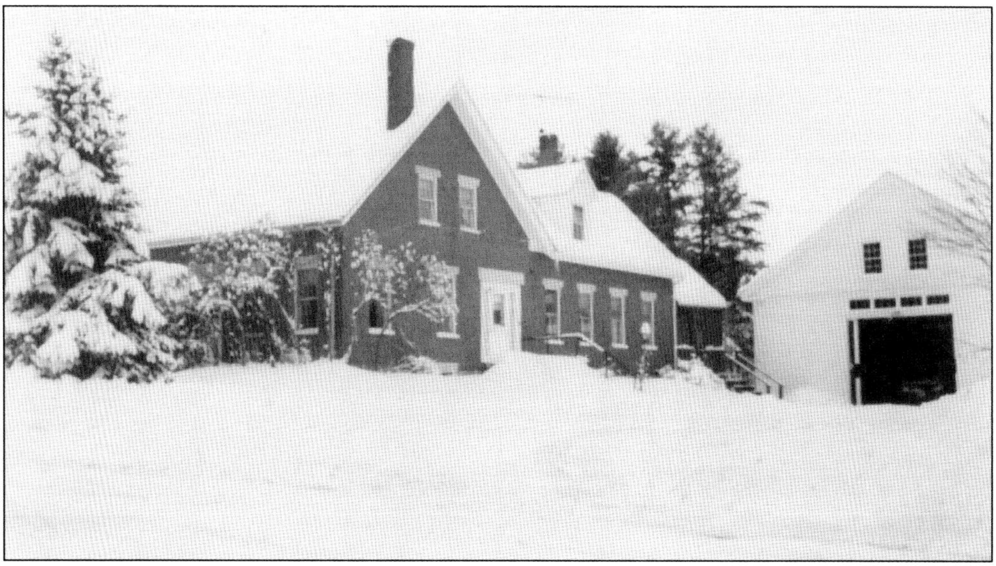

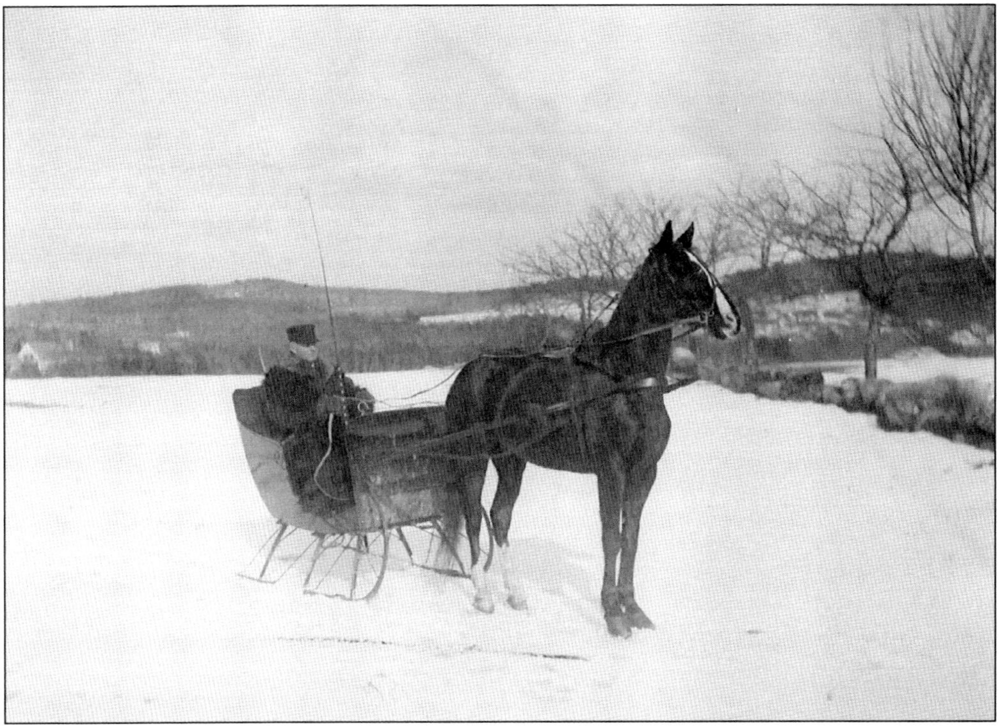

Dr. Leland Poor was for many years one of the most widely known physicians of southern Maine. Well established as a community leader, he was superintendent of the town's school system and chairman on the board of health. An old-school country doctor, he made his rounds under any conditions.

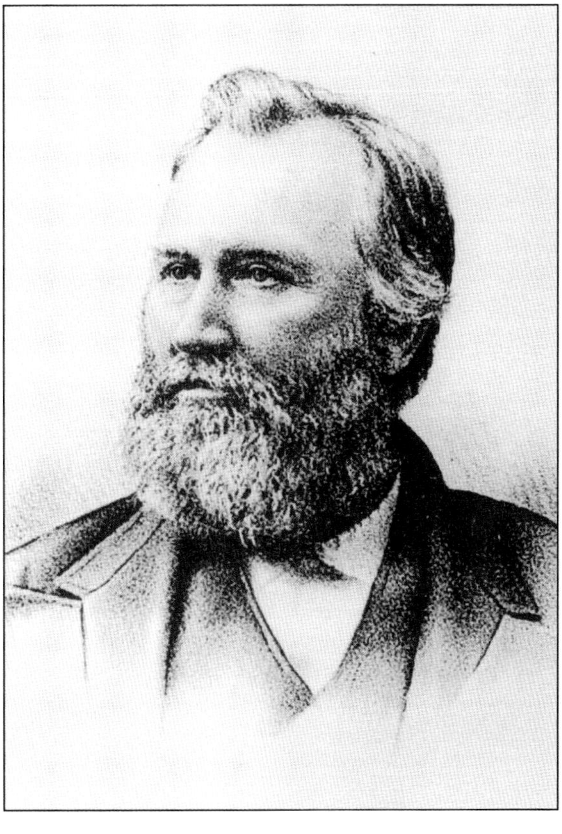

Dr. Albion Cobb moved to the Webbs Mills area of Casco around 1860. Entering the army in 1862, he was an assistant surgeon of the 4th Maine Volunteers. He was the father of four sons, all of whom became prominent in the world of medicine.

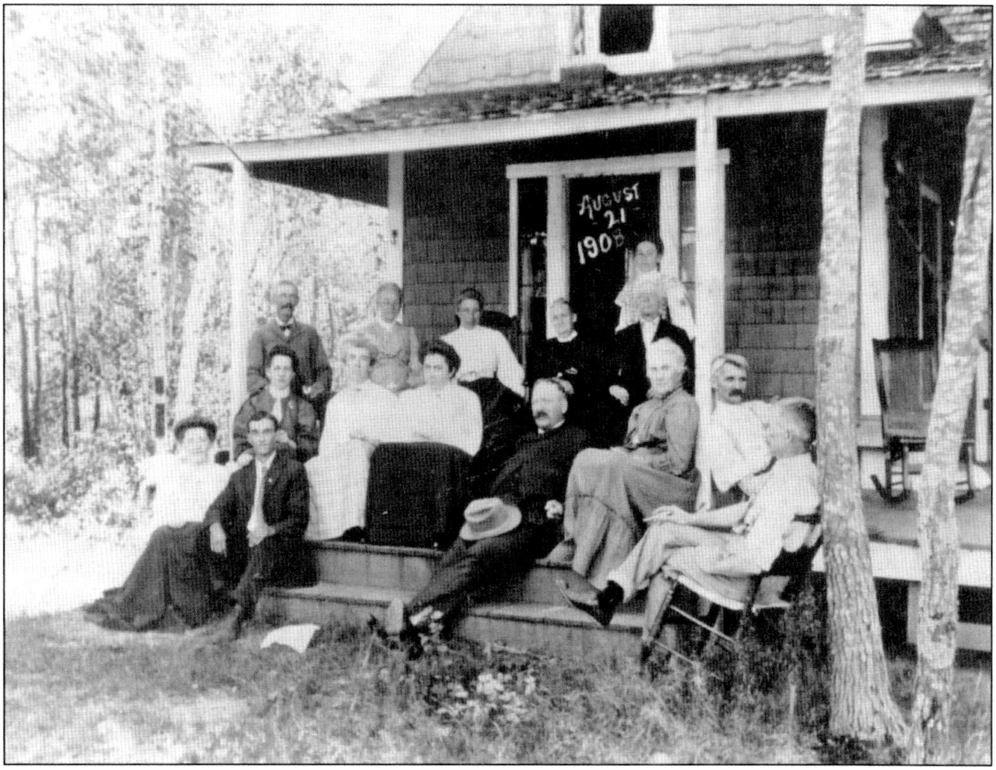

A Winslow family reunion was held in 1908 on an island on Crescent Lake that was about 2.5 acres in size. This island, surrounded by white sand, was 300 yards offshore opposite Camp Agawam. Cad Winslow built the family cottage here about 1900.

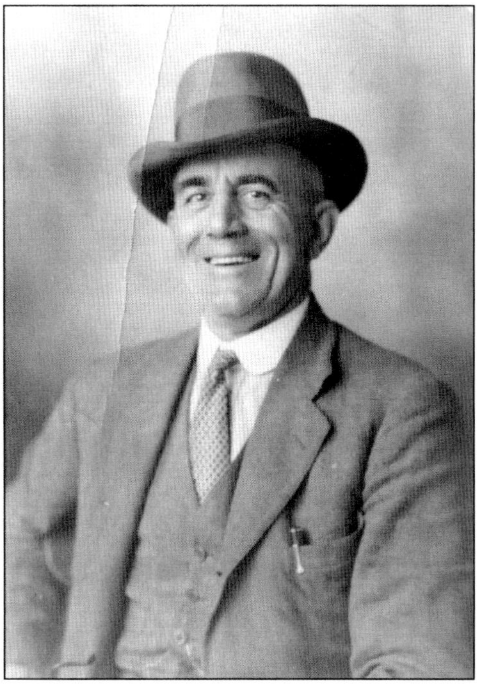

Hamden Tripp was born in Casco in 1874. He was a well-known photographer here for more than 30 years. He lived across the road from the church on Route 85, and his studio was beside his home. His photographs ranged from schools and summer camps to many of the local people and their businesses. He was a pioneer artist in photography, working often with his panoramic camera. He worked mostly with five-by-seven glass plates, and the local museum is fortunate to have possession of some of his plates.

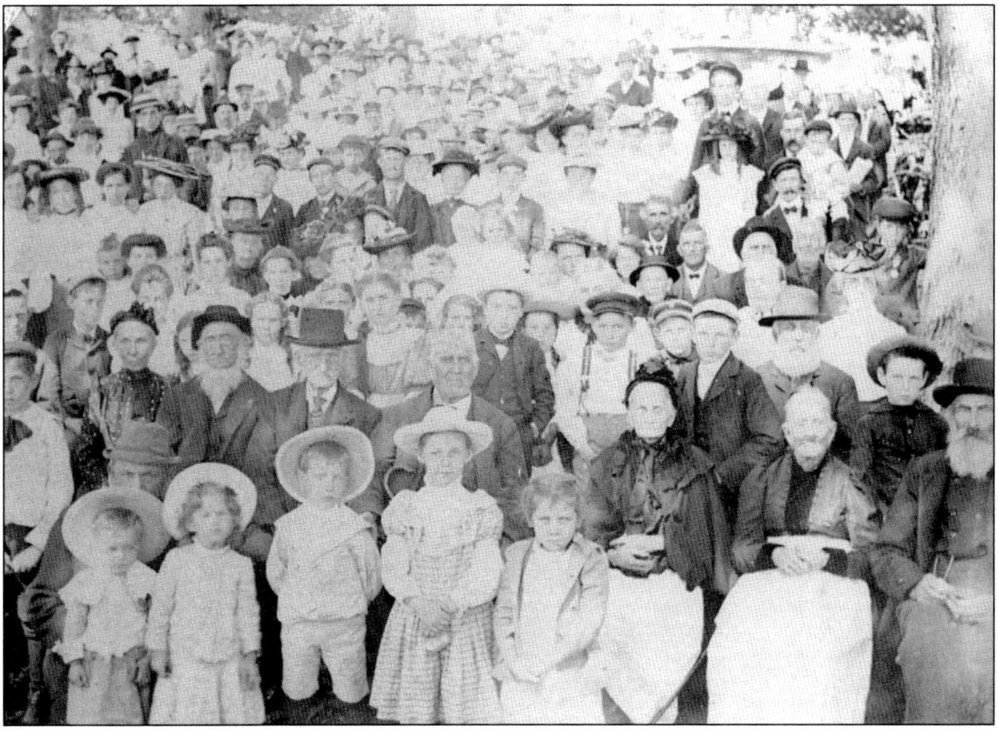

Born in 1852, Cyrus Winslow Spiller married Susanne D. (Edwards) Spiller. They lived off Route 11 up the Spiller Road in Webbs Mills. "Spiller Heights" was the family farm on the northerly slope of Rattlesnake Mountain. Gathered together at the old home place for a picnic are the Spiller, Winslow, and Edwards families.

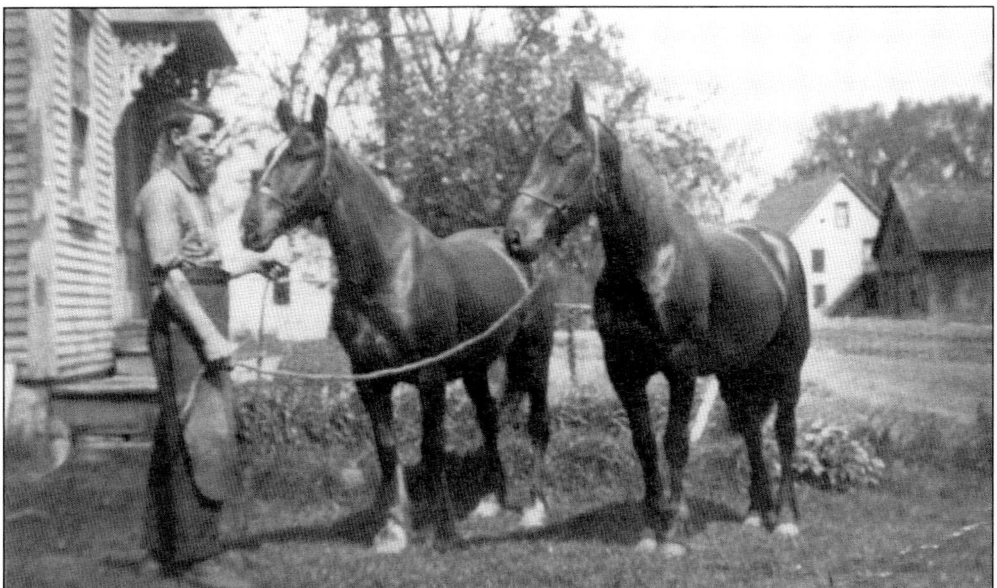

In the village of Webbs Mills, John Polland had a blacksmith shop next to his home. This blacksmith shop was located close to the road on Route 11 and was torn down in the late 1980s. John also had a portable sawmill that he operated with his sons around 1942.

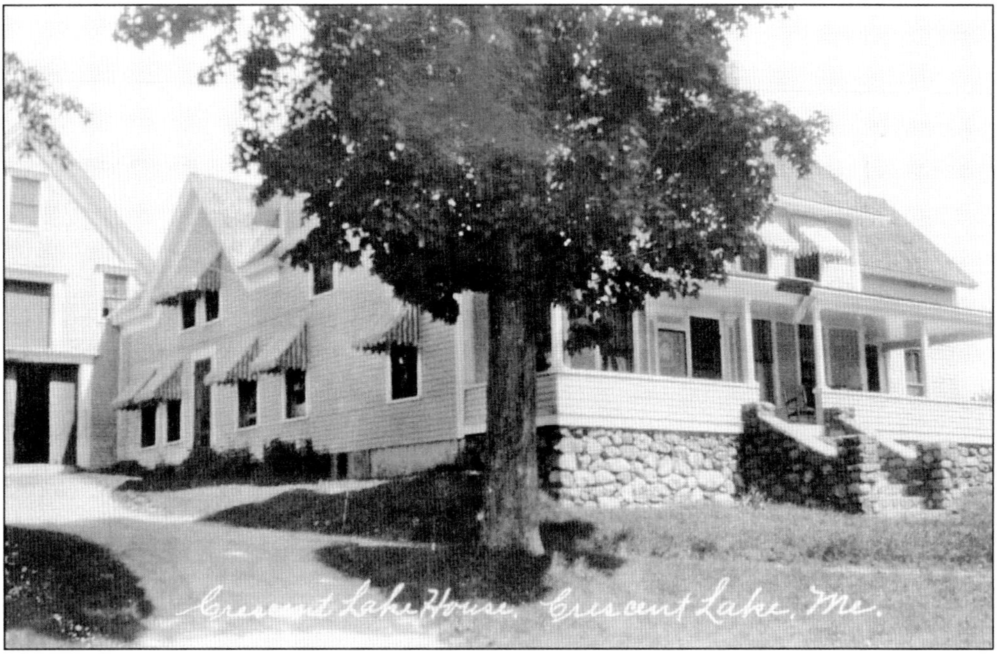

The Crescent Lake House was located in Webbs Mills on Route 11, where the Mitchell home is today. At the time of this picture, John Symonds owned it. Along with the house for guests, they had overnight cabins. It burned in the summer of 1931.

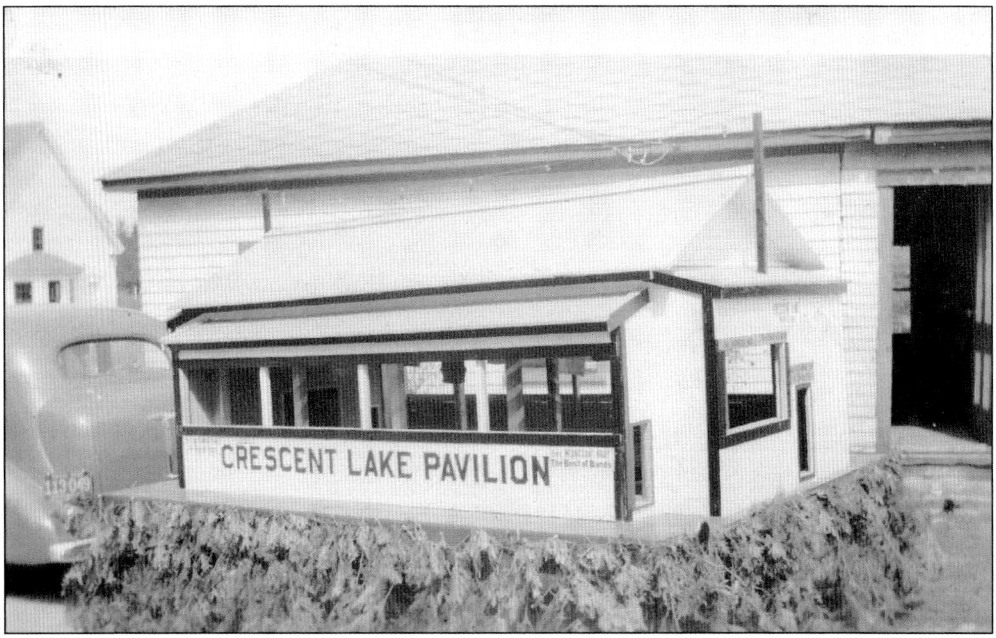

The Crescent Lake Pavillion on Route 11 at Crescent Lake was built in 1927 as a dance hall and roller skating rink, catering to high-class tourists with its big band music of the 1930s. The property was sold, and Camp Netop opened in 1956. The dance hall was turned into Camp Netop's main dining lodge.

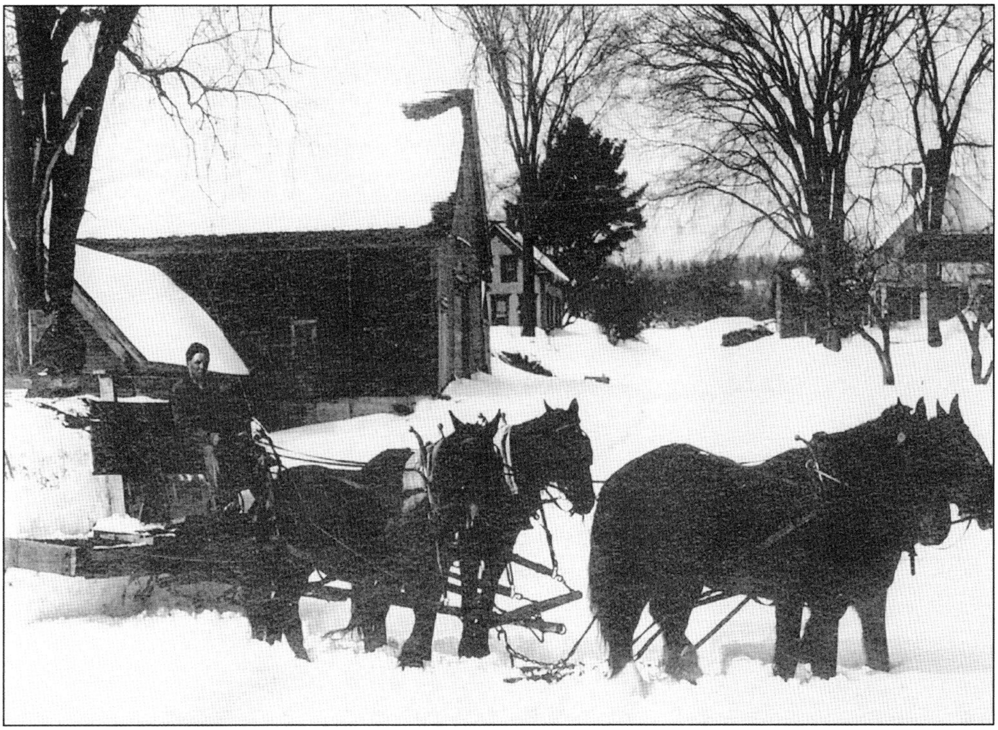

In the 1920s and 1930s, the roads were not plowed; they were rolled. The snow roller was a wooden cylinder about 6 feet around and 15 feet long. It was filled with fieldstones and usually pulled by four horses. This packed the snow down hard and made for easier traveling. (Paul Edes.)

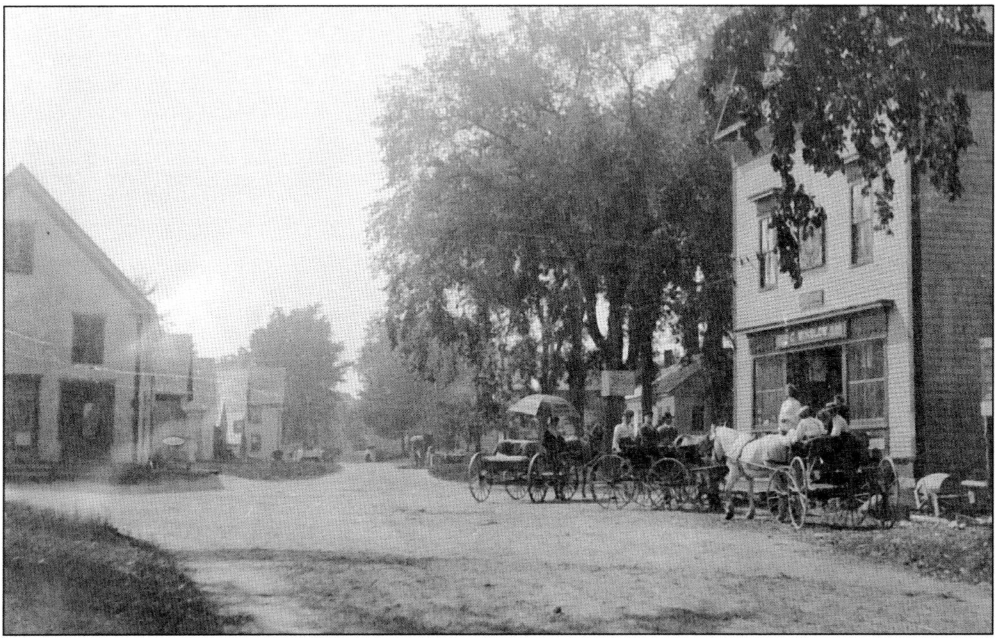

In the years before engine-powered transportation, the horse-drawn carriage was the only way to go. As one can see here, the local folks are out purchasing their dry goods from the Winslow store on Route 11 in Webbs Mills. (Paul Edes.)

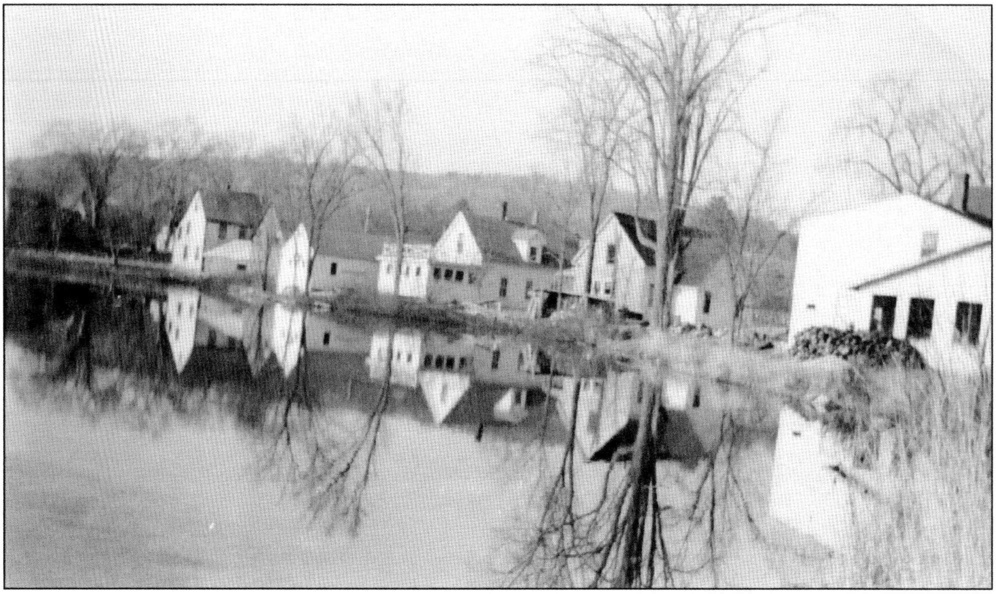

The tranquil waters of the millpond in the 1920s reflect a beautiful scene in the center of Webbs Mills. At that time, there were 121 people living there in 38 houses. The buildings are, from left to right, Jed Wilson's house, the back of the Webbs Mills Post Office, Ruth Courtney's house, Lil Peterson's place, and Stuart Plummer's house, which was originally a corn shop.

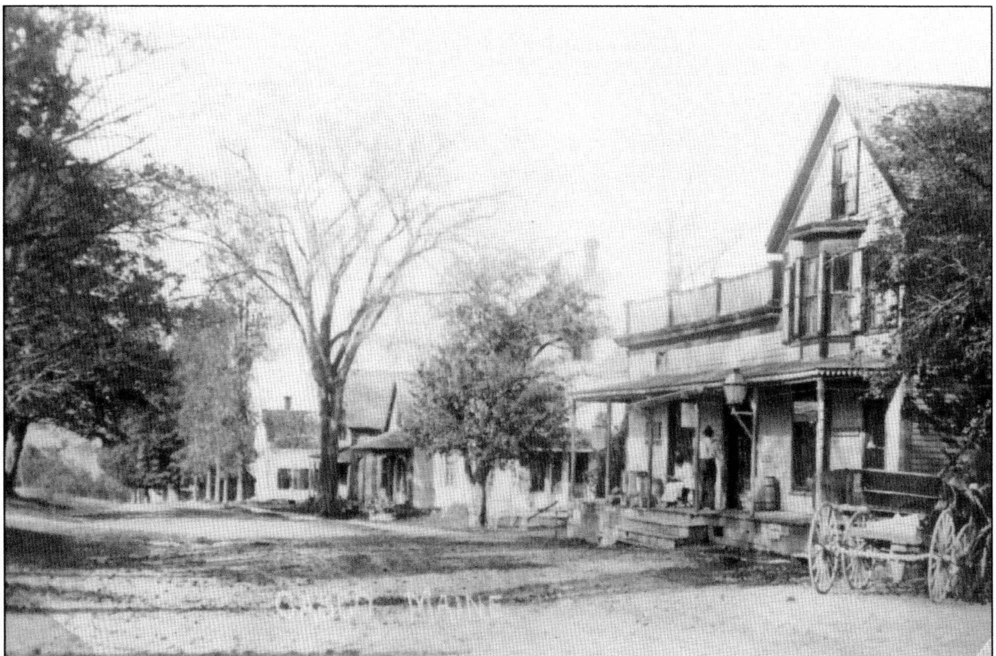

The Holden family came to the area of Casco Village in the early 1800s. The store on the right, carrying all the necessaries of the day for the local folks, is one of many businesses built by the Holdens. Cyrus Henry Holden built a mill on Mile Brook on Edes Falls Road that opened up work for many of the local people. The Holdens were a great influence in the building of Casco.

The church in Casco Village was built the same year Casco was incorporated, 1841. Congregationalists and Baptists worked together to build this new church, and to honor this feat, it was called the Union Church. Money from the sale of pews and contributions made by the citizens went into the building fund. Now called Casco Village Church, it is a member of the United Church of Christ.

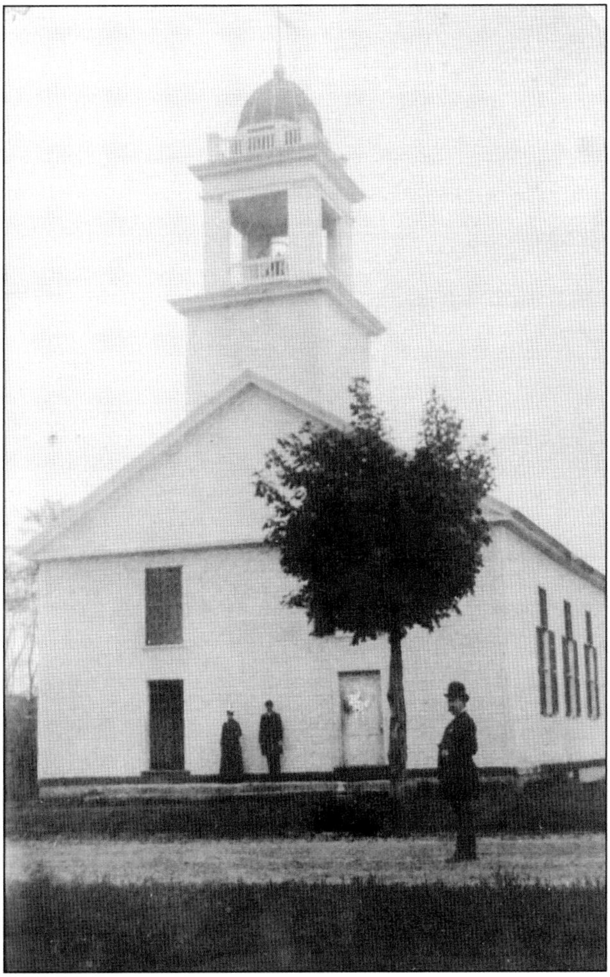

The long building at left is the Mayberry Stock farm, built in 1888. At 303 feet long, it was considered the longest building in the state of Maine at the time. The barn housed 30 trotting horses and had indoor facilities for exercising the thoroughbreds raised there. Several of these trotters were well known on some of the most famous tracks in New England. Today, what remains of this building is used for Casco Days.

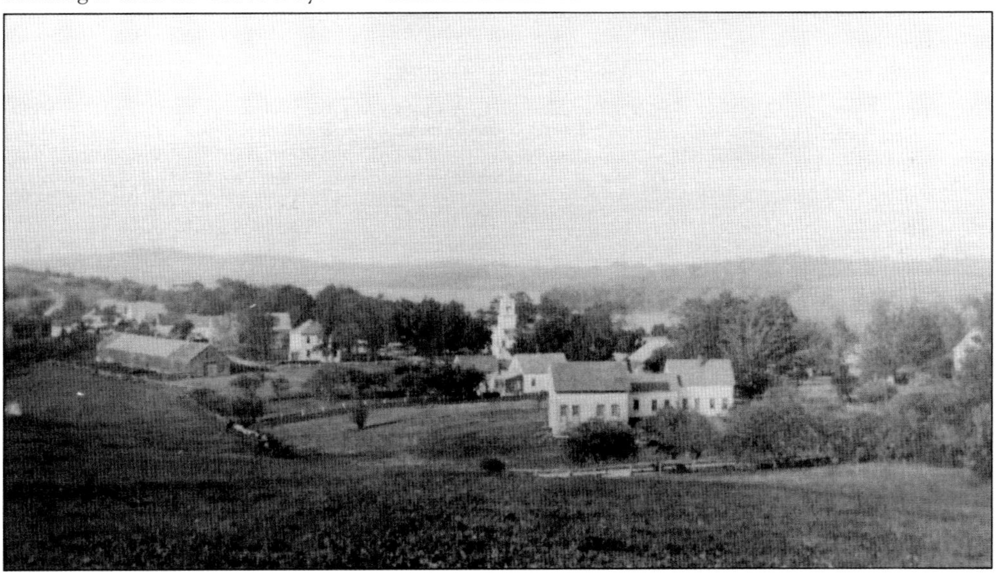

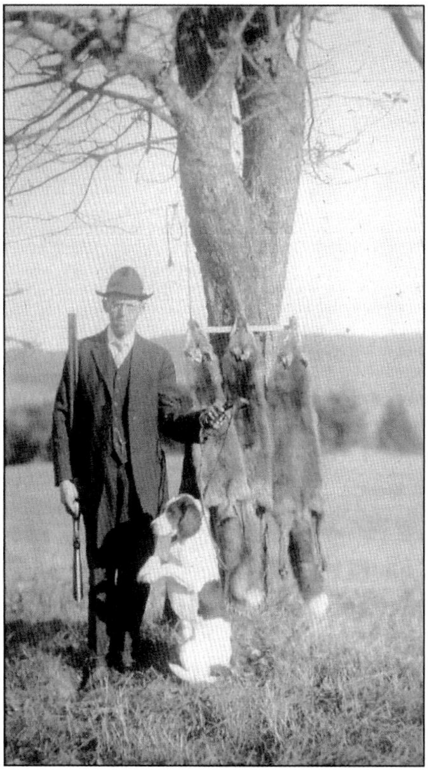

Cyrus Leach was a farmer who lived with his family on Leach Hill Road. Fox hunting with dogs was big sport back in the 1920s and 1930s. A good hunting dog could cost up to $100. Hunters would go out all day in the fall or winter, stopping to build a fire to get warm and cook their lunch. Pelts like these would bring good money and would be made into muffs or stoles.

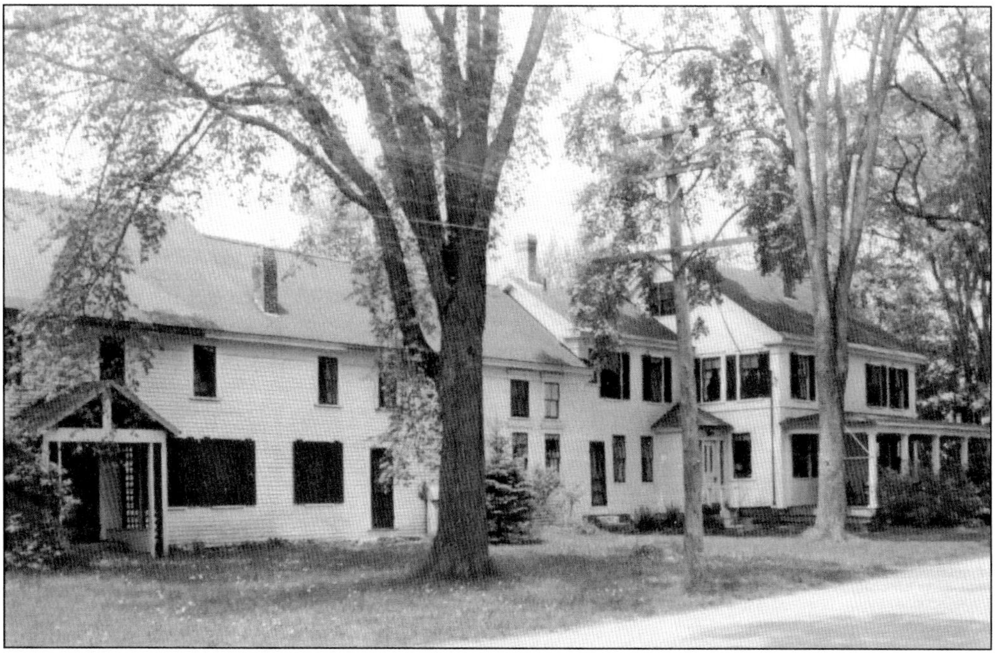

This familiar landmark in Casco Village near Pleasant Lake was once the home of the Mayberry family. Gardner Cole purchased this property in 1928 and converted it to the Casco Inn, a popular vacation spot. Cole was also the principal of Casco High School from 1925 to 1948. Later, it was run by his son Phil Cole and his wife, Bessie Mae. Today, it is a residential care facility for the elderly.

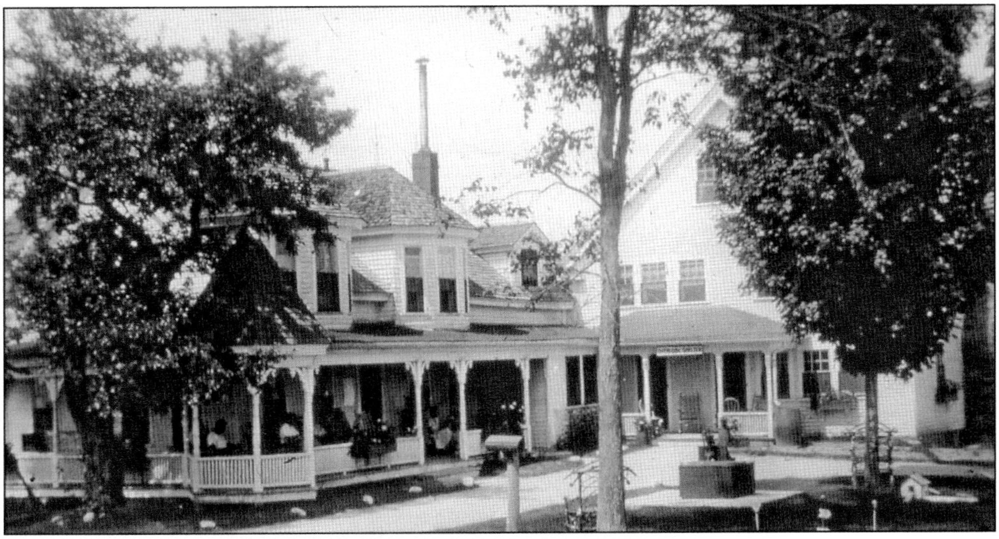

One of the more beautiful homes of Casco that turned into an inn was Overlook Farm on Mayberry Hill. Charles and Angie Walker operated it as an inn and restaurant beginning in the 1930s, catering mostly to the parents of children who were attending one of the local summer camps. Since the late 1970s, it has been a preschool.

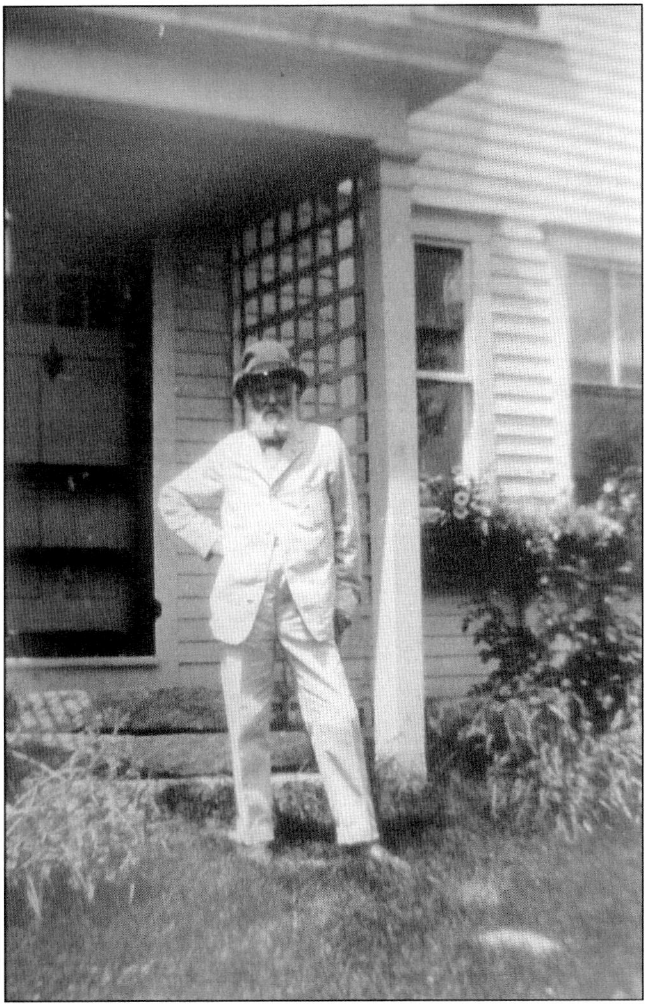

Alonzo S. Mayberry, son of Capt. Oliver A. and Rebecca (Bodge) Mayberry, was born on the family farm on Mayberry Hill in 1836. Alonzo and his wife, Charlotte, summered in Casco for a number of years. After his wife's death, his daughter Edith bought a house on Mayberry Hill for herself and Alonzo so they could spend their summers here.

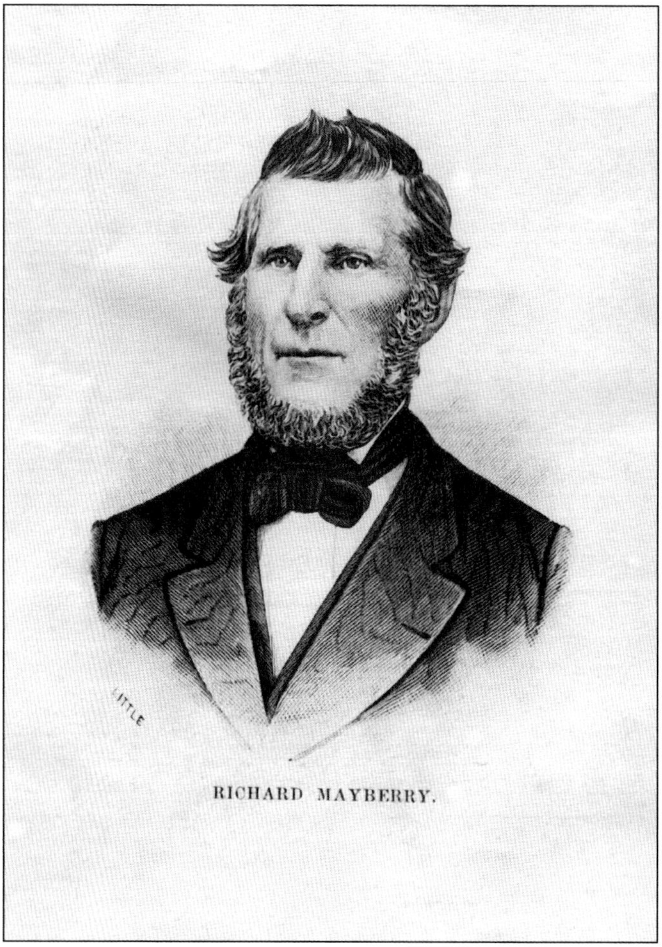

Richard Mayberry was born in 1811. For 10 years in his youth, he was a peddler traveling the roads. After moving back home, he became involved in town affairs, becoming postmaster, tax collector, and treasurer of the town. He served one term as a representative in the Maine state legislature. Richard also served in the Battle of Bunker Hill, where his son William was his body servant.

In 1837, John Holden III settled at the north end of Casco Village on Route 121 and built a dam at the outlet of Pleasant Lake. This mill furnished power for both a gristmill and a sawmill. Holden farmed and ran his mills. When prosperity made it possible, he built his beautiful home, which has since become known as Pleasant Lake House.

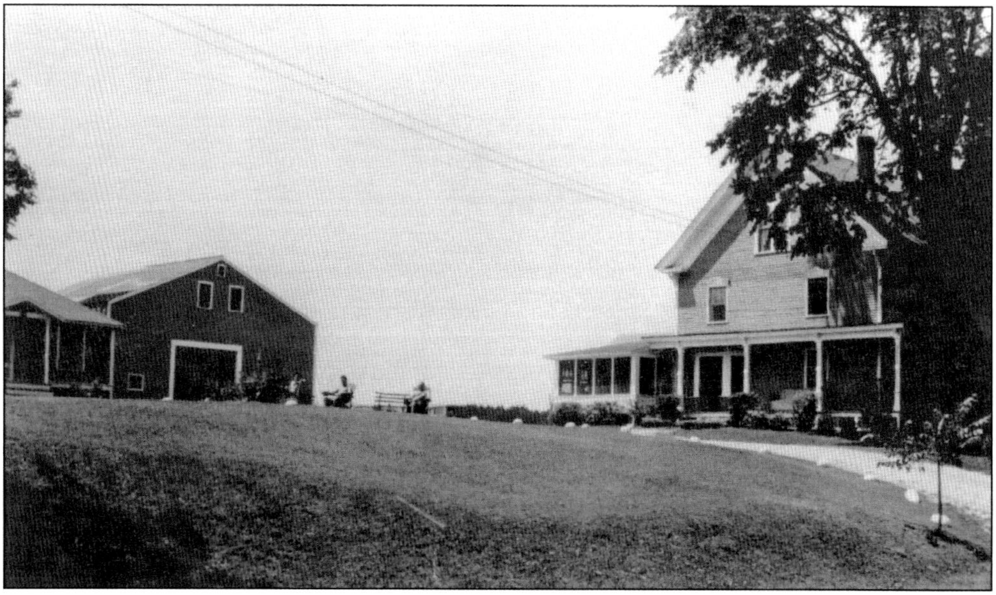

Born in 1811, Alpheus S. Holden was a public-spirited citizen always ready to promote the prosperity of his native town and its advancements in education, religion, and morals. This reputation led him to become a member of the Maine House of Representatives in 1843 and 1865 and the Maine Senate from 1845 to 1846.

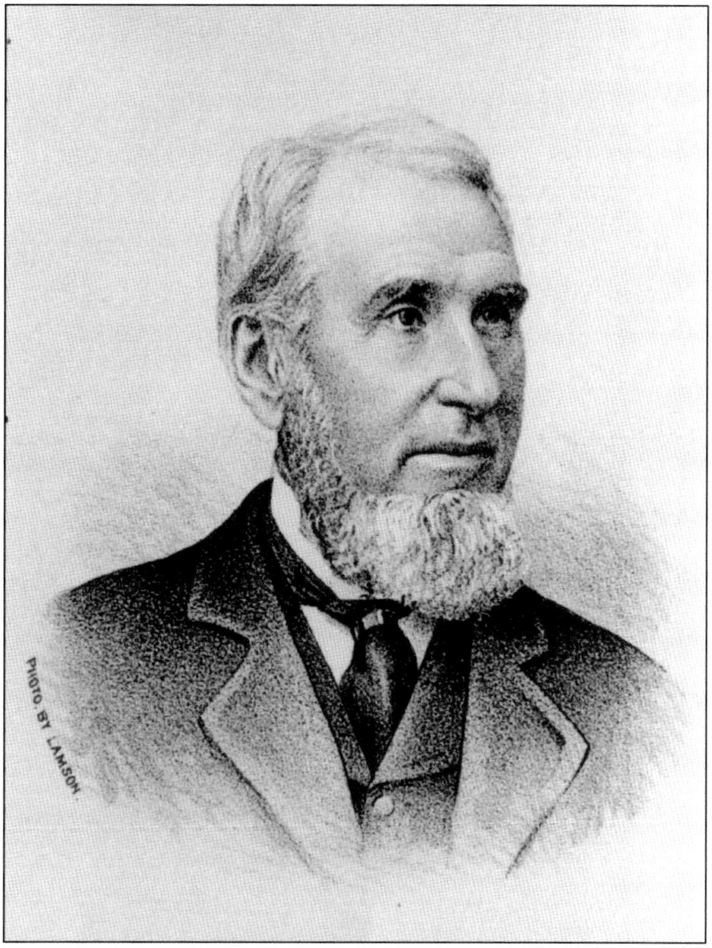

This store in Casco Village was located beside the Grange Hall. Around 1919, Harry Parry ran the store. Parry was the town clerk, and when his store burned, all the town records that he kept in the store were burned as well. The building was rebuilt and held the post office and a garage.

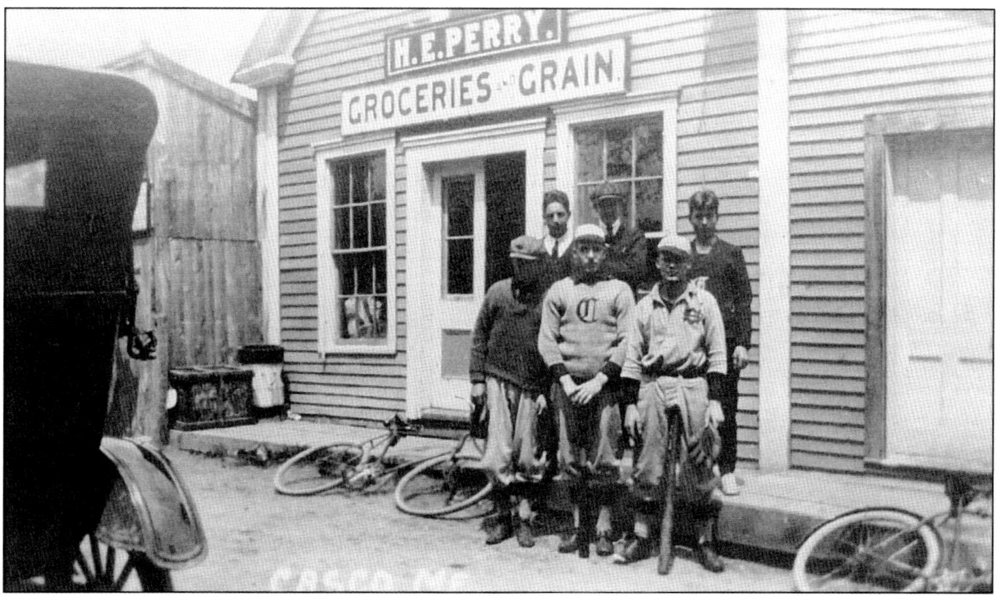

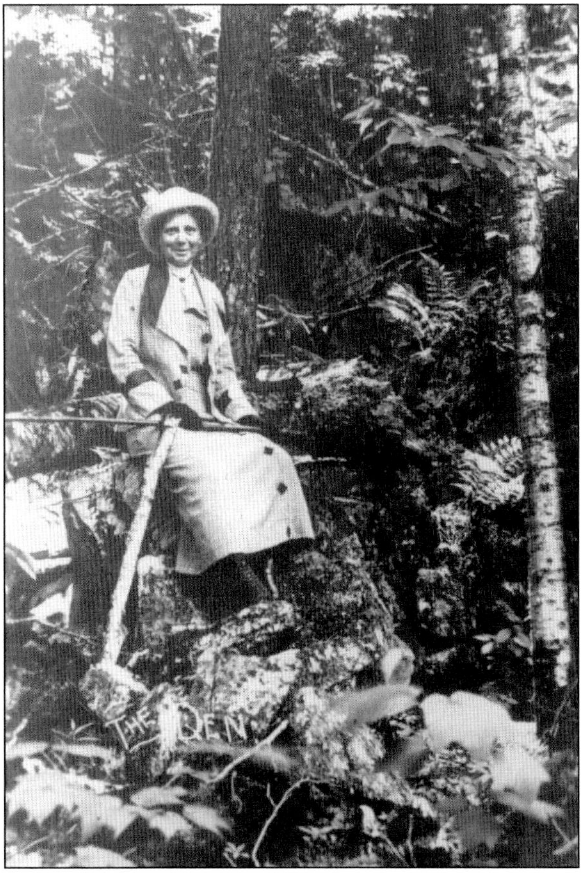

Cecelia Compton was not a native of Casco; however, her love for it was so great that she considered it her town. Coming here around 1905, her brothers were the Comptons of *Compton's Encyclopedia*, and her allowance to live here was furnished by them. She was a naturalist who loved animals, birds, and flowers. She wrote and published *Nature Studies in Casco, Maine*, and *Minerals and Rocks of Casco, Maine*.

Mark L. Leach was a farmer who held many prominent positions in Casco and was very well liked. He lived on the family's 100-acre farm on Leach Hill and raised large quantities of sweet peas and corn. Mark Leach and Cecelia Compton were known for their sweet peas, which they took to Poland Spring to sell.

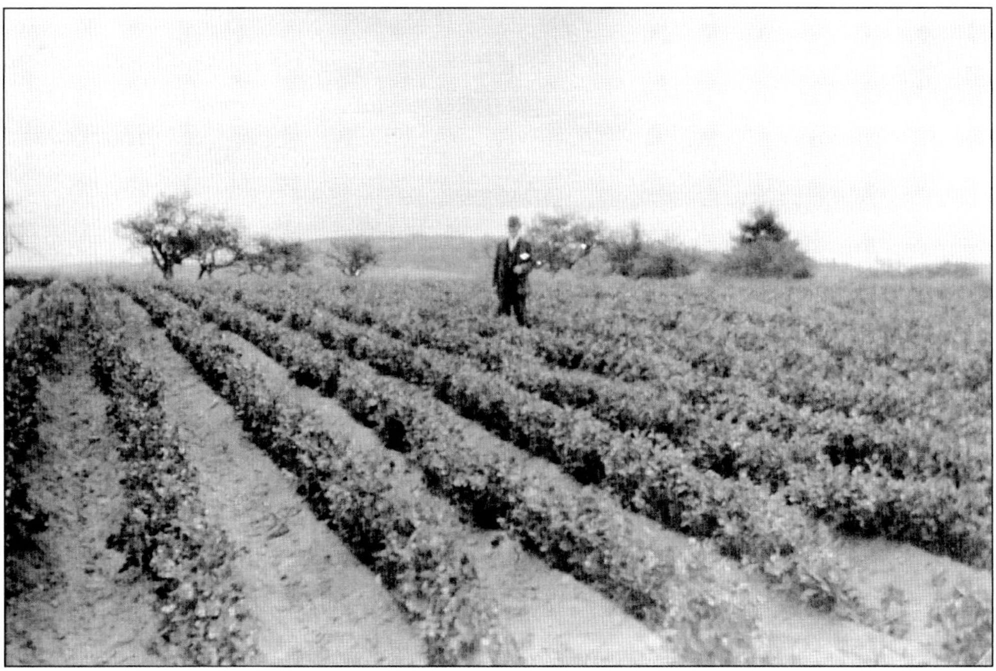

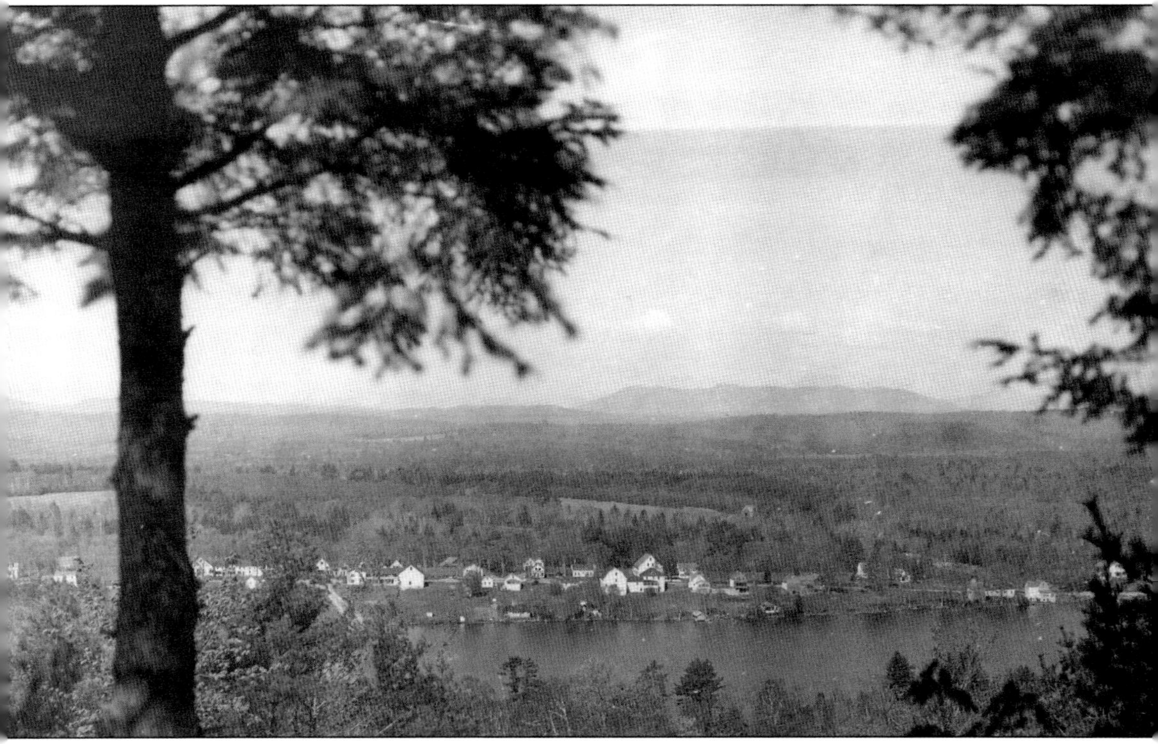

This striking scene is of Casco Village, which was photographed in the early 1900s from the top of Mount Quito by nature lover Cecelia Compton. Nestled between the hills on the shores of Pleasant Lake are the homes and businesses of some of Casco's early citizens.

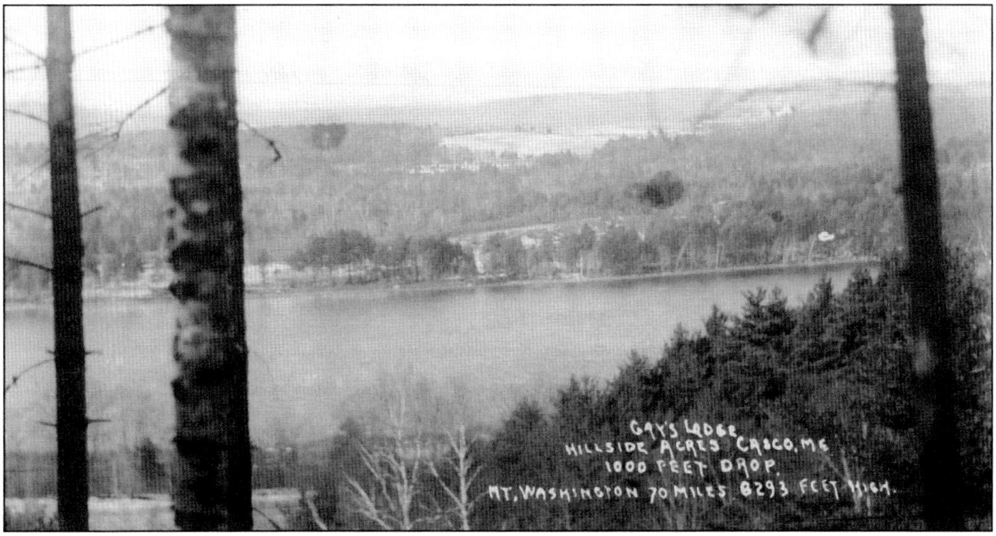

Built in the 1930s by Bessie Gay, Gay's Lodge on Mayberry Hill was a popular vacation spot for tourists from all over the country. Bessie was an exceptional cook and prided herself on the meals she served her guests. Her husband, Mert, expanded their trade by building three cabins across from the lodge on the shores of Pleasant Lake. They also had a small ski slope behind the lodge on Mount Quito.

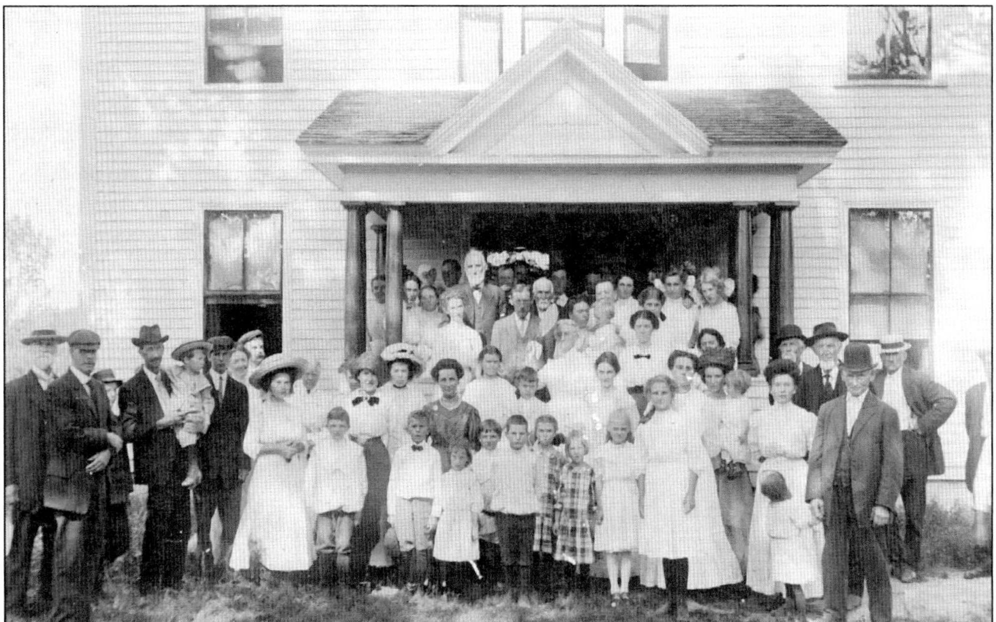

Built in 1903, the Grange Hall in the village hosted Casco Old Home Days in 1911. Among those pictured are, in no particular order, Dr. Wight, Charles Lord, Fred Lombard holding a baby, Ernest Nichols, Helen Cook, May Hancock, Minnie Lombard, Forrest Nutting, Ethel Leach, Beryl Leach, Harold Bennett, Marjory Mayberry, Mildred Harmon, Mark Leach Sr. Cecelia Compton, Frank Jordan, William Cook, Ella Reed, Win Chute, Mary Holden, Ethel Mayberry, Inez Tenney, Sumner Hancock, Dora Jordan, Maria Jewell, Milton Hancock with baby, Mary Gove, Louise Prescott, and Ella Hall.

For many Casco people, manning the operations post was a major part of their contribution to the war effort. "The Aircraft Warning Service" was located in the field behind Grange Hall in Casco Village. Residents took turns watching for airplane activity from 1941 until 1944. Up to 150 planes a day headed for Europe were spotted from this post.

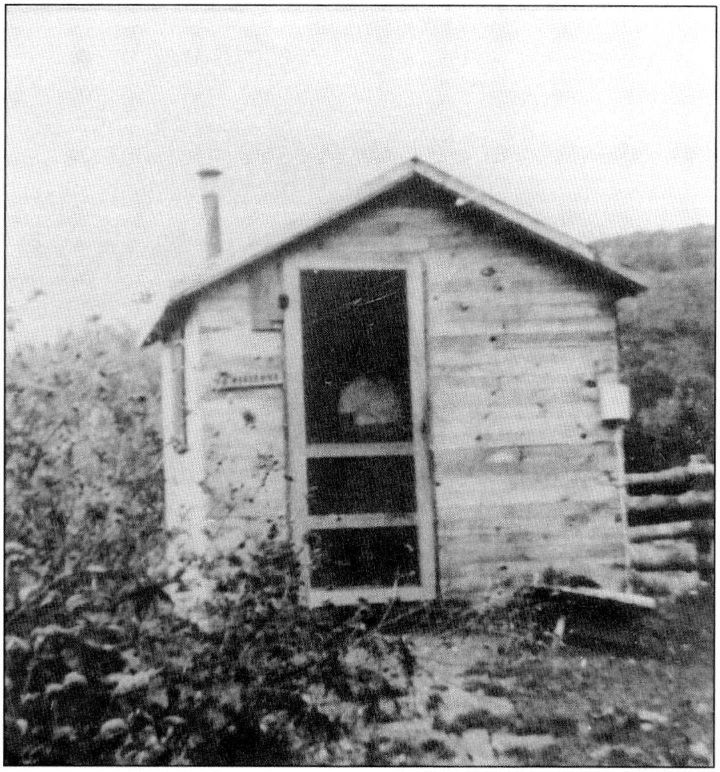

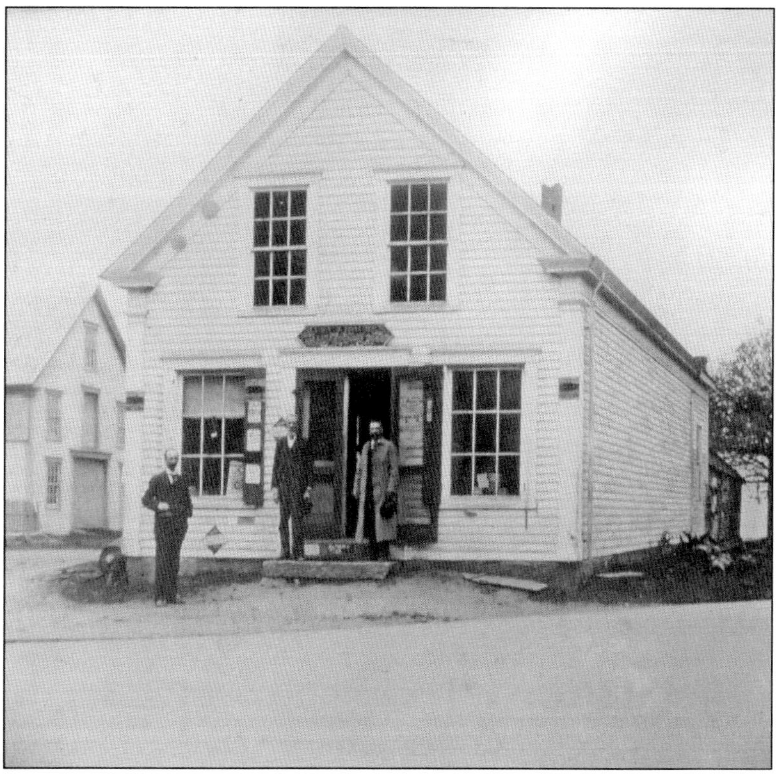

Richard Gay and his wife, Grace (Spurr) Gay, had part ownership of the Holden and Gay Store on Route 121 with Richard's uncle Lyman Holden. Richard was the postmaster, keeping the post office in the store. He was appointed postmaster in 1902 and, in 1941, he received a prize for being the longest-serving postmaster, for a record 39 years. Later, the store became Gay's; today, the name of the store is Casco AG.

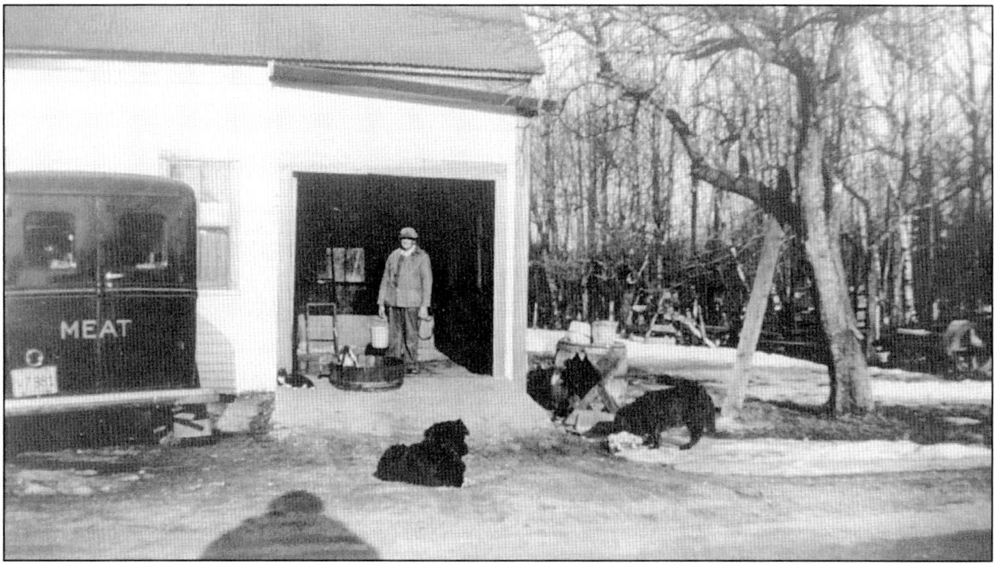

Walter Perris built a store on the corner of Route 11 and Route 121 in 1911. Originally a grain store, it eventually became a general store. Walter's son Arthur and his wife continued this business, and he built a butcher shop across the road. Arthur drove around Casco and neighboring towns selling meats from his wagon.

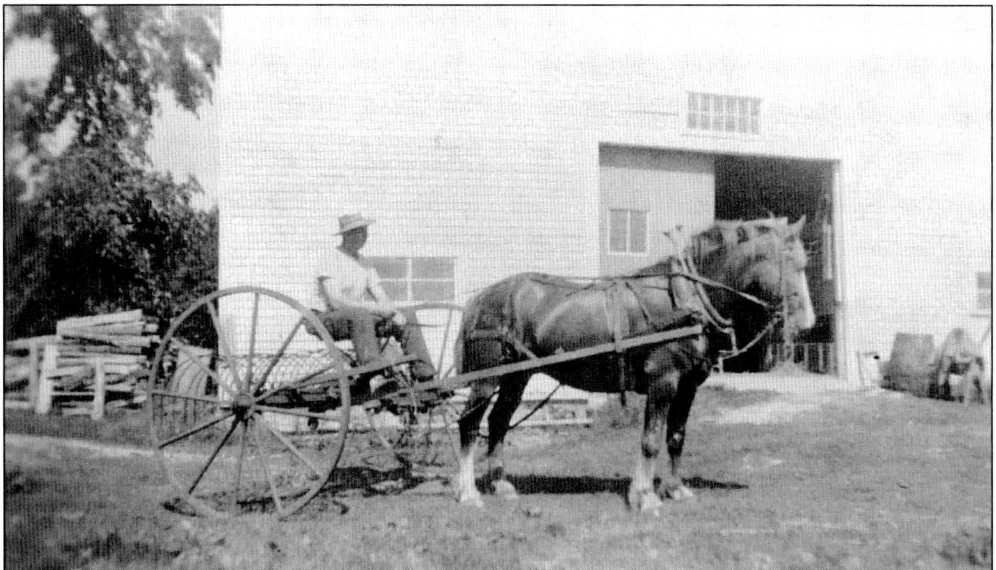

Shown at Arthur Perris's place on the corner of Route 11 and Route 85 is George N. Burgess, with his horse Lucky. Burgess and his wife, Olive, lived on the family farm on Burgess Road. He was a farmer and a rural-route mail carrier for 35 years. He graduated in the first class of Casco High School in 1916 and was a veteran of World War I.

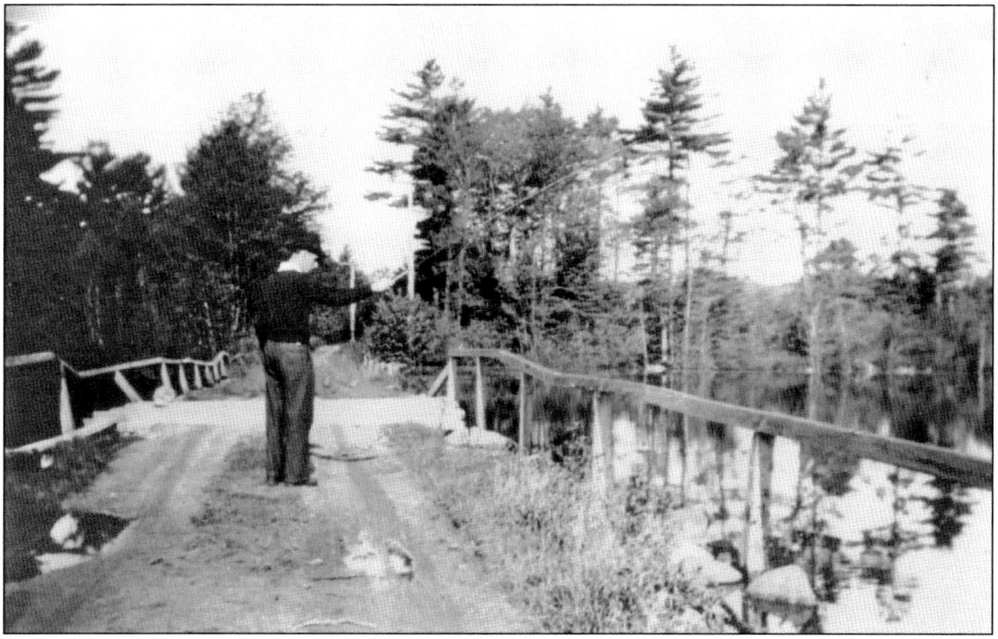

In 1941, Gus and Alice Poulin moved to Heath at the south end of Thompson Lake. At that time, there were only two camps there, with a one-track road going over a rickety plank bridge. They built a home in 1943 and, later, four camps on the water's edge. Gus built the first house on Heath Island for a Reverend Boyd, thus earning the name Parson's Point for that area.

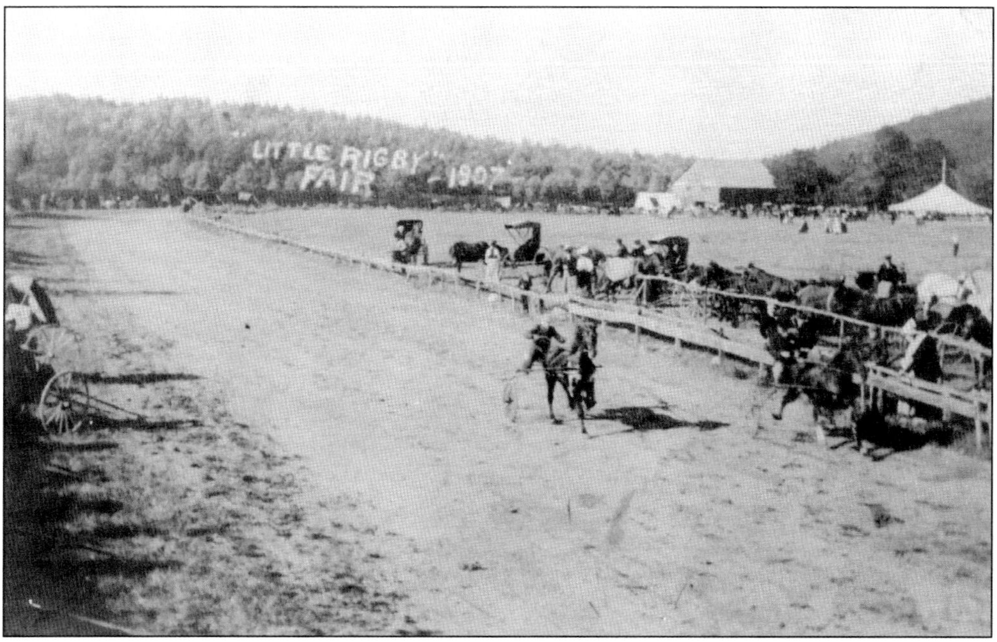

In the early 1900s, a group of men formed an organization called the Little Rigby Park Agriculture Association. This popular country fair was held on the corner of Route 11 and Route 121. It had all the exhibits and events of the day. Most popular was a half-mile oval track for horse racing. The two-story exhibition hall, horse stalls, and cattle sheds were on the lower end of the field, and the main entrance was on Route 11. The last Little Rigby Fair was held in August 1916.

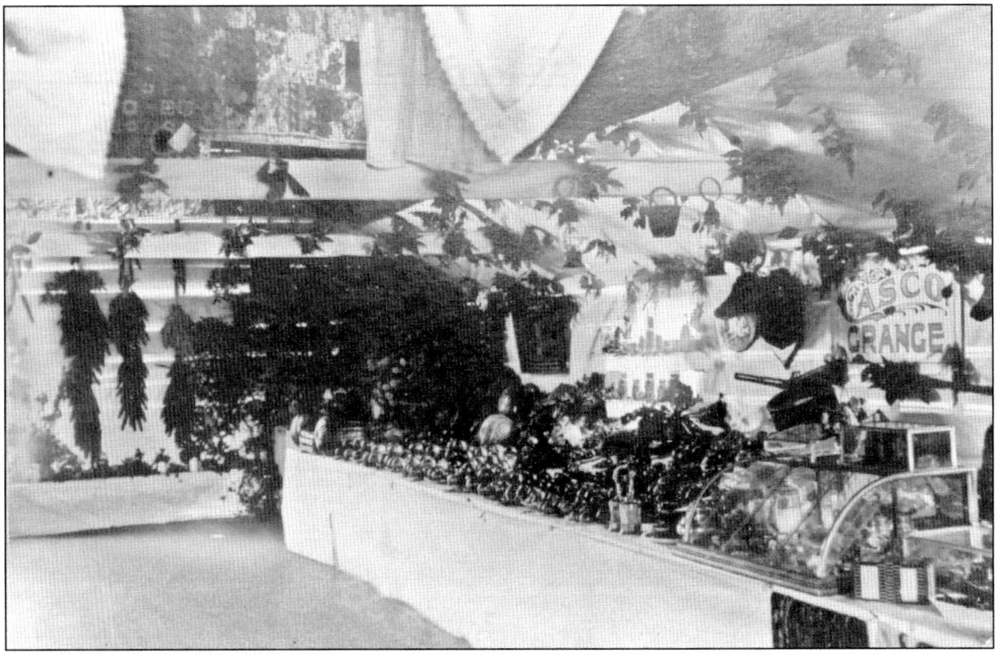

The exhibition hall of the Little Rigby Fairgrounds in the early 1900s held colorful displays of canned berries, jams, jellies, fruits, and vegetables. Another section was for the women to show off their handiwork, crochet doilies, knitted mittens, and hats, all hoping to win a ribbon for their efforts. Beautiful hand-made quilts of many designs adorned the walls.

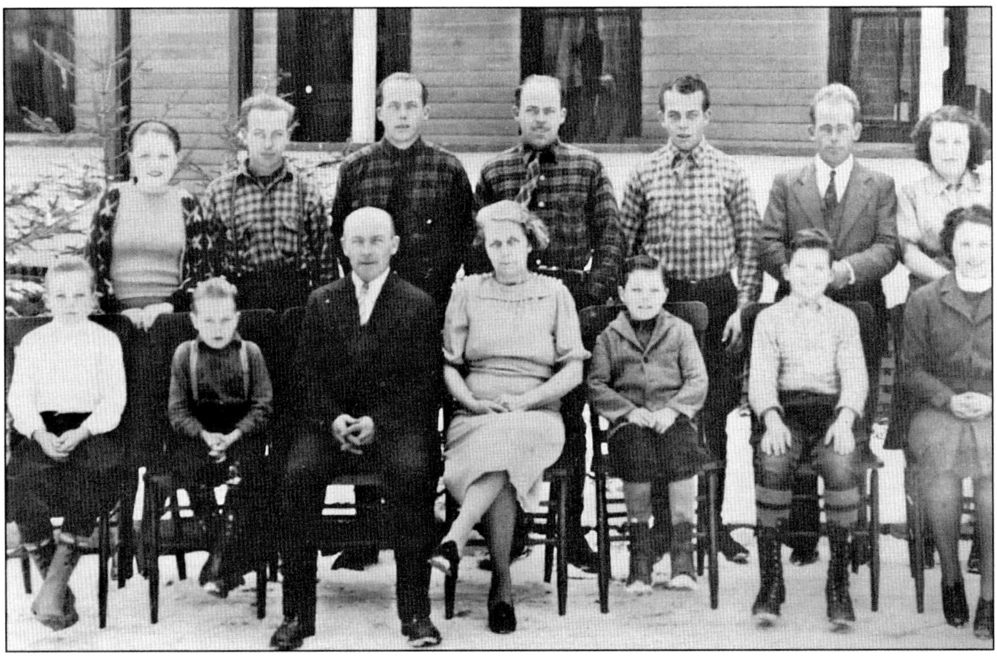

The Everett and Lucy (Edwards) Berry family are at the farm on Route 11. Everett purchased the property that was Little Rigby Park. Those pictured are, from left to right, (sitting) Floyd, Bryant, Everett, Lucy, Calvin, Leon, and Emma; (standing) Pheobe, Archie, Dexter, Philip, Clifford, Stillman, and Jenny. Everett was a lumberman for many years. This is a genuine, homespun Maine family.

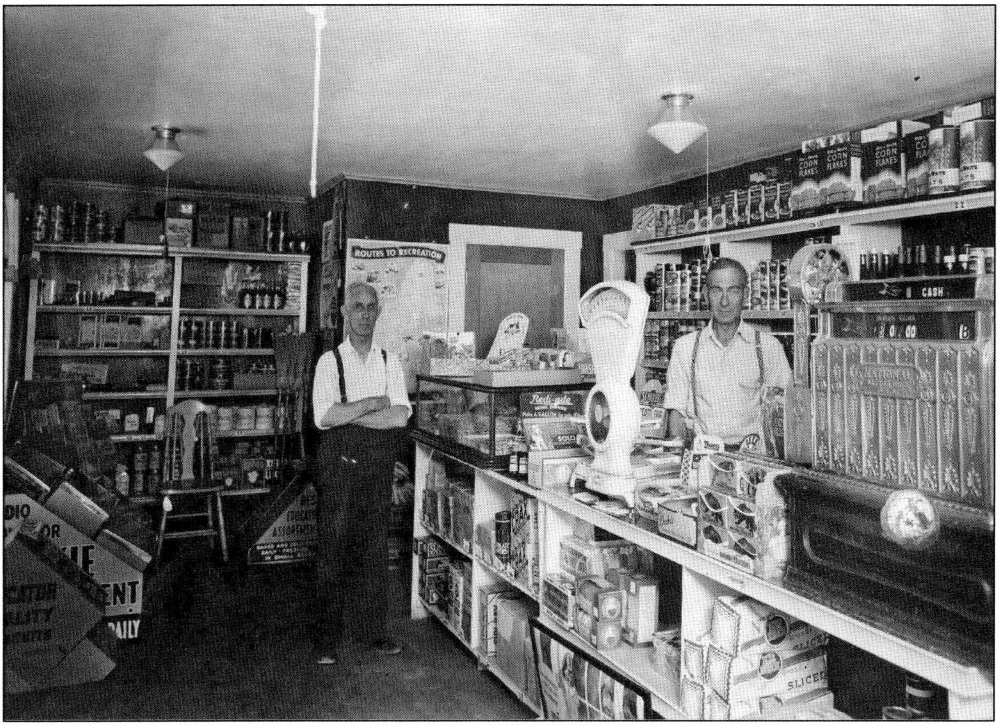

Ben Smith and Edward Heizman built the Pikes Corner Store in Casco in 1937. The Smiths ran the store, and Ed Heizman was the mechanic. It was later run as the Red and White Store by Bessie Combes, daughter of Ben and Flossie Smith, and her husband, Herman Combes. Today, this store is known as Crossroads Country Store.

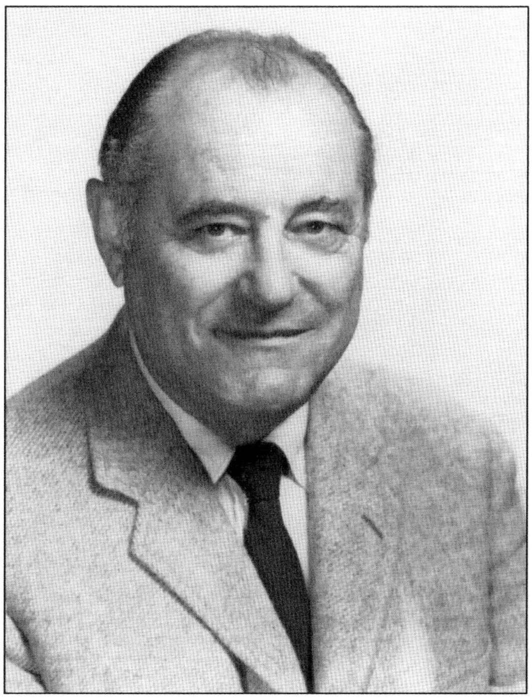

Having had fond memories of Maine from camping here as a boy, Martin Dibner settled in Casco in the 1940s. A local celebrity of sorts, he was the author of numerous books, including novels and thrillers, on subjects ranging from World War II to Maine. His naval experience provided plots and characters for his novels, the first being *The Bachelor Seals*, published in 1948. *Deep Six* was published in 1953 and made into a movie. He also wrote *Sleeping Giant*, *A God for Tomorrow*, *Seacoast Maine*, *The Admiral*, and many more. (Eric Dibner.)

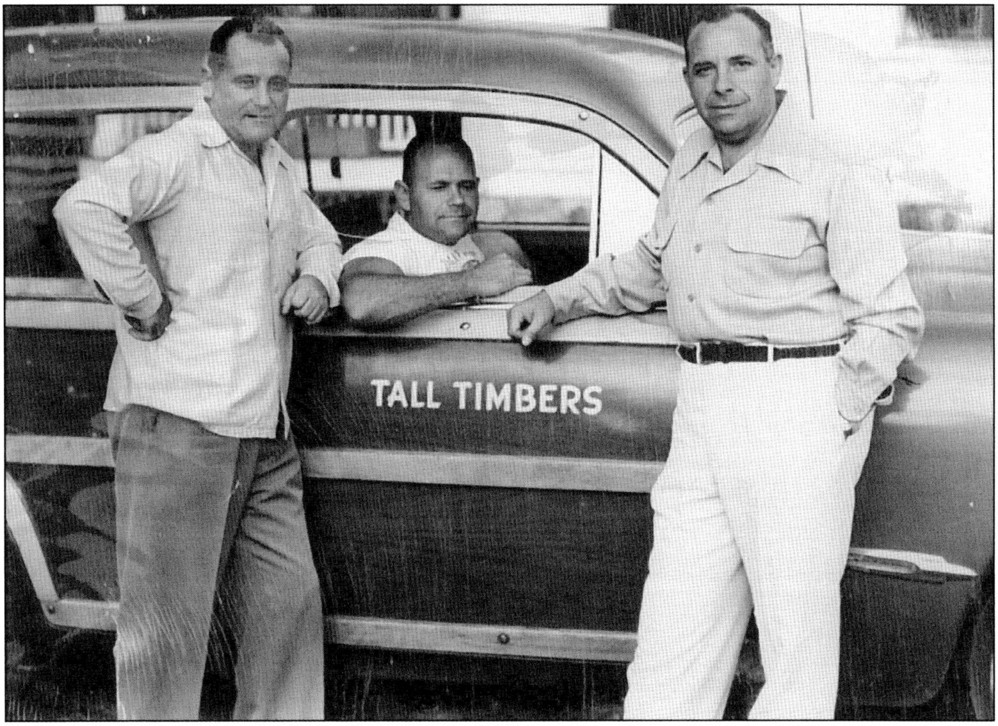

In 1946, the Dibner brothers bought what was Barter Camp on the east shore of Pleasant Lake. Martin, Paul, and Edward Dibner, along with their families, made the necessary repairs and were ready the following year to open their boys' camp, Tall Timbers. In their third season, they had 85 boys for their summer session. Martin retired from the business in 1954. (Eric Dibner.)

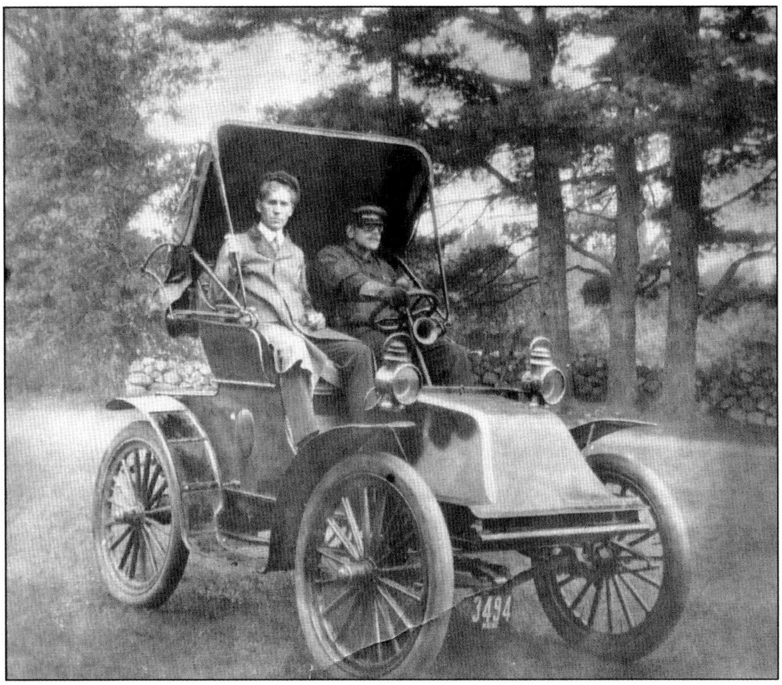

Alf Gould, with Newell Whitney as his passenger, is driving one of the first cars in Casco on Quaker Ridge between 1905 and 1910. Drivers did not use their automobiles in the winter at this time. People would put them up at the first snow and not use them again until April, after the mud season ended.

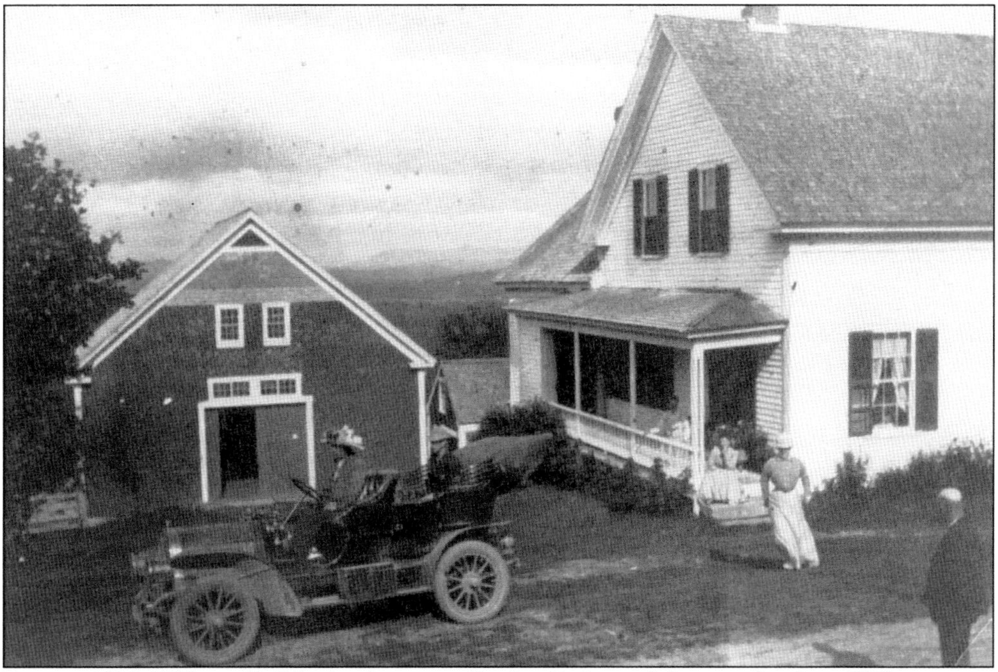

Born in 1808, William Hall built a home on Quaker Ridge with his son Stephen. William was a farmer and a joiner. Since a joiner was a carpenter, people often asked him to make coffins. The constant construction of coffins is what started the Hall family in the funeral home business, which has continued today into its sixth generation.

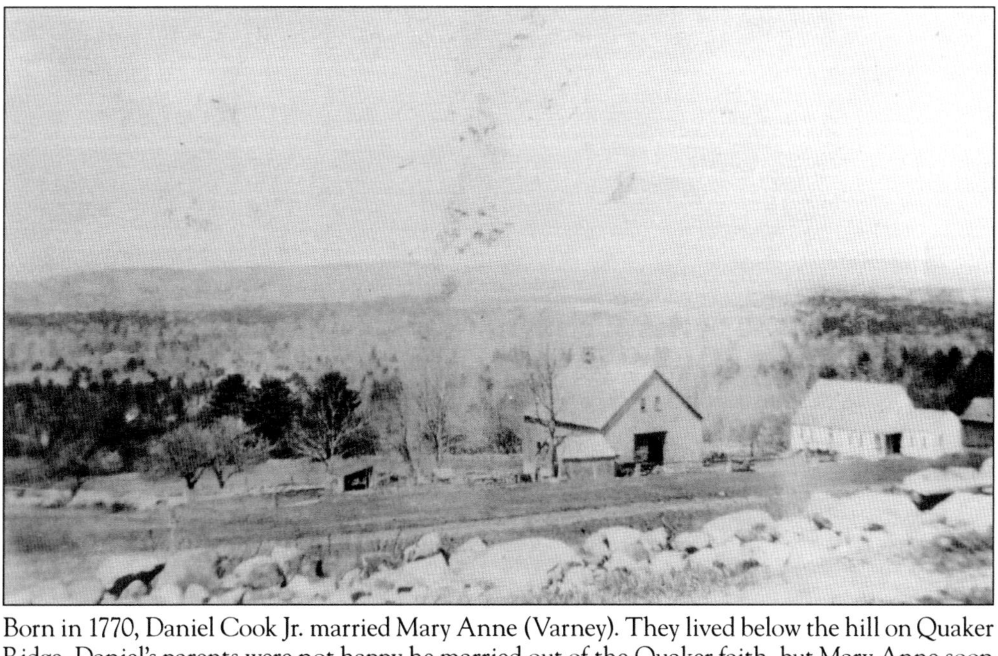

Born in 1770, Daniel Cook Jr. married Mary Anne (Varney). They lived below the hill on Quaker Ridge. Daniel's parents were not happy he married out of the Quaker faith, but Mary Anne soon converted, and meetings were held in their home. In 1814, Daniel sold a piece of property to the Quakers so that a meetinghouse could be built. His farm is now known as the Tenney place.

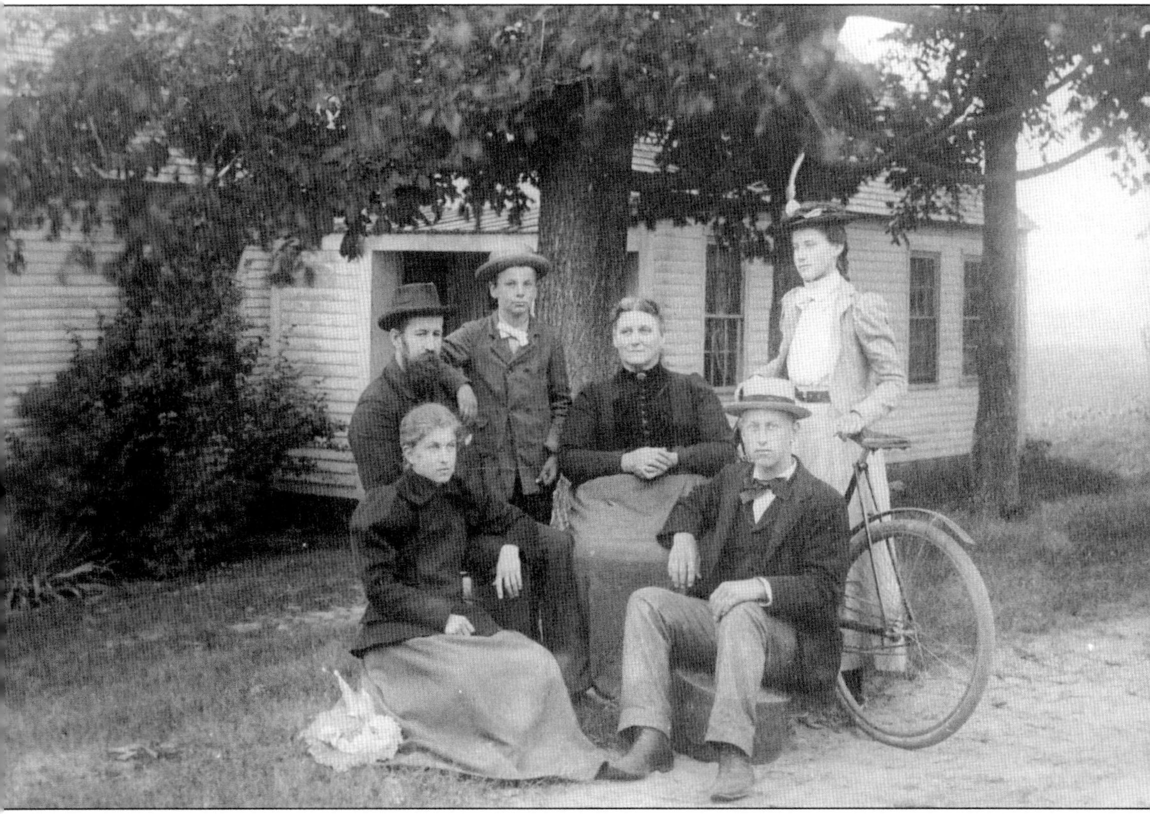

Born in 1850, Rufus M. Gould was the grandson of Obadiah Gould, the first settler on Quaker Ridge. Rufus married Rachel E. Hall, and they lived on the family farm with their four children, Lizzy, Alpheus, Ellen, and Charles, none of whom ever married. They were a frugal and self-sufficient family, supplementing their farming income by various other means. Ellen was a teacher for many years, Alph had an oil business, Charles was a mill operator, and for many years, Alph and Charles operated a cider mill at the family farm.

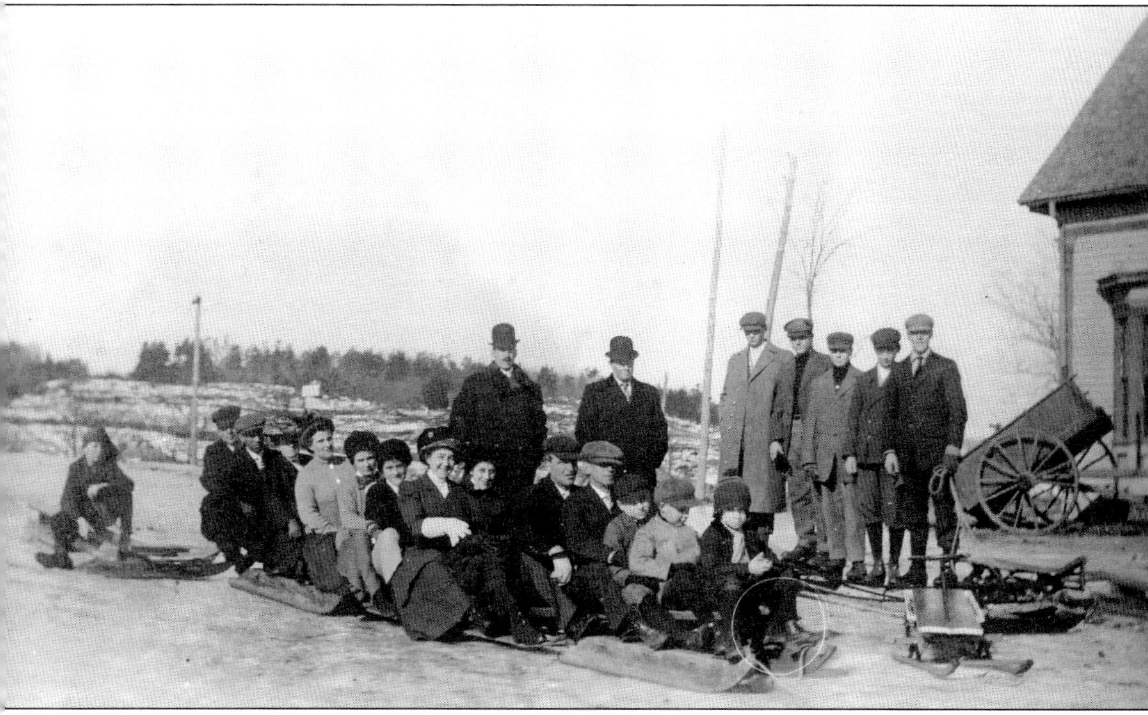

With little to no traffic on Quaker Ridge, sledding was not as dangerous in the past as it would be today. Two single sleds were held together from front to back with a long board connecting them to make a bobsled. Pictured here are Angie and Myron Hall and their neighbors.

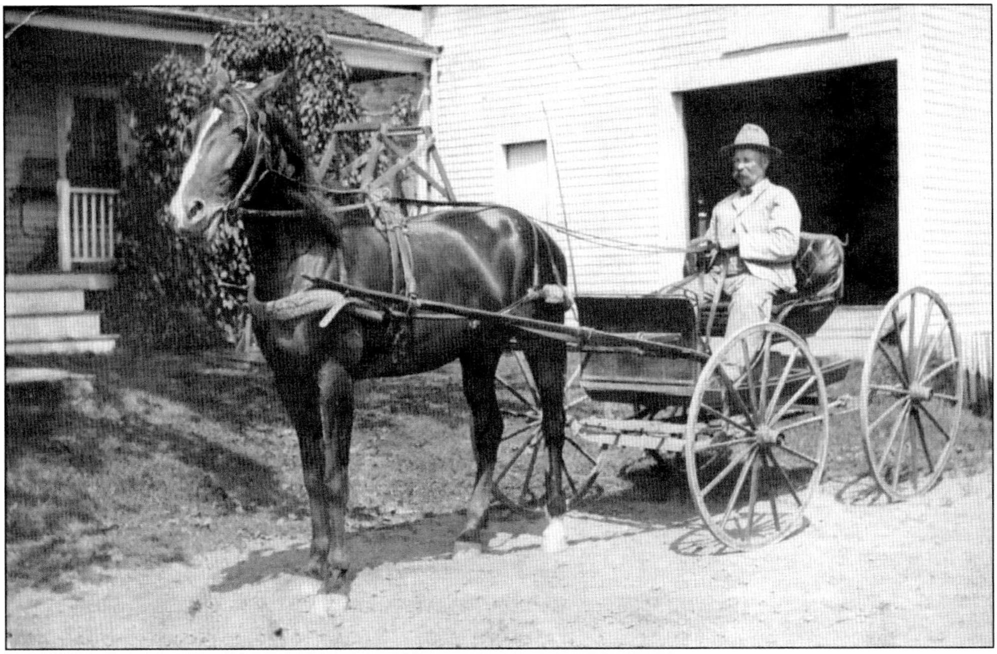

Born in 1861, Hall A. Edwards married Elizabeth Smith. He operated a large farm where he produced almost everything they needed. He was also the local tax collector. The homestead, once belonging to an S. Smith, was on Jim Small Road. The farm was torn down about 60 years ago, and the site was never built on.

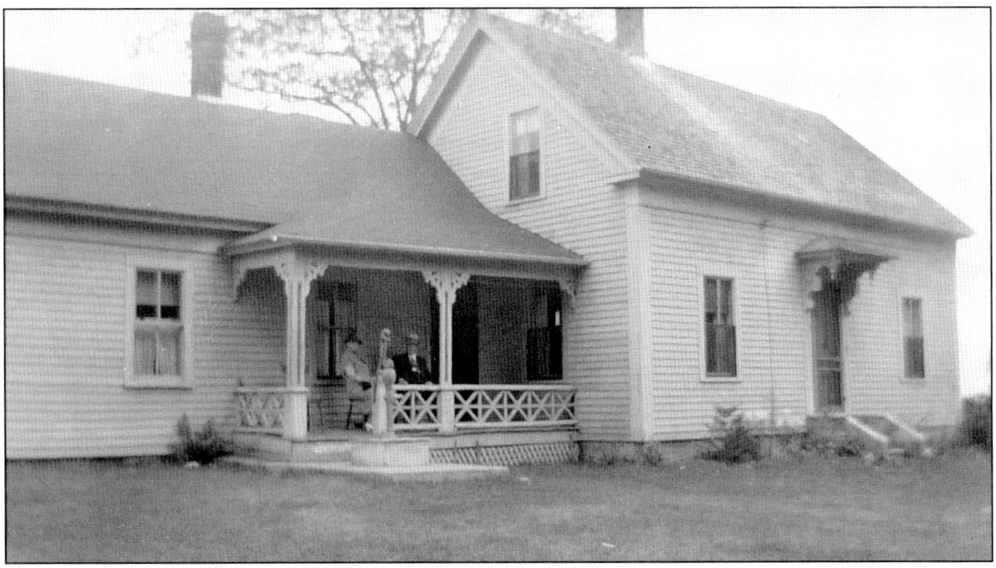

Mark Whitney, a grandson of Moses Whitney, one of the first settlers in Casco, married Maria Watkins. Maria lived on Libby Road, and Mark lived on Bridgton Road. Around 1882, he bought this home and moved his family to Quaker Ridge, where he was a farmer. Today, this is the Bogdahn home.

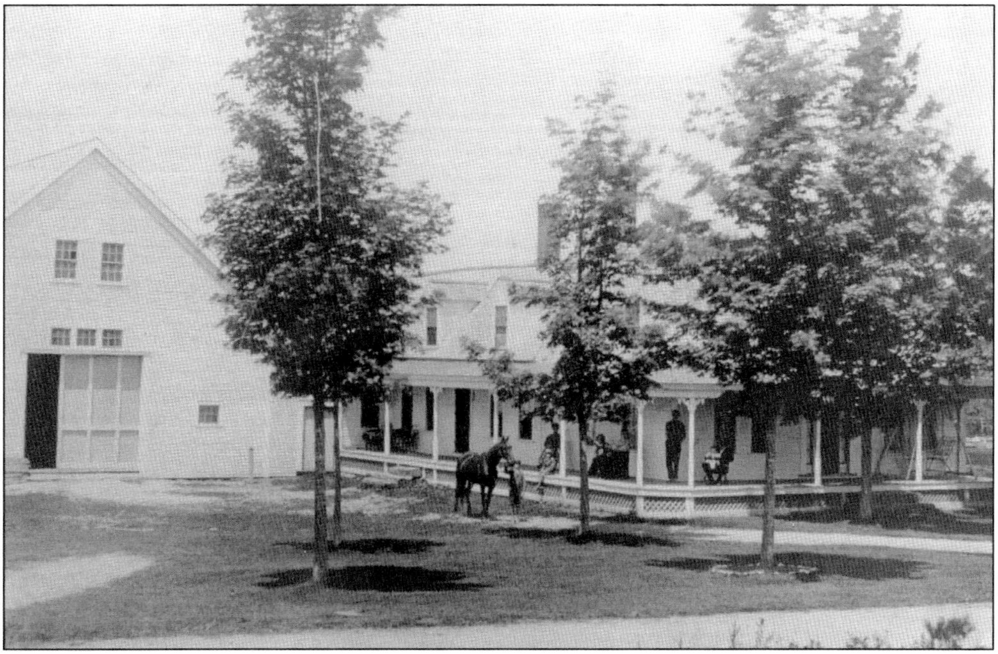

Born in 1832, Joshua C. Cook married Elizabeth H. Cook in 1856. He was a cobbler who went to Rattlesnake Mountain every year to kill rattlesnakes for their oil to use on the cowhide boots he made. His cobbler's shop sat near the road of his family's home on Quaker Ridge. His original home burned, and has since been rebuilt; his great-grandson's family, the Hanscoms, live here today.

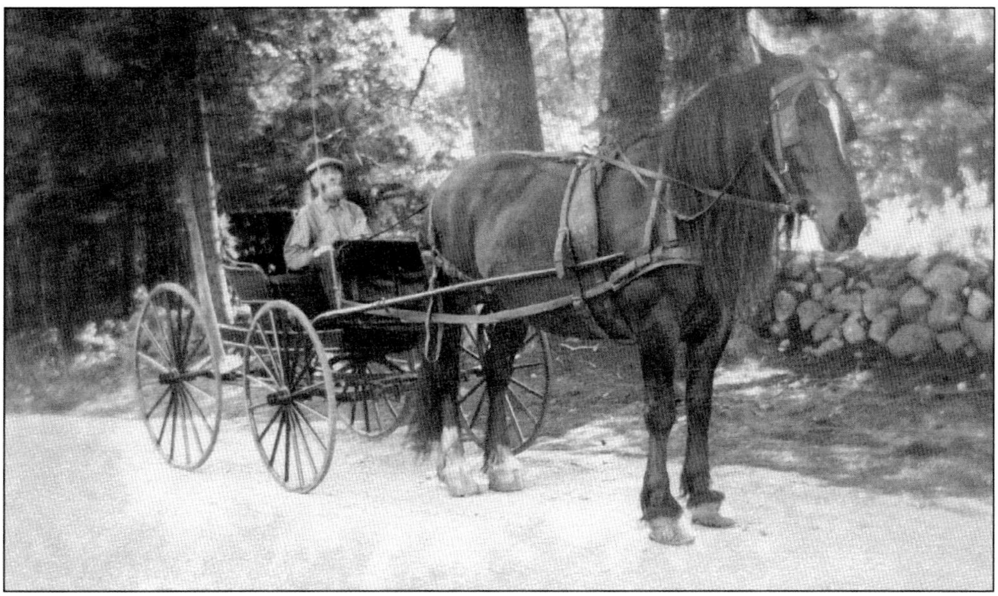

Charlie Wilbur married Nellie Jordan, and they lived on the homestead that had been his grandfather's in the 1880s. This home was Daniel Fickett's place, located off Quaker Ridge on what is now called Farm View Road. Charlie was one of nature's great mechanics, running a one-man sawmill and doing custom work for the government during World War I. He was a little odd as well. Only taking a bath once a year on the hottest day of the summer, he would strip down, scrub up, and call it good for another year!

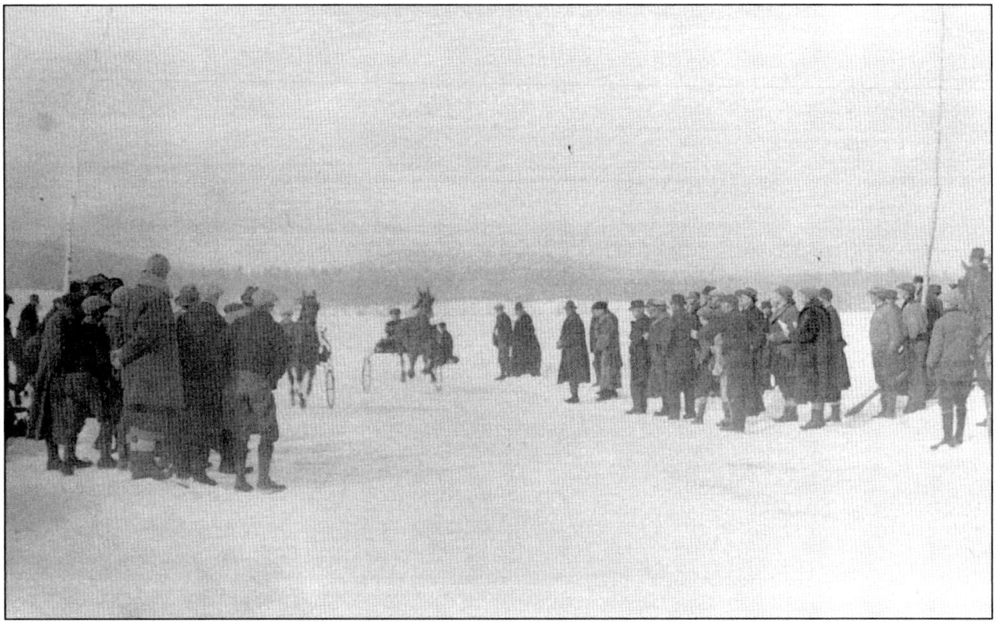

Many men in Casco had prime racehorses in addition to their working horses in the 1920s. Their pride in them and their spirit of competition led to local races. When they were not racing on dirt tracks in the warm months, they shifted to the ice. This picture shows a good-sized crowd gathered on Thomas Pond to cheer them on. One of the favorites was Albert Watkins driving Gordon Tenney's horse, Bonus Castle.

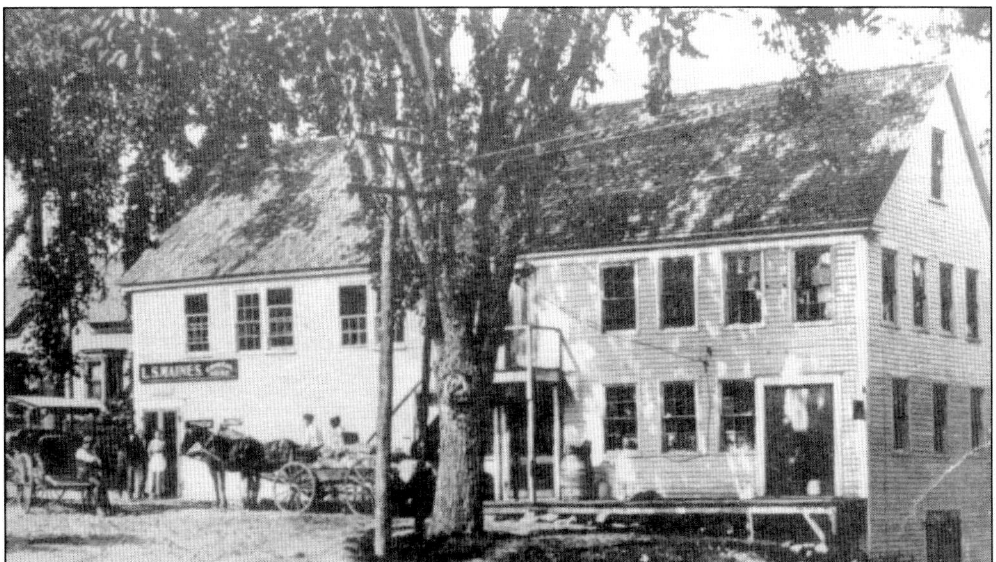

Otis Watkins established this store in 1848. William Dingley Jr. became his partner in business in 1851, naming the store Dingley Watkins. William's son Fred ran a coat shop in the upstairs of the store. After Otis's death, Loring Mains was a partner and eventually ran the store with his son Fred and his wife, Shirley. Mains General Store operated until the late 1950s. The upstairs became the South Casco Community Center. This building was the center of the community for well over 100 years. It was torn down in 1997.

In early days, the men in town maintained roads. All roads were divided into sections, and one man was appointed surveyor in charge, with the other men living in that section contributing their help. This earned them money that was paid toward their taxes each year. Maintenance included digging ditches, keeping roads passable during mud season, and shoveling drifts of snow, such as shown here by the men of South Casco.

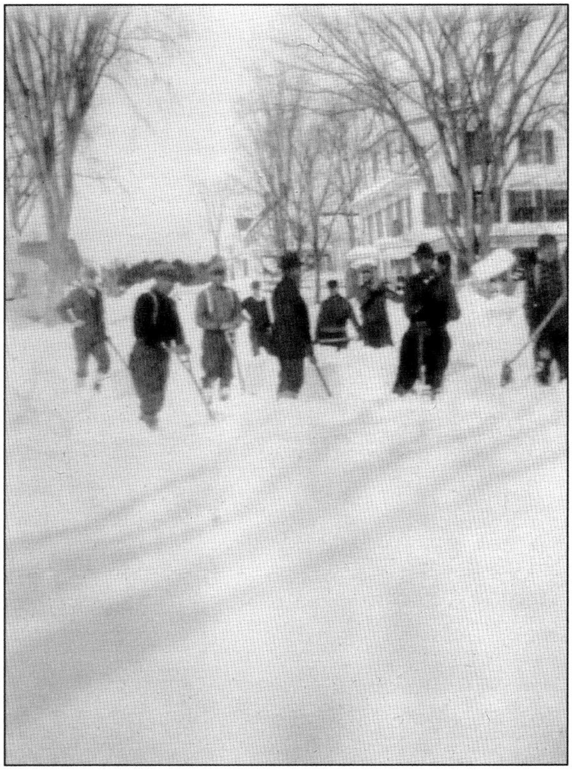

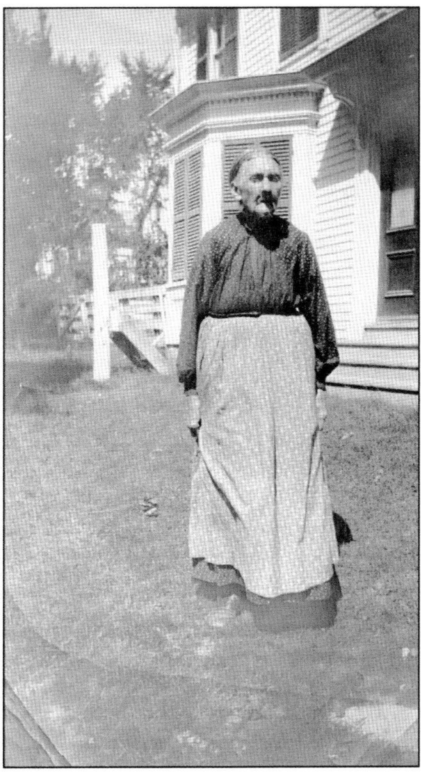

Born in 1826, Eliza M. Watkins, daughter of Jacob and Maria Watkins, married William Dingley Jr. They built the Thomas House in 1874, but it is not known when they took in boarders. It has been said Eliza has walked the rooms of her beloved home even after her death in 1911.

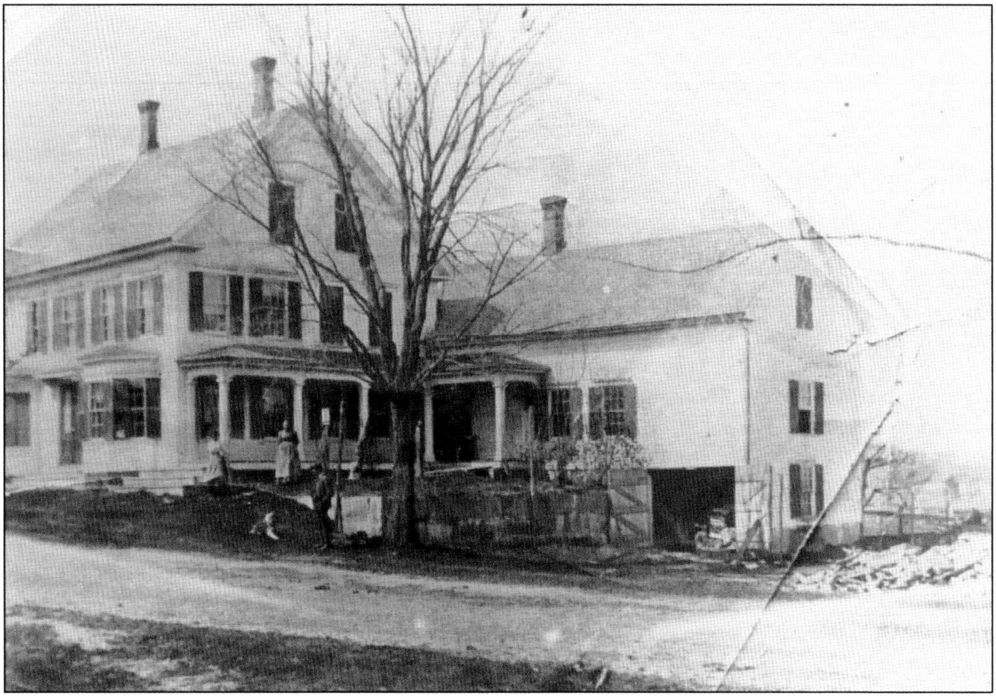

Born in 1820, William Dingley Jr., son of Samuel and Margaret (Jordan) Dingley, settled in South Casco and began a mercantile business with his wife Eliza M. Watkins. He was a large landowner and farmed extensively. He held many town offices and was postmaster in South Casco for about 30 years. In 1874, he built his home, which became the Thomas House.

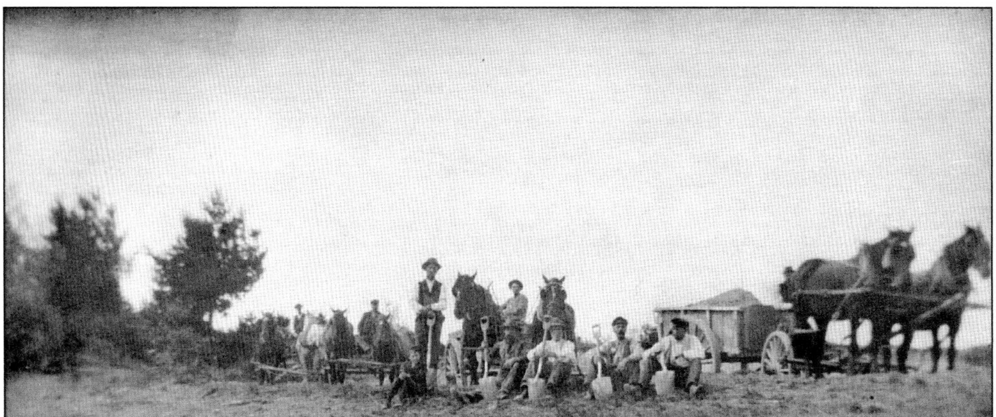

Building the state road on the Bridgton Road, Route 302, is pictured here around 1910. One of the men shown here is Silas F. Jordan, with his son Philip. Silas was very active in town affairs and was road commissioner for seven years. The Jordans of Casco are descendants of Dominicus Jordan.

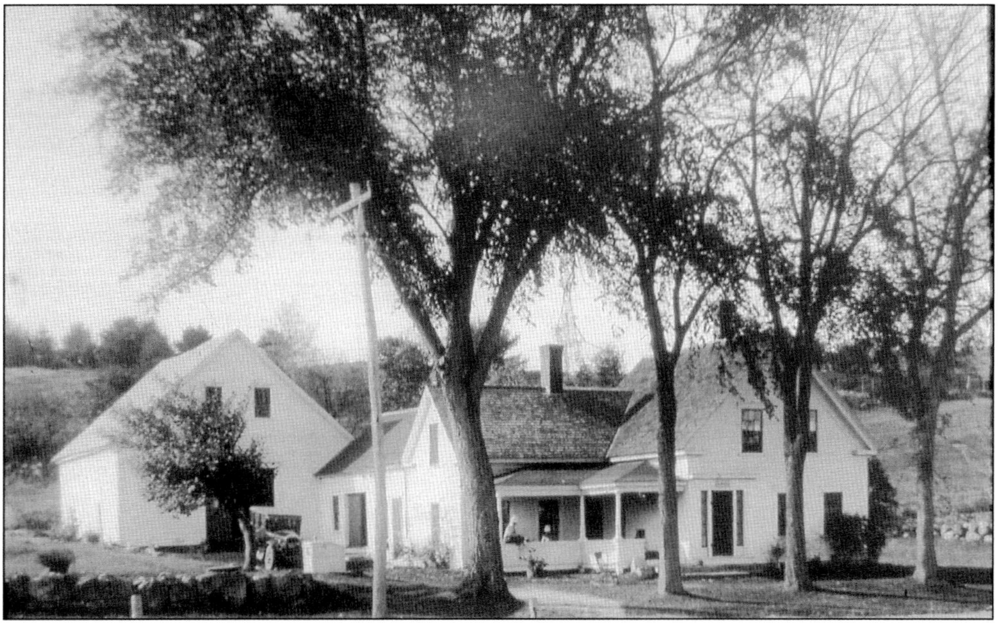

Born in 1831, Orrin Watkins, son of Jacob and Maria Watkins, married Harriett Varney. He was a canal boat operator and later became a manufacturer of ready-made clothing. They lived in this house on Quaker Ridge, called "Elmdale." Later, Jim and Angie Watkins owned this house. Angie operated a gift shop here in the summers.

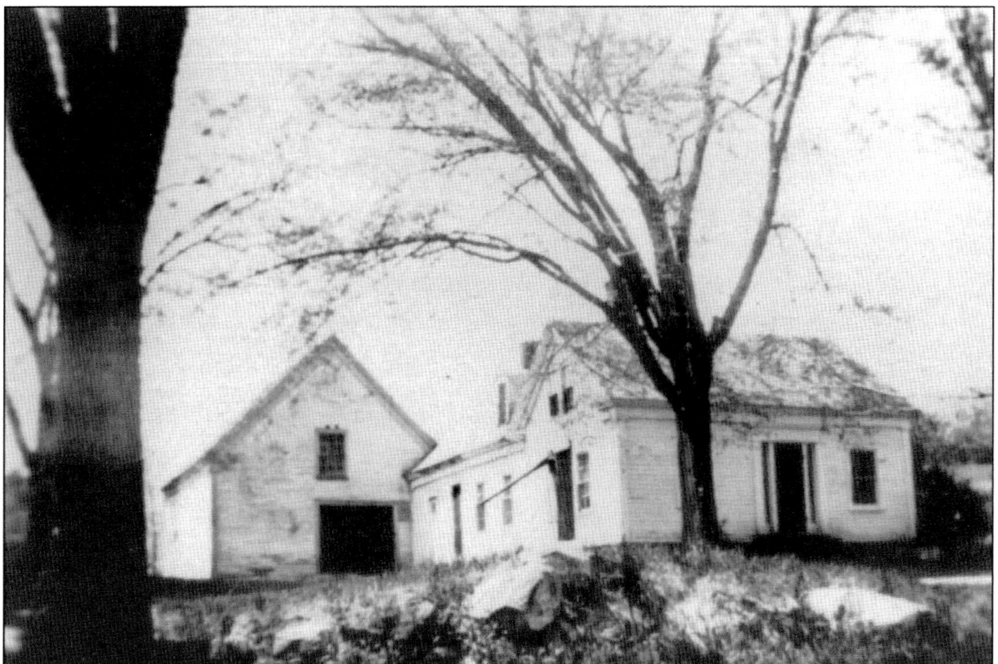

Lorana Watkins's house was in South Casco, between the end of Quaker Ridge Road and South Casco Village Road. When the new Route 302 was built in the mid-1950s, this house would have been right in the middle of it, so it was moved to Windham.

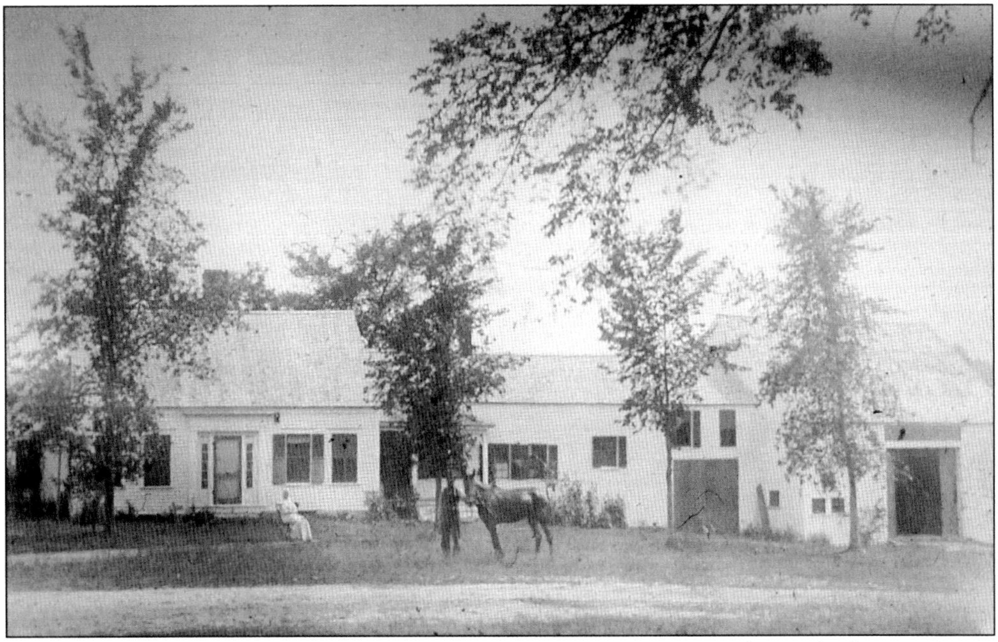

In 1780, Capt. Joseph Dingley, the first settler to claim land in Raymondtown, built a new home by his mill site at Dingley Brook on Raymond Cape Road. At this time, he turned his home on Roosevelt Trail, Stone Bridge Farm, over to his son Samuel. Samuel married Keziah Proctor, and they had eight children. These buildings once made up the terminus of the Murch stagecoach line.

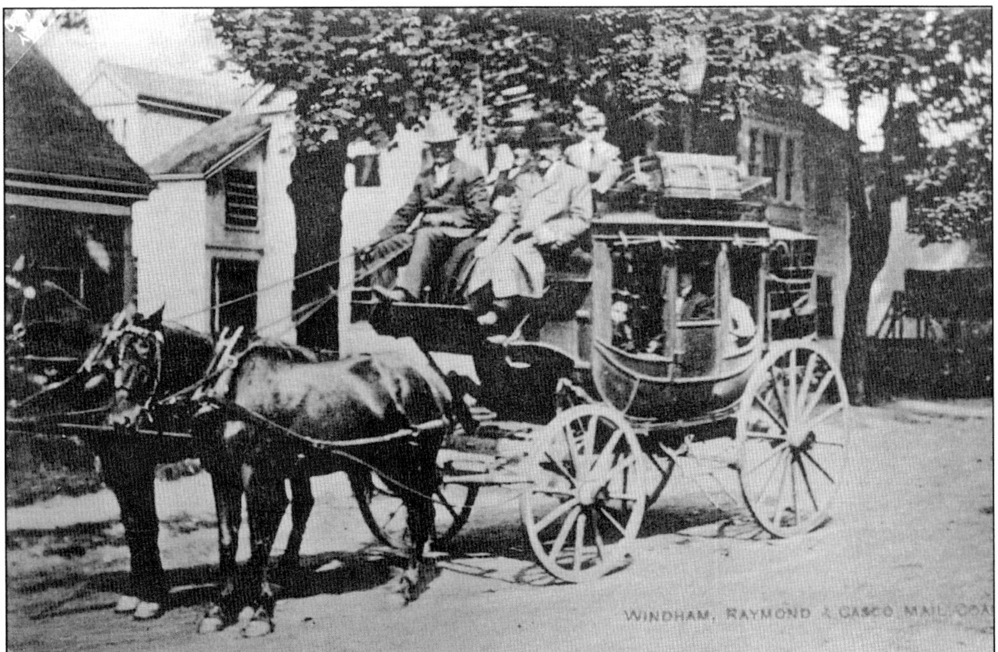

At the age of 17, Albert Murch bought a stagecoach from a man called "Slipper Toe" Davis from Poland. In the year 1886, bids were made for the stagecoach route from Portland to South Casco, and Murch won the bid. He drove his stage for transportation and mail deliveries every summer until automobiles made the stagecoach obsolete.

Lumbering and farming continued to be the main occupation for many in Casco until the last years of the 19th century. Then residents catered to spring fishermen and summer vacationers. Albert and Amy Watkins took in boarders in their home, along with any overflow of guests from the Thomas House. Amy took great pride in keeping her boarders happy with her home cooked meals of fresh fish caught from Thomas Pond.

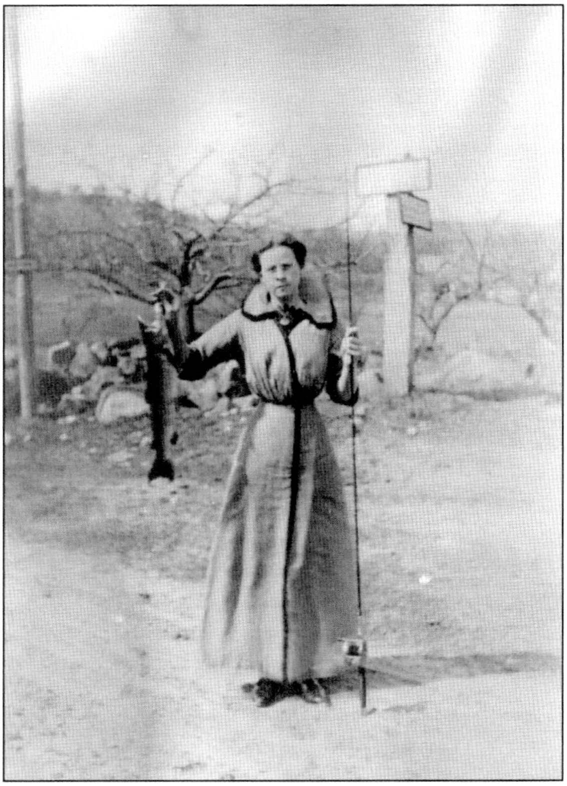

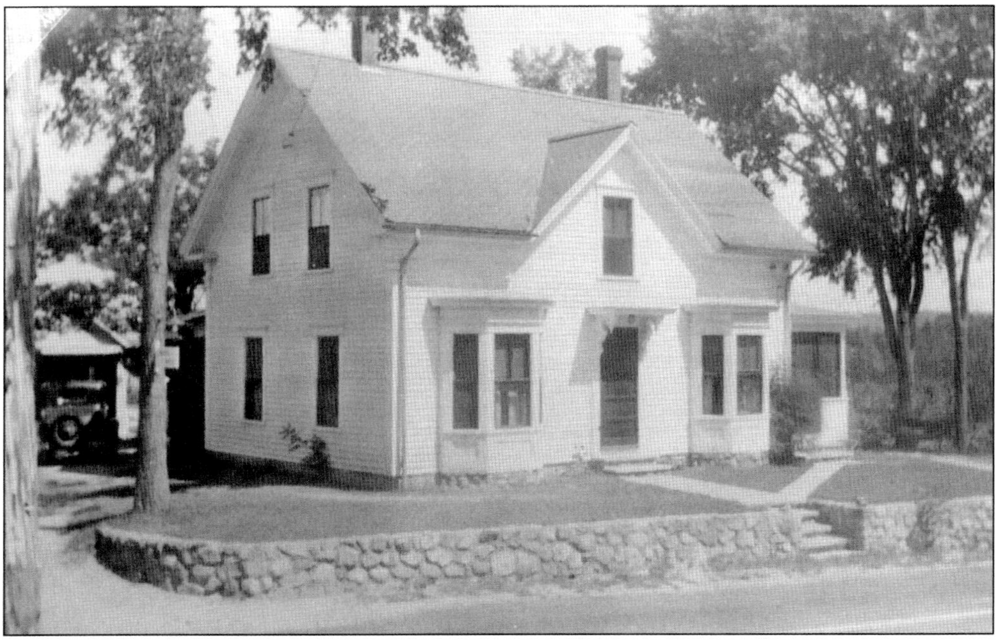

Built in 1835 by Ira Shaw and his son, this house is located on the corner of Quaker Ridge Road and South Casco Village Road. Albert C. Watkins and his wife, Amy, lived in this home in the early 1920s. This beautiful home has the last stone wall made in Casco with what was called a raised joint done by local mason Howard Shane.

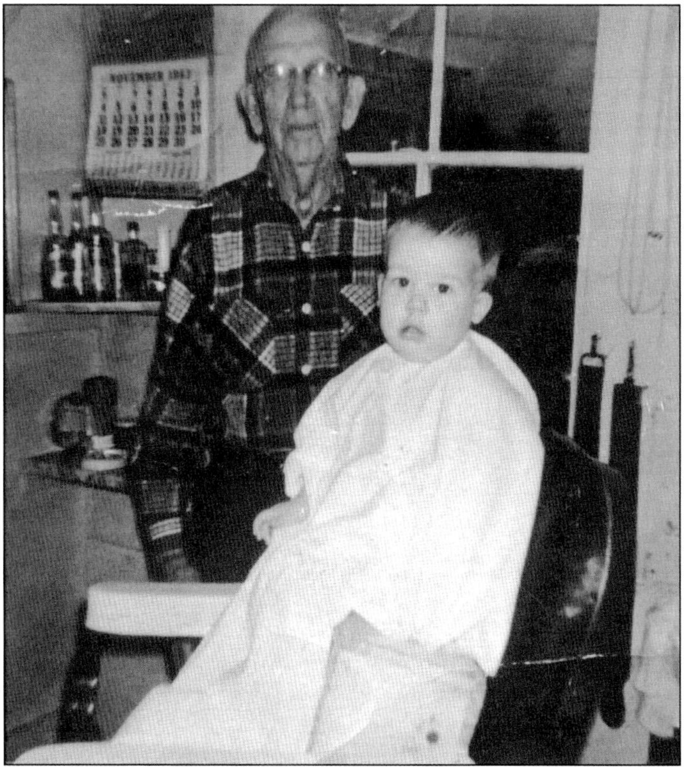

Albert C. Watkins was a blacksmith like his father, William, starting when he was only 15 years old and continuing for over 40 years. He was also a farmer, selling his own eggs and milk. What he is best remembered for is being the local barber. He had his barber chair in a room in the shed of his home and cut hair here from the 1920s until the late 1960s.

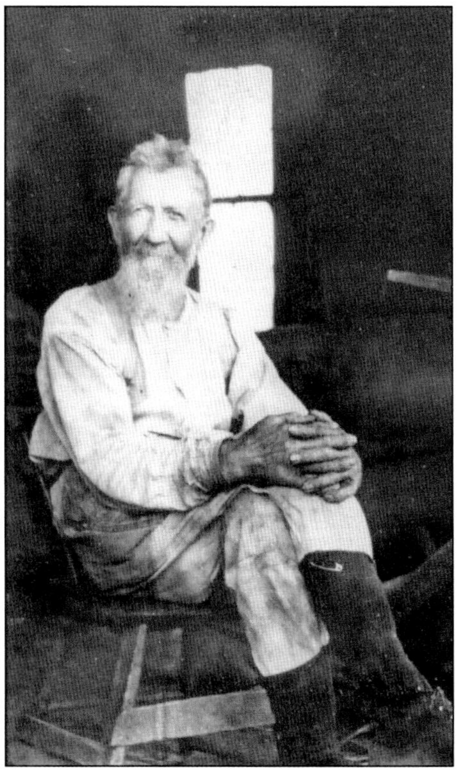

William "Bill" Watkins was a blacksmith in South Casco. Living here all his life, Bill loved his family, his job, and his community. He also loved a good yarn. On warm summer afternoons, he would often sit on the porch where he could see everyone pass by, often inviting people to come up and set a spell. He was asked one time "where does this road go?" and his answer was "I've lived here a long time, and it has not gone anywhere yet!" (Sharon Plummer.)

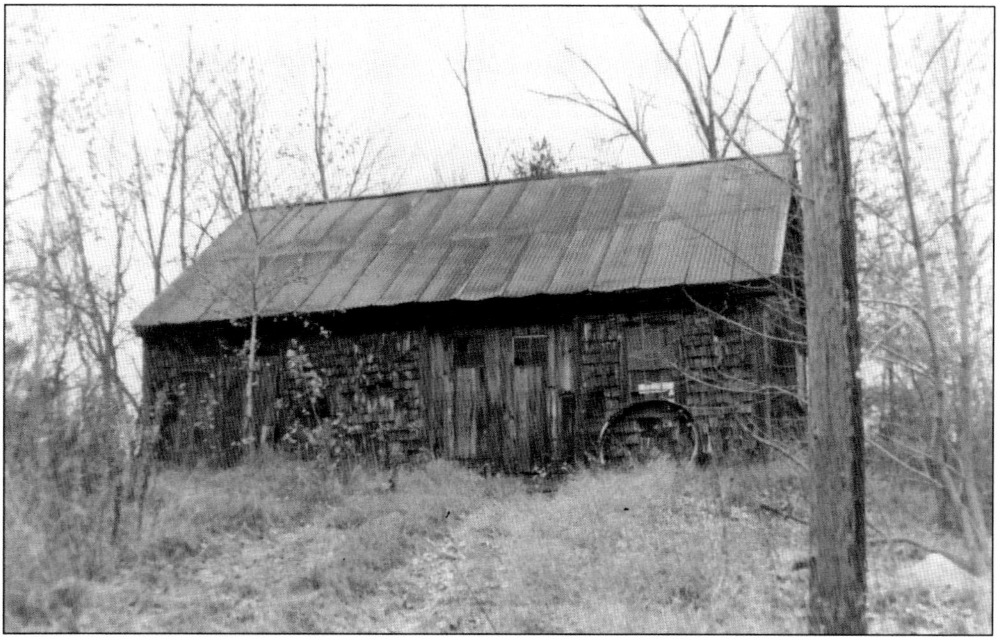

In the early days, a blacksmith was an important part of the community, and William Watkins filled that position proudly. He built his shop in 1874 after working for his relative William Dingley for 10 years. For 55 years, he continued working as a blacksmith, making his own horseshoes, ox shoes, and nails. Overgrown with bushes and in poor condition, his shop still stands at the south end of Quaker Ridge Road near Route 302. (Sharon Plummer.)

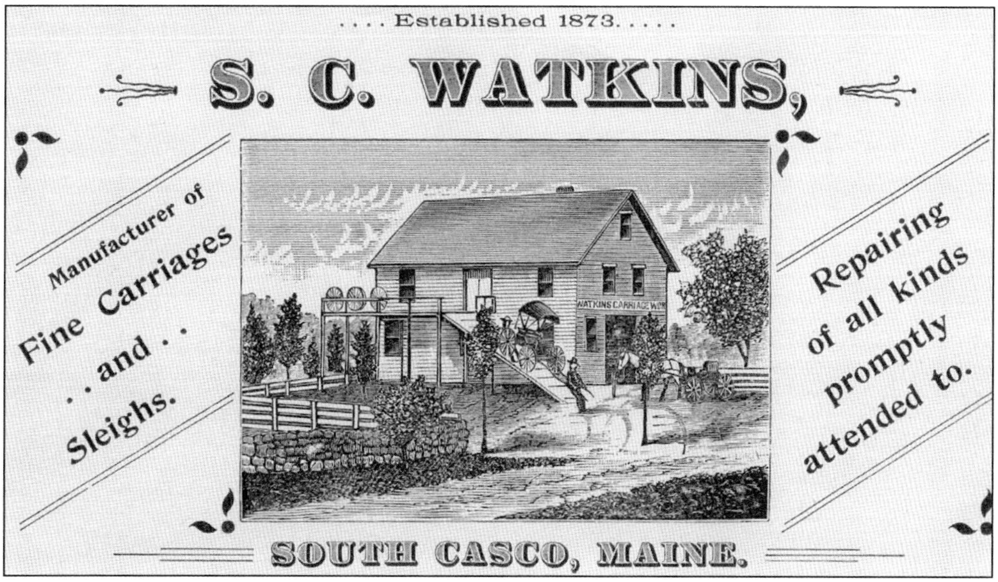

Born in 1851, Sumner C. Watkins had a carriage shop in South Casco, located on Raymond Cape Road about half a mile in from Route 302 on the right, in 1873. It had a large outside ramp from the second story to the ground for the finished custom-made carriages, carts, and wagons. His shop served local customers, as well as those from Portland and as far away as Bath. The business continued until his death in 1907. The building sat unused and rotting, eventually tumbling down.

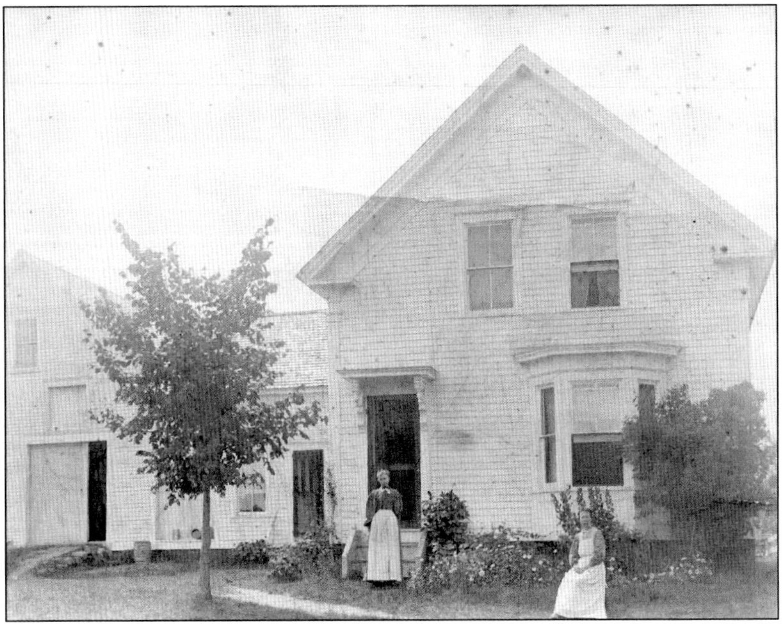

Born in 1849 to Henry and Louisa Graffam, Samuel married Helen "Nellie" Dingley, the daughter of William and Eliza M. (Watkins) Dingley. Graffam was a cooper in South Casco, and they lived in the house on Route 302 that is known today as the gift shop Cry of the Loon.

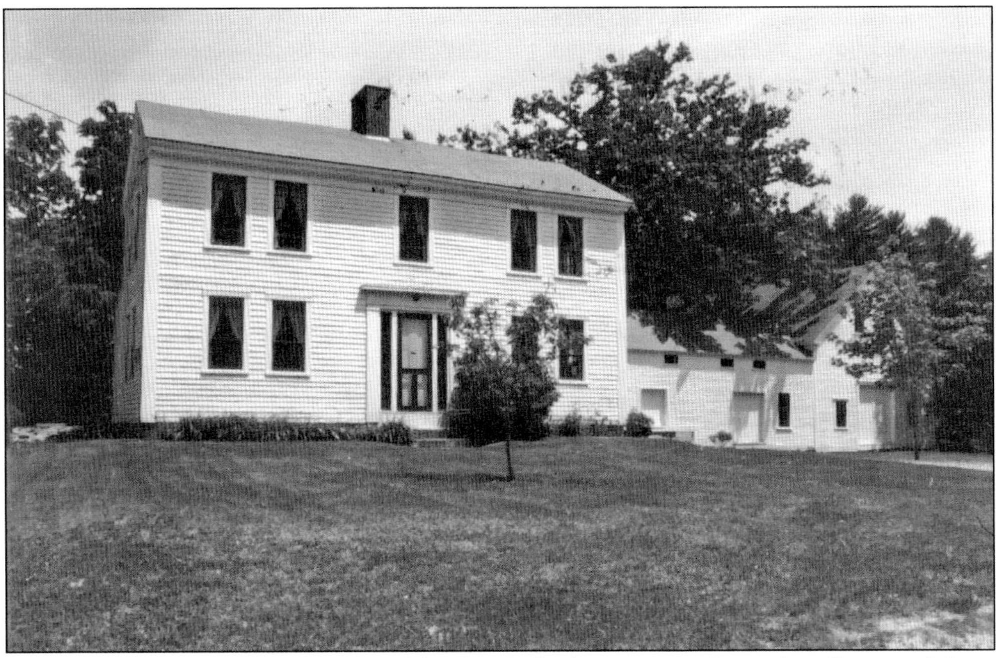

The house of Sumner C. Watkins and his family, built in 1810, is located on Raymond Cape Road, across from his carriage shop. His son Charlie S. Watkins rented cabins and lived at the family home until his death in 1974. At one time, this property extended all the way to Thomas Pond. This house is one of the oldest in the South Casco Village area. It is listed on the National Register of Historic Places.

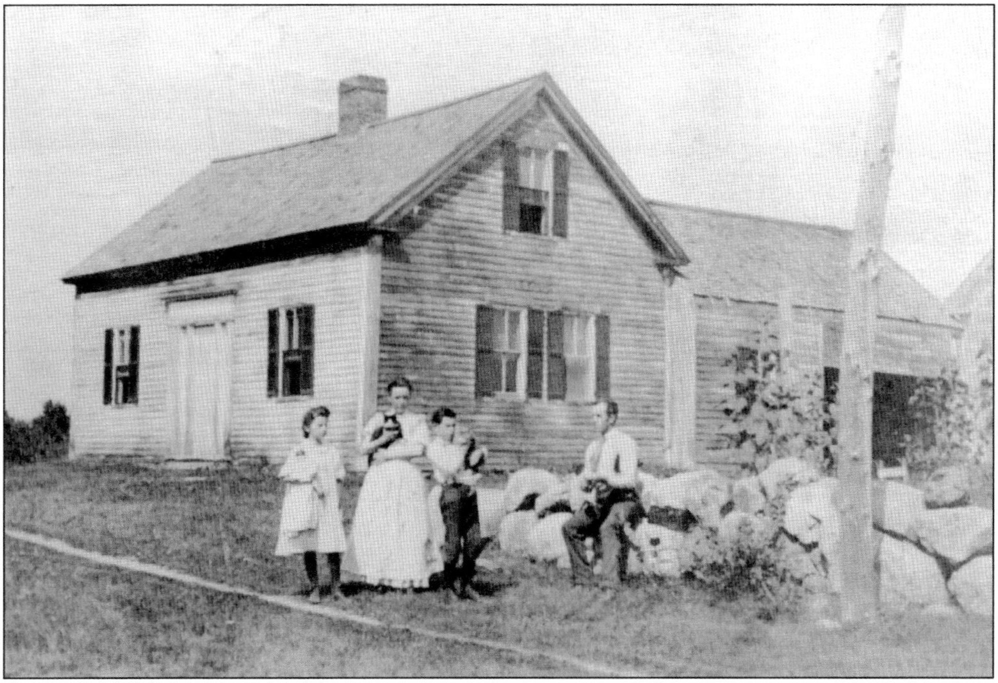

Born in 1809 to Jacob and Maria Watkins, Clark Watkins married Mary Jane Jackson. This picture shows Hamden Tripp and his family living in Clark's home. This house, built in 1837, is located beside the Murch Cemetery on Raymond Cape Road in South Casco.

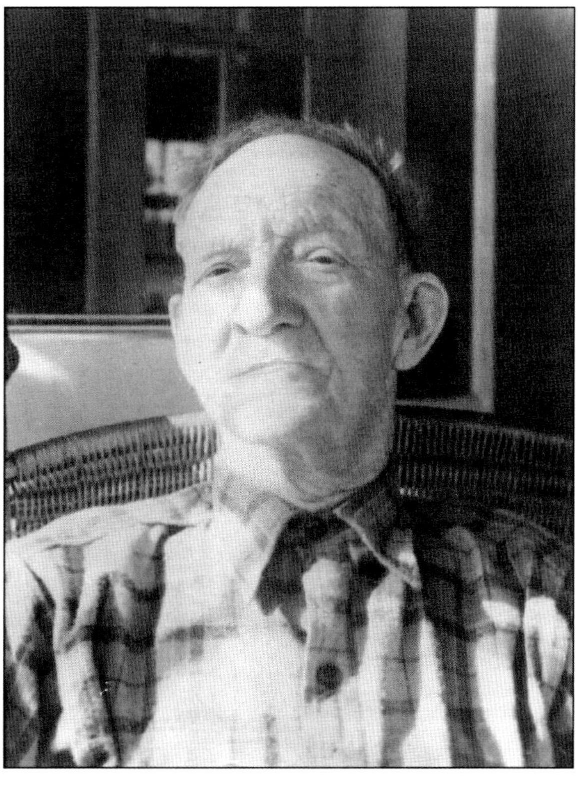

Born in 1846, Nelson Mann lived on Route 302 near where Stone Bridge Farm was located. He had one of the largest and finest gardens around, doing all the cultivating, planting, and harvesting himself. After winning a contest for making the most wooden hoops in a day, he was known as the "Champion Hoop Maker" of Casco and the surrounding towns. In his youth, he was the best clog dancer for miles around. He was an ardent fisherman and one of the first guides on Sebago Lake. (David Proctor.)

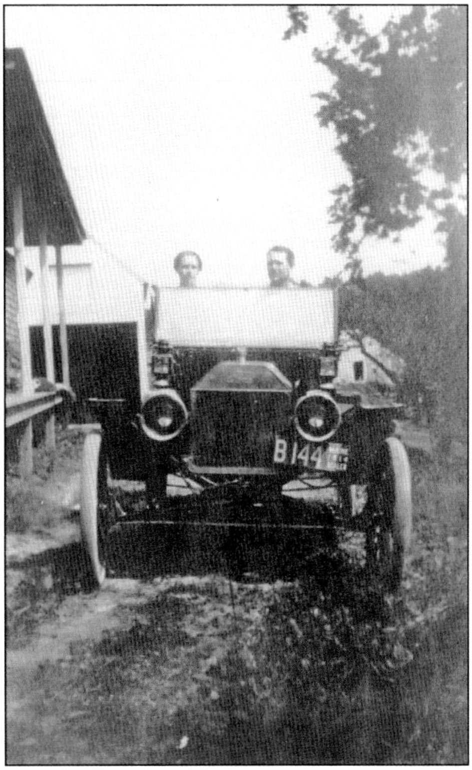

Shown here going for a Sunday drive in their first car in 1914 are Clarence Dana and Mary B. (Tenney) Watkins. They lived on Quaker Ridge on the family farm, which was often called the "Mae Danie" place. It was located below the hill on the shores of Thomas Pond in South Casco. They hosted summer camps called "Old Homestead Camps" that were operated until the mid-1950s. The farm was passed down from Jacob Watkins to his youngest son, Royal S., to his son, Clarence D., and then to his son, Owen Dana Watkins.

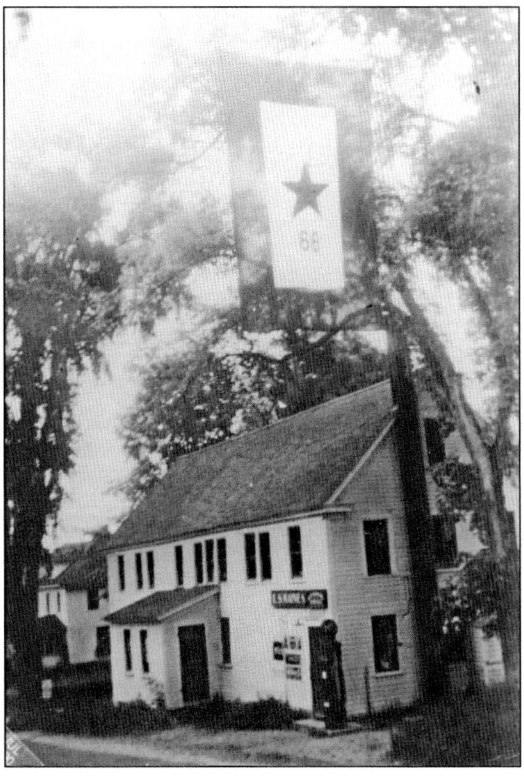

This service flag hung in South Casco on the old Route 302 by the old general store. The number on the flag told how many men were serving in World War II. Casco was fortunate that of these 66 men, women, and boys who fought for their country, the lives of only 3 were taken: Dexter Berry, Raymond Shane, and Robert Murch.

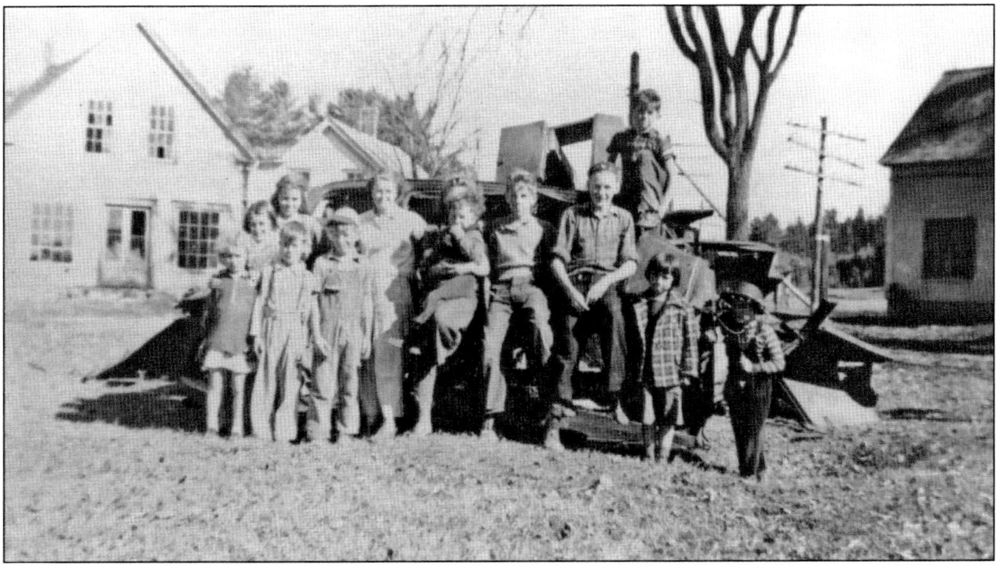

The World War II scrap drive in Cooks Mills was a community effort, with every age participating. All the scrap was hauled to the Casco Village schoolyard. In 1942, it was estimated that 200 tons of scrap metal was collected in Casco, one of the most successful small towns in the state of Maine. Shown here is Gilbert Avery, fourth from right, with his friends and a pile of scrap metal that they had gathered for the war effort.

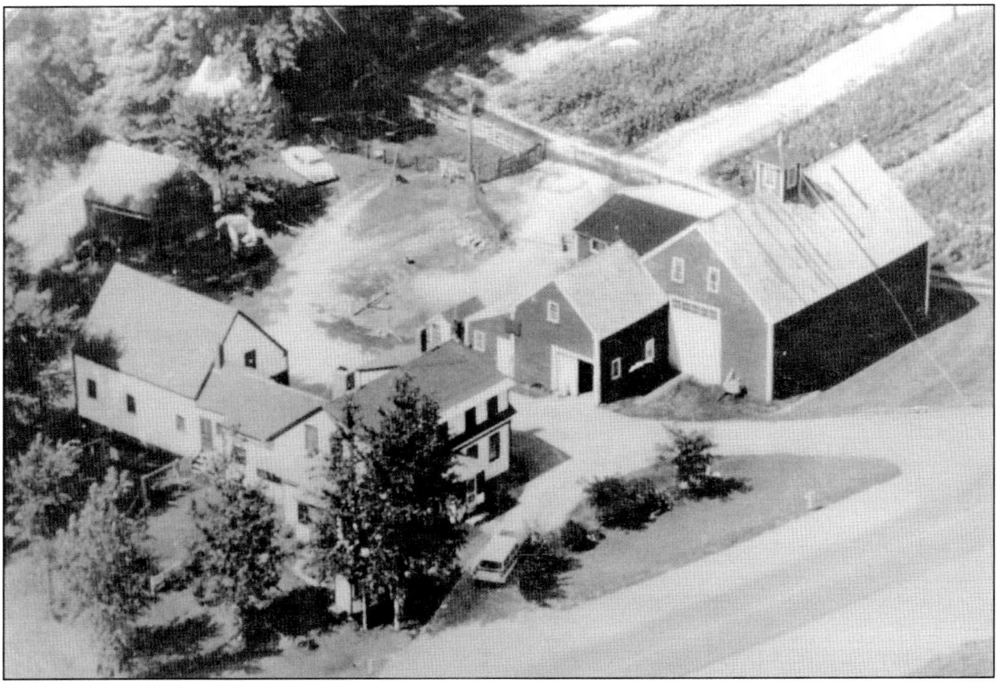

The Watkins farm on Route 302 in Casco, between Raymond and Naples, has been a landmark for tourists and visitors for years. Carolyn (Hartford) Watkins, the wife of Perley Watkins, ran a produce stand here for over 60 years, selling to campers and tourists from all over the world. Carolyn worked the land from morning until night, starting at 4:00 a.m. before the heat of the day. She instilled a great work ethic in her family and others.

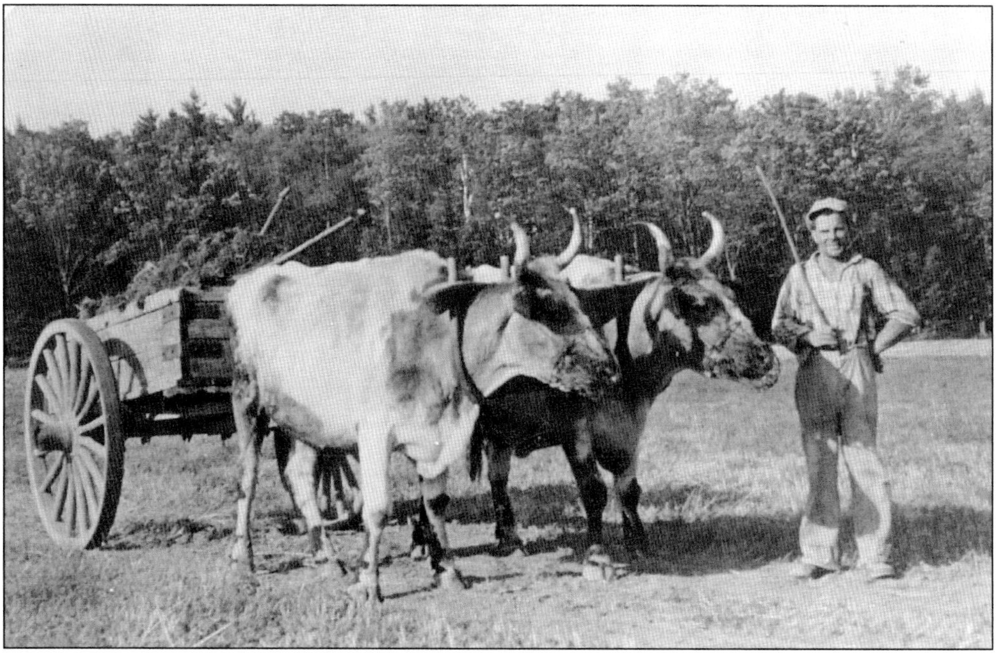

Henry Perley Watkins is out dressing the fields in 1940 for the growing of hay and produce on the family farm on Route 302 in Casco. This was before machines were available, and this job was a one-man show. The Watkins family has lived on this property for 150 years and continues to live there still to this day.

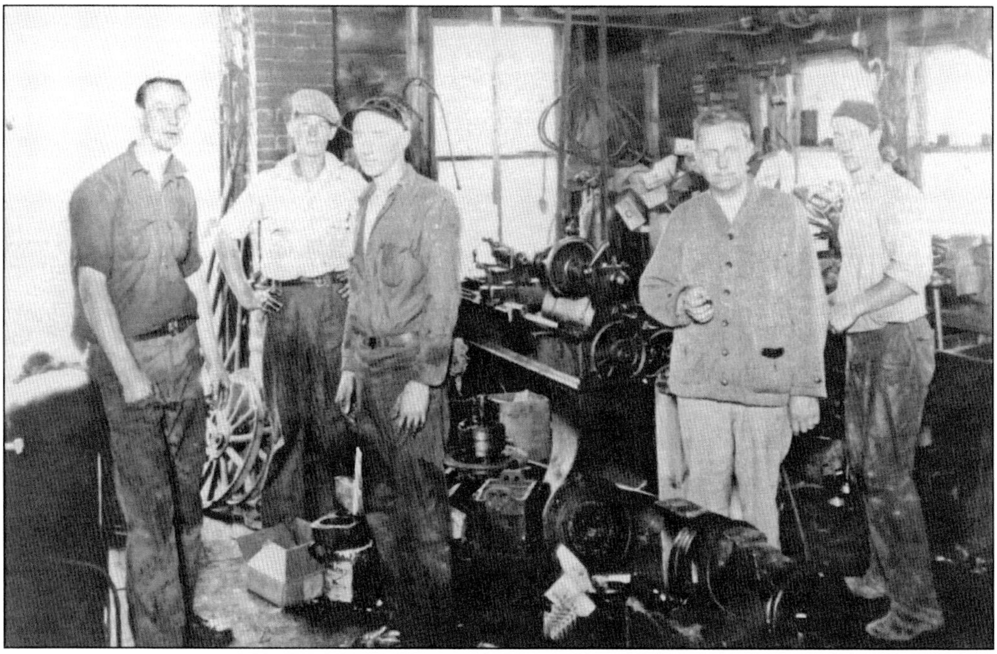

Ernest Lombard's Garage, bought from Lew Welch, was located beside the blacksmith shop at the end of the Quaker Ridge Road. It was a popular hangout in the 1930s. Shown here are, from left to right, Wess Lombard, mechanic; Wyman Watkins; Eldrid "Dutch" Spiller, gas jockey; grease monkey Wilbur Hoyt; and Richard Shane. Ernest also sold Chevrolet cars here.

Eugene Harmon was born in 1867 and lived on Roosevelt Trail in South Casco. He was a farmer, historian, major league baseball player, sheriff, and US deputy marshall. Appointed in 1914 as an officer of the law for the government, his territory was statewide. His career included seizing the luxury liner *Kronprinzessen Ceceile* in 1914 with its $14 million in gold bullion in its hold, arresting a suspected German spy in Washington County, breaking up illegal whiskey stills, and arresting smugglers. Eugene's carefully kept diaries spanning 52 years have been an invaluable record of history. (Audrey Galarneau.)

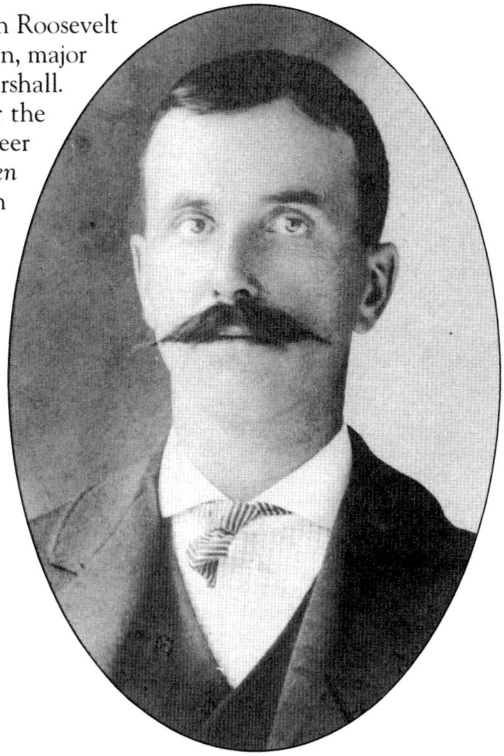

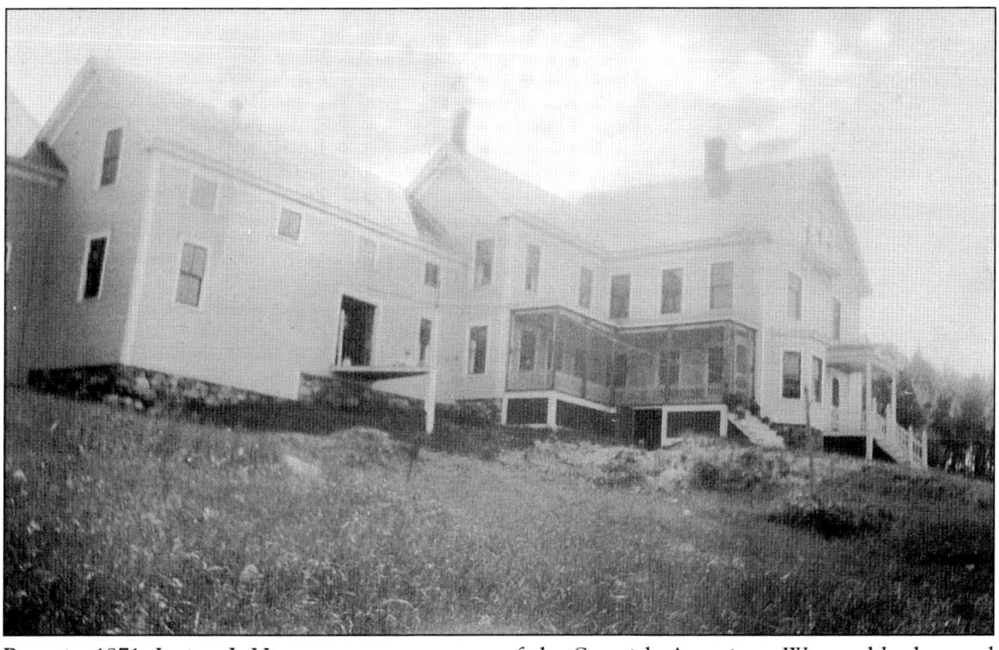

Born in 1871, Irving J. Harmon was a veteran of the Spanish American War and had served two years in the Philippines. After the war, he learned the shoemaking trade and worked for the Norway Shoe Company. Around 1912, he started to build the big set of buildings that would be his home. Local men worked on this house for over 20 years, and everything was beautiful inside and out. This house is on a side hill on Route 302 near Watkins Farm.

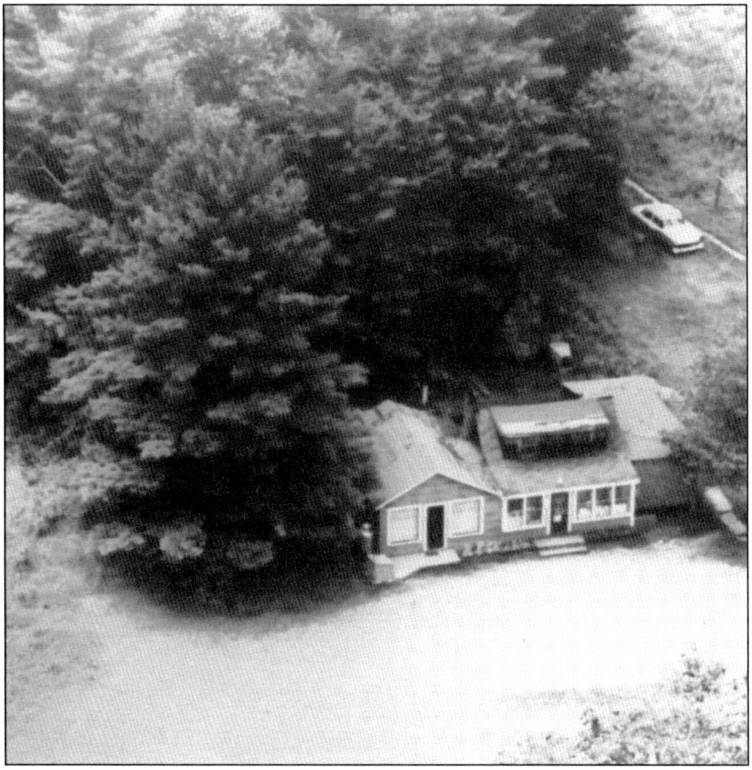

Born in 1902, Alice Spiller, the daughter of Ralph E. and Blanch (Hasty) Spiller, married Lewis L. Merrill, and they lived on Roosevelt Trail in South Casco next door to Eugene Harmon. Lewis was a grader of lumber, painter, and a carpenter and served as tax collector and constable for seven years. Their son Marvin began Merrill's Market in this home. Selling it to his mother, Alice became the proprietor of this store for almost 20 years.

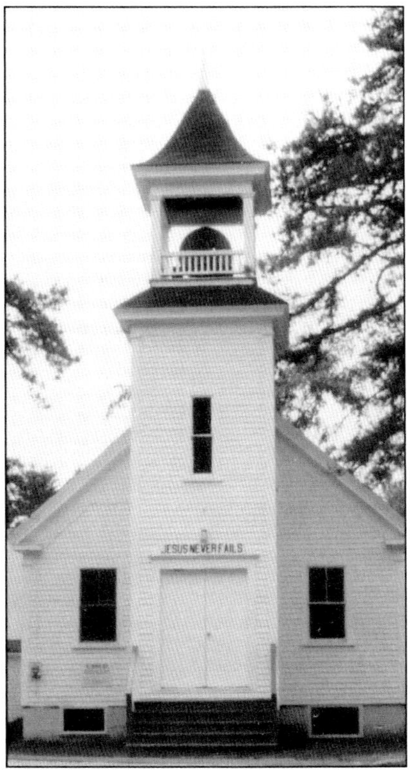

The Bridgton Road Church, located on the corner of Route 302 and Point Sebago Road, was built in 1914. Called at that time the General Provisional Baptist Church, the land was donated by Robert Dingley. The church community, along with other generous parties, pulled together, and built this beautiful little church in 142 days. In 1954, a parsonage was built across the road on land donated by Willard Chute. Although a new and bigger church was built behind this church in 1978, the original still stands as a symbol of the dedication of the congregation.

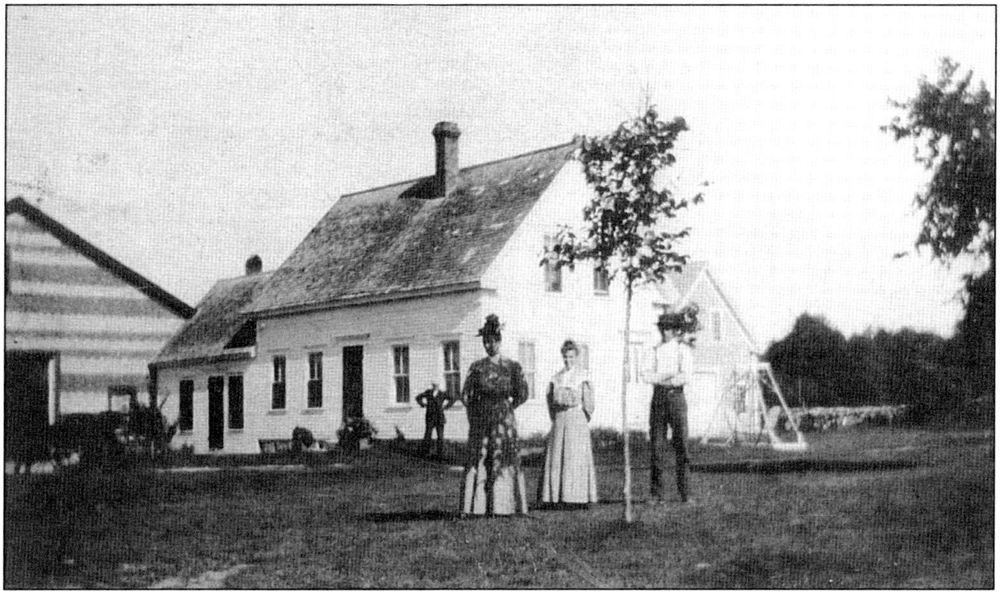

Wilber F. Tenney was born on Tenney Hill in 1860. By persistent hard work, he increased his acreage and built up a paying lumber and dairy business. Despite a heavy workload of 16-hour days, six to seven days a week, he found time to serve as a selectman for the town for several years. Today, this home belongs to the Russos.

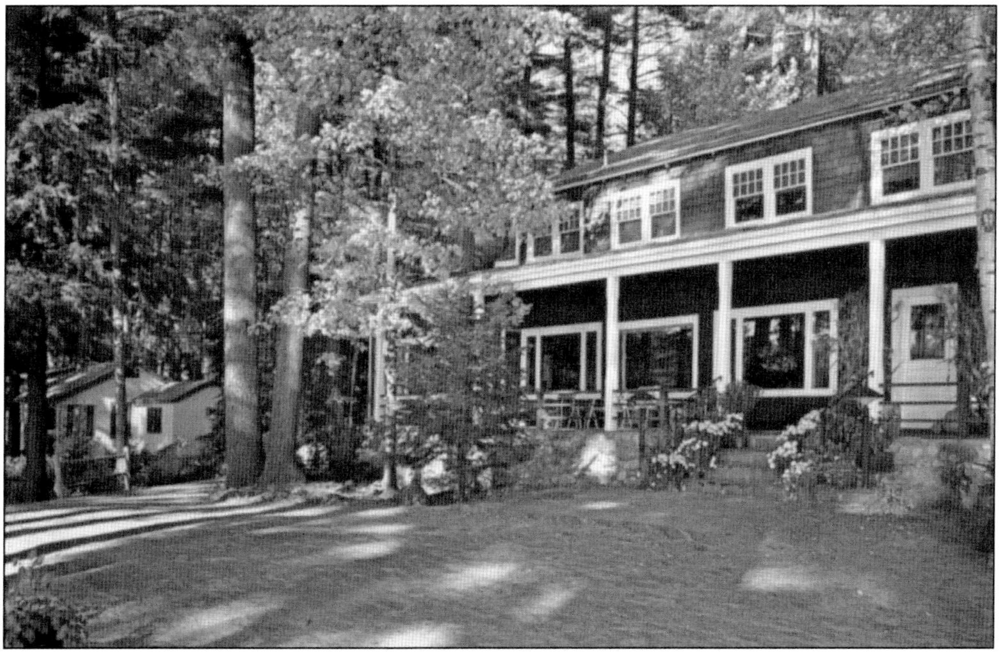

Sporting camps were built in South Casco in 1916 on the shores of Sebago Lake for people wishing to stay on the lake to fish, relax, or enjoy the views. These camps were called National Camps, and the founder of Wohelo, Charlotte Gulick, purchased the camps in 1924. The name was changed to Migis Lodge. In 1968, Sherman and Mabel Crockett owned the property. Today, under the ownership of the Porta family, Migis Lodge is one of the most prestigious and widely known resorts in the country.

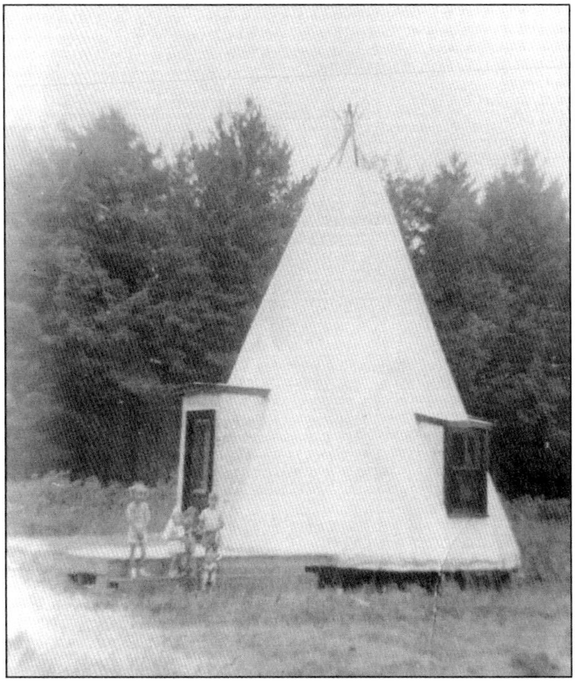

In the mid-1940s, a Penobscot Indian lived in Casco. Princess Golden Rod, also known as Dorothy Ranco Beatty, was the daughter of Chief Ranco, of the Indian colony at Old Town, Maine. She operated a craft and gift shop on the corner of Brown Avenue and Route 302 with her husband, Chief Half Moon. Many people still fondly remember them and their gift shop, a full sized tepee.

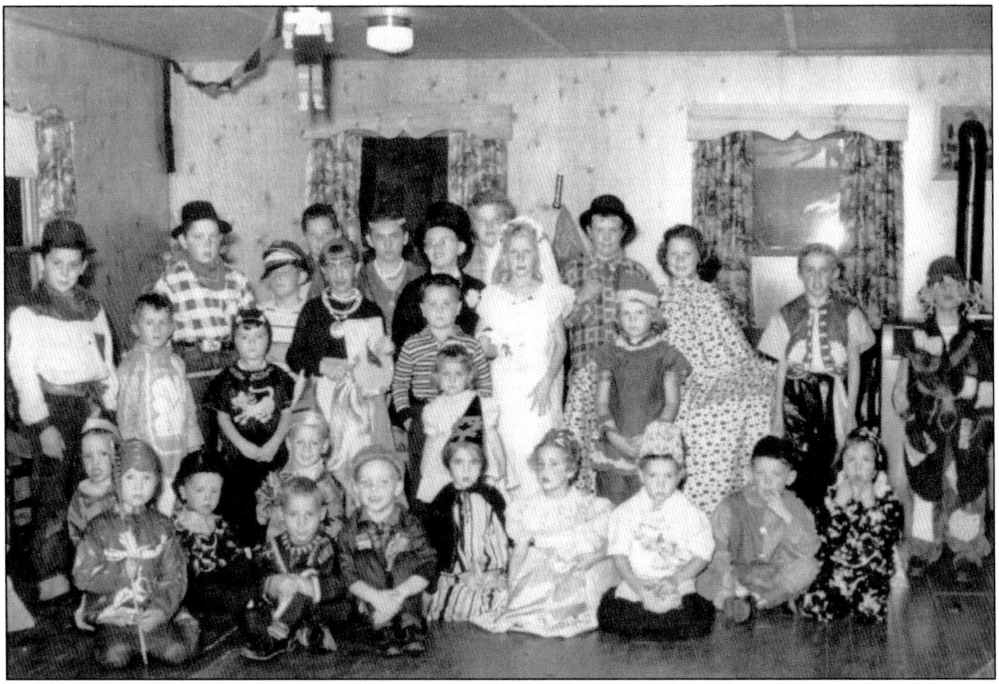

The kids of South Casco are at a Halloween party in South Casco Community Hall in 1955. Those pictured are, from left to right, (kneeling) Barry Lombard, Randy Varney, Reggie Watkins, Gary, Larry and Barry Lombard, Pam and Becky Watkins, Darryl Watkins, Mark Carson, and Linda Lafontain; (standing) Dana Durgin, Carol Mains, Mark Proctor, John Watkins, Debbie Watkins, Mary Jane Moore, Calvin and Karen Nutting, Sharon Dingley, Betsy Proctor, Marjorie Lombard, Sheila Tenney, Joanne and Bonnie Mains, Jennifer Carson, and Dana Watkins.

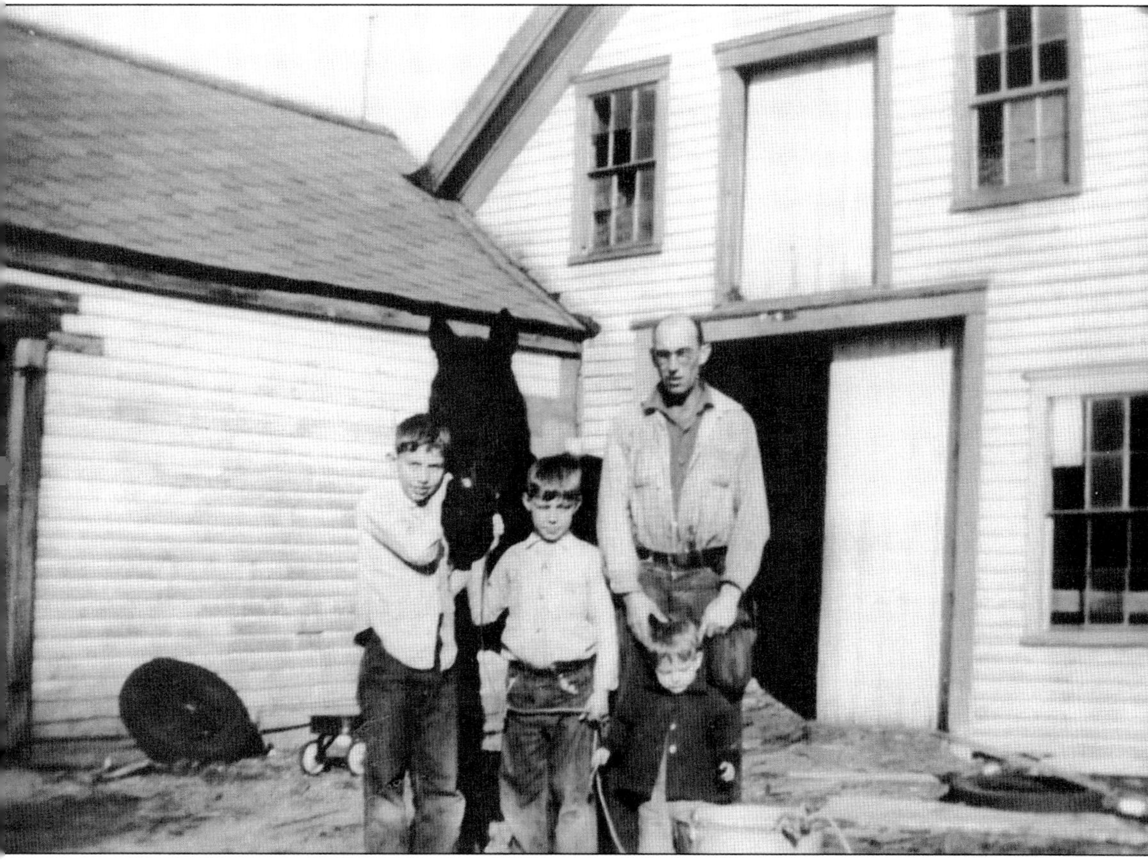

Built in 1860, the old Wilbur Watkins place was burned down in the mid-1950s when Route 302 was built. The new road would be right at the doorstep, so a new house was built farther back in the field. Shown here are Wilbur's grandson Arthur Proctor and Arthur's sons, from left to right, Jim, David, and Mark. David has been invaluable in sharing his knowledge of history pertaining to our towns.